T0334052

AIDING AFGHANISTAN

PAUL ROBINSON & JAY DIXON

Aiding Afghanistan

*A History of Soviet Assistance
to a Developing Country*

HURST & COMPANY, LONDON

First published in the United Kingdom in 2013 by
C. Hurst & Co. (Publishers) Ltd.,
41 Great Russell Street, London, WC1B 3PL
© Paul Robinson and Jay Dixon, 2013
All rights reserved.
Printed in India

The right of Paul Robinson and Jay Dixon to be identified as the
authors of this publication is asserted by them in accordance
with the Copyright, Designs and Patents Act, 1988.

A Cataloguing-in-Publication data record for this book
is available from the British Library.

ISBN: 978-1849042390

This book is printed using paper from registered sustainable
and managed sources.

www.hurstpublishers.com

CONTENTS

v

CONTENTS

LIST OF TABLES AND FIGURES

ACKNOWLEDGEMENTS

The authors would like to thank all those who have helped to make this book possible. Special thanks are due to Valerii Ivanov for sharing his time and knowledge; to Viktor Korgun for putting us on the right track at the start of this project; and to the staff of the Russian State Archive of the Economy. In Canada, we are particularly grateful to our research assistant, Alfia Sorokina, for her excellent work in tracking down Soviet-era materials; to Chione, for the loan of her library of Afghan-related books, and for her editing skills; to Nipa Banerjee and Christoph Zurcher for their comments on earlier versions of this work; and to Marina Dmitrieva for transcribing the interview with Valerii Ivanov. *Spasibo bol'shoe!*

NOTES ON STYLE

Transliterations from Russian follow the U.S. Library of Congress style except where there is a commonly accepted alternative—thus "Yeltsin" not "El'tsin." The spelling of Afghan names generally conforms to that used by the Soviets. Citations from the Soviet archives follow the format *fond, opis'*, *delo, list* (f., o., d., l.).

1

INTRODUCTION

For nearly sixty years Afghanistan has intermittently been one of the largest recipients of foreign aid yet it remains one of the poorest countries on the planet. At the time of writing, Western states are again pouring billions of dollars into Afghanistan in the form of development assistance and humanitarian aid, in the hope of stimulating economic growth, winning hearts and minds, and strengthening the national government against insurgents. So far they have received few benefits from their enormous efforts. As Andrew Wilder comments, "Instead of winning hearts and minds, Afghan perceptions of aid and aid actors are overwhelmingly negative. And instead of contributing to stability, in many cases aid is contributing to conflict and instability."[1] Given the decidedly patchy record of foreign aid programs throughout the world over the past sixty years, this should probably come as no great surprise. Unfortunately, the governments leading the effort have paid little attention to past attempts to "fix" Afghanistan, despite their obvious relevance to the present time. The lessons from the Soviet Union's economic and technical assistance to Afghanistan, in particular, have been ignored, even though the Soviet Union was the most significant provider of foreign aid to Afghanistan for almost four decades.

From 1953 to 1991, the Soviets launched around 270 major construction projects in Afghanistan, 142 of which were completed (see Annex I). Finished projects included roads, electric power stations and power lines, irrigation canals, factories, housing, grain elevators, bakeries, automotive repair plants, airports, educational institutions, and others. The Soviets also trained tens of thousands of Afghan specialists, and distributed food, seed and medical aid. Apart from Egypt, Afghanistan received more Soviet aid per capita than any other country.[2] By the mid-1980s, over half the paved roads in Afghanistan had been built by the Soviet Union, and some 60 percent of Afghanistan's electricity came from Soviet-built power stations or via power lines bringing electricity from the Soviet Central Asian republics. Factories built by the Soviets made up some 75 percent of Afghanistan's industrial production, and the Soviet-established gas industry provided the Afghan state with much of its tax revenue. Soviet geologists were responsible for discovering and charting the great majority of Afghanistan's mineral deposits, some of which are only now being opened up for exploitation (sensational press reports in 2010 of finds of up to a trillion dollars of mineral deposits in Afghanistan for the most part merely repeated what the Soviets had documented decades ago). The history of Soviet assistance to Afghanistan, with both its successes and its failures, forms an important part of the history of Soviet-Afghan relations and of the history of international development more generally. It is a story which holds lessons both for current aid programs in Afghanistan and for development programs elsewhere.

Economic growth is arguably the most important tool for raising the people of the developing world out of poverty and increasing the well-being of humanity. It not only leads to material prosperity, but also, as Amartya Sen pointed out in his book *Development as Freedom*, creates choices and opportunities for the population.[3] Because of the importance of growth for hundreds of millions of poor people, figuring out how economies grow and how to stimulate growth in them is one of the great challenges in modern economics.

During the Cold War, both communism and capitalism were judged by their ability to raise living standards. The West and the socialist bloc believed in the moral superiority of their systems with equal conviction: the Soviets touted communism's emphasis on social and economic justice, while the West emphasized the freedoms inherent in capitalism. But both sides knew, as Bertold Brecht said, that morals followed the feast ("*Erst kommt das Fressen, dann kommt die Moral*"). In the developing world, each system would be judged on its ability to (literally) deliver the goods.

Until at least the 1980s the contest was yet to be decided. The West was richer, but the Soviet Union's rapid industrialization from lower levels of development appeared more relevant to the developing world. Even Western observers who were hostile to Stalinism's brutality conceded its ability to deliver growth, at least within the Soviet Union. Many otherwise anti-communist leaders in the developing world expressed open admiration for, and drew inspiration from, Soviet central planning.[4]

Both West and East initially agreed on the mechanisms of growth. The key was believed to be building capital and the human skills to use it. The primary problem facing developing countries was thus seen as a lack of capital: roads, rails, cables, buildings, machinery, and equipment. The solutions were to remove the barriers to accumulating capital, and/or to overwhelm the barriers with aid.

The analysis and the prescriptions proved to be faulty. The West and the Soviets provided much aid and advice to developing countries, but the results were poor. China and Ethiopia's Soviet-inspired economic policies produced devastating famines in the 1960s and 1980s, respectively. Soviet growth turned out not to be durable. As their economy stagnated in the 1980s, the Soviets desperately searched for models of reform, and developing countries increasingly turned to the West instead for assistance and advice. Unfortunately, however, the capitalist system also failed to operate as well in developing countries as it did in Europe and North America. In countries that followed the advice and accepted the assistance provided by the industrialized world, the results ranged from disappointing to disastrous. Latin America initially grew rapidly under programs of import substitution, but stagnated in the 1970s and 1980s. India posted a consistent rate of growth of 4 per cent among its Hindu population, but this was not enough to lift the country's rapidly growing population out of poverty.

Countries that thrived were neither capitalist nor socialist in a Western sense: Japan, the Asian tigers (South Korea, Thailand, Indonesia, and Malaysia) and post-Mao China followed a more or less capitalist path, but incorporated less-than-free market elements. Asian governments routinely allocated credit and guided investments. China grew rapidly during the 1980s and 1990s after abandoning communism in all but name, but did not formally guarantee property rights until the new millennium.

The apparent failure of both Western capitalism and Soviet communism in developing countries has now led to a re-evaluation of the sources of growth. The Soviets began first. In the 1970s some Soviet economists started to note the difficulties for development presented by culture and customs, and put forward the idea that the complexity of developing countries' experiences was the reason for Soviet failures in the developing world.

The West followed with its own rethink somewhat later, leading in the late 1980s and early 1990s to the so-called "Washington Consensus," which laid out a series of prescriptions for developing countries, including fiscal discipline, privatization, and trade liberalization. Recent disappointment with the Washington Consensus has caused economists to rethink yet again, and to look at the "nature" of developing countries that has made them so resistant to economic wisdom. Many have concluded, as Dani Rodrik notes, that:

The encounter between neo-classical economics and developing societies served to reveal the institutional underpinnings of market economies. A clearly delineated system of property rights, a regulatory apparatus curbing the worst forms of fraud, anti-competitive behavior, and moral hazard, a moderately cohesive society exhibiting trust and social cooperation, social and political institutions that mitigate risk and manage social conflicts, the rule of law and clean government—these are social arrangements that economists usually take for granted, but which are conspicuous by their absence in poor countries.[5]

In this way, today's development economists have shifted their gaze away from capital accumulation towards the study of institutions, reflecting the growing belief that the primary cause of economic troubles in the Third World is not a lack of capital but poor leadership and weak institutions. The history of Soviet economic and technical assistance to Afghanistan bears out this belief, showing that the reasons why the flood of Soviet assistance failed to substantially boost the Afghan economy were as much political and institutional as economic.

This book explains the failure of the Soviet effort by placing it in the context of evolving Western and Soviet theories about the appropriate means of development for Third World countries. The evidence shows that Soviet economic and technical assistance was more well- intentioned than Western commentators have assumed, but that the Soviets were often economically naive. Contrary to Western claims that Soviet assistance was meant to reduce Afghanistan to a position of dependence, it is clear that the Soviets did genuinely intend their help to stimulate economic growth. However, this growth did not materialize. To their credit, the Soviets were aware very early on of the importance of institutions in economic development, which put them in some respects ahead of their Western counterparts. But while their critiques of Afghan institutional failings were often astute, they struggled to find better structures, and in the end their efforts to solve Afghanistan's political and institutional problems only made things worse.

INTRODUCTION

Soviet Assistance to Afghanistan—An Unexamined Subject

In December 1979 troops of the Soviet 40th Army crossed the Amu Darya River which marked the border between Afghanistan and the Soviet Union. The soldiers moved easily south into Afghanistan, rapidly occupying the major population centers. But their initial success did not last long. Like so many invaders before and after, the Soviets found that while overrunning Afghanistan might be easy, holding it is not. Over the subsequent ten years, thousands of Soviet soldiers were killed and tens of thousands more were wounded; the war added to the already severe economic strains on the Soviet Union, and the international prestige of the Union of Soviet Socialist Republics (USSR) suffered irreversible damage.

The conduct of the Soviet war effort has tended to overshadow everything else the Soviets did in Afghanistan during that decade and the preceeding thirty years. Books covering the war years rarely acknowledge the economic and technical assistance provided by Soviet civilians during the 1980s, and when they do it tends to consist of no more than a passing mention. For instance, Henry Bradsher's 1999 book *Afghan Communism and Soviet Intervention* devotes a mere two pages to Soviet economic and technical assistance.[6] Similarly, Gregory Feifer's 2009 book about the Soviet occupation of Afghanistan, *The Great Gamble*, mentions on one page that "Moscow sent thousands of economic advisers to oversee major new construction projects, including the building of hospitals and power stations and expansion of Kabul airport," and then spends the rest of its 300 or so pages recounting military operations.[7] We are thus provided with a hint that something significant was going on, but are never told exactly what it was. The most recent English-language book on the subject, Rodric Braithwaite's 2011 work entitled *Afgantsy*, is somewhat better in this regard, but it still leaves a lot to the imagination. The author devotes a whole chapter to the Soviet civilian effort in Afghanistan, and gives a more positive spin to Soviet motivations than was the case in Cold War-era publications. But his emphasis is almost entirely on the personal experiences of the Soviet citizens who served in Afghanistan. He provides very little detail of what they actually did in terms of economic development.[8] This is very much par for the course.

Feifer and Braithwaite at least mention the economic effort of the war years. Many earlier accounts focused exclusively on the military occupation. As noted in a recent report produced by the Canadian Department of National Defence, "economic development in Afghanistan in the 1980s is largely overlooked by analysts and rarely discussed in the extant literature."[9] This, the Department of National Defence points out, is important as "it was not on the battlefield where Soviet strategy failed but in their efforts to influence Afghan social dynamics and to address crucial economic sustainability issues facing the government of Afghanistan."[10]

Interestingly, the neglect of the subject is as true of Soviet and subsequent Russian publications as it is of Western ones. Although military operations have been well covered by books such as General A.A. Liakhovskii's *Doblest i tragediia Afgana*[11] and the Russian General Staff's study of the war (published in English under the title of *The Soviet-Afghan War*),[12] with the exception of several book chapters by authors such as L.B. Teplinskii,[13] almost nothing has been written by Russians about Soviet economic aid to Afghanistan either during the 1980s or before.

With all this being said, there are some exceptions to this lack of interest. For instance, a 1986 book on the occupation by J. Bruce Amstutz devoted considerable attention to Soviet economic assistance,[14] as did a 1985 country study by American University in Washington, DC,[15] and a handful of scholarly articles produced in the mid1980s.[16] Since the end of the Cold War, however, almost no work has been done on the subject, either in Russia or in the West. The notable exceptions are a short paper published by the Afghanistan Analysts Network comparing Soviet and American state-building experiences,[17] and the above-mentioned study produced by the Canadian Department of National Defence in 2007.[18] Entitled *Economic Development in Afghanistan during the Soviet Period, 1979–1989*, the latter is indicative of a renewed interest in the subject, but it is limited in its coverage. The subject clearly remains under-researched.

Unfortunately, Cold War biases taint much of the literature concerning Soviet assistance, on both the Soviet and the Western sides. Most of the Western commentators viewed Soviet aid in an almost totally negative light, while such Soviet and pro-Soviet writing as exists on the subject tends to consist of little more than a catalog of completed aid projects peppered with propagandistic statements about the fulfillment of "internationalist duty." An early example of this is a 1958 book chapter by L.B. Teplinskii on the subject of the history of Soviet-Afghan relations. According to Teplinskii:

The economic aid provided by the Soviet Union to Afghanistan has a disinterested character. The same principle guides the Soviet government in its relations with other countries. ... The Soviet Union provides disinterested, active help to economically underdeveloped countries, so that, by liquidating their backwardness, they can become economically stronger. The Afghan people know that the Soviet Union, when it provides them with economic aid, will meet their requests and will not put any conditions. The aid provided by the Soviet Union is distinguished from the "aid" given to Afghanistan by Western powers. The capitalist countries, as a rule, do not want to give weakly developed countries credits to develop industry, so that these countries can eliminate their backwardness.[19]

Thirty years later the tone remained the same. Lev Nikolaev, in a book published in English in 1987 in Moscow, celebrated the economic achievements of the Democratic Republic of Afghanistan (DRA) which built on projects completed by the USSR: "the chemical fertilizer plant in Mazar-i-Sharif … 1,600 km of modern motor roads … several power stations … a few agricultural farms. A mechanical plant, a housebuilding combine, a bread factory, and new housing developments," and others. "No few large enterprises that are pillars of the national economy were built with Soviet assistance," concluded Nikolaev.[20] A pro-Soviet book published India in the following year echoed Nikolaev's theme. According to the author, R.B. Gaur, "During the five years 1981–1986 the national income [of Afghanistan] rose by 11 per cent," despite enormous problems caused by the war. "Afghanistan could overcome all these hurdles," claimed Gaur, "only because of the selfless help rendered by the Soviet Union."[21]

Unsurprisingly, the Soviet press was equally enthusiastic about the selflessness of Soviet aid and the benefits it brought. As well as lists of completed development projects and ringing declarations that "Many industrial objects have been created in Afghanistan with the brotherly assistance of the Soviet Union,"[22] newspaper articles praised Soviet specialists working in Afghanistan who "fulfill their internationalist duty with all their strength, generously sharing their experience with Afghan workers and engineers."[23] Suitable quotations from grateful Afghans supported these assertions. The newspaper *Sotsialisticheskaia Industriia*, for instance, cited one Dzhomadin Zozai, an Afghan employee of the joint Afghan-Soviet transport company the Afgano-Sovetskoe Transportno-Ekspeditsionnoe Obschestvo (AFSOTR), as saying, "The sincere aspiration of the Soviet people to give their experience, to teach advanced methods of labor and industrial organization, is our society's most priceless capital. We are strongly convinced that with the help of our Soviet friends we can soon stand on our own feet."[24]

It is easy to mock such Soviet writings as pure propaganda, but there seems little reason to doubt the 2006 claim by Viktor Korgun, head of the

Afghanistan Faculty in the Institute of Oriental Studies of the Russian Academy of Sciences, that many of the Soviets who worked in Afghanistan "sincerely wished to help the Afghan people in the socio-economic and cultural spheres."[25] As Rodric Braithwaite points out, "Many of the Soviet advisers genuinely believed in their mission to help the local people and were wholeheartedly enthusiastic about it."[26] Perhaps because of that sincerity, while modern Russian officials and historians have been very willing to criticize the conduct of the Soviet Army in Afghanistan, Russians have yet to conduct any similar critical analysis of Soviet economic aid projects. The prevailing view remains, in Korgun's words, that, "From the moment that troops entered the country in 1979, Soviet specialists enjoyed the deep respect of simple Afghans, regardless of the official line adopted by the leadership of both countries. A true friendship cemented many of them together."[27] Similarly, Valerii Ivanov, former secretary of the Permanent Soviet-Afghan Commission on Economic Cooperation, said in a December 2008 interview with one of the authors of this book that, "The most unsuccessful thing was the arrival of the army, but all the rest went not at all badly."[28]

Needless to say, the view of the few Western authors who have chosen to comment on Soviet economic assistance to Afghanistan has been very different. The focus is overwhelmingly on the 1950s and 1960s, and Soviet aid projects are most often viewed through the prism of the later invasion and occupation, being discussed primarily as a means of explaining growing Soviet influence and interest in Afghanistan prior to the decision to invade. For instance, the fact that the Soviet Army eventually used much of the infrastructure the USSR had built in Afghanistan for military purposes is seen as evidence that the infrastructure was constructed with the aim of facilitating an eventual invasion.[29] As M.S. Noorzoy wrote, "In the views of the Afghan public and foreign observers, this highway [between the Soviet border and Kandahar] ... was constructed less to accommodate normal commercial traffic, but, rather to support heavy (Soviet) military traffic."[30] This is despite the fact that the Soviets had absolutely no plans to invade Afghanistan until late 1979, and even during most of 1979 the USSR rejected numerous pleas by the Afghan government to intervene before eventually doing so in December. Just as it would be foolish to analyze American aid to Afghanistan prior to 1979, including the building of roads in the south of the country and the construction of Kandahar airport (now, of course, a major NATO base), through the lens of the American arrival in

Afghanistan in 2001, taking all construction as evidence that the Americans had been preparing the way for military operations for decades, it would be foolish to allow the Soviet invasion of 1979 to color one's perceptions of everything that the Soviets did before that date.

In general, Western writings on Soviet aid are descriptive rather than analytical. In most cases, little or no effort is made to determine what the economic impact of the aid was, what succeeded and what failed, and why. In other instances, little information is provided to substantiate the assessments that are made. A few authors are willing to admit that some Soviet projects did occasionally bring some positive results. Martin Ewans, for instance, comments that "Some of the projects were less than successful, but others made a positive contribution to Afghanistan's infrastructure."[31] Similarly, J. Bruce Amstutz points out that, "Not all Soviet projects were of low quality, however. The paved roads built by the Soviets were uniformly good, notably the 425 mile highway between Kandahar and Herat… On balance, Afghans believed that Soviet trade and economic aid were beneficial."[32]

Most authors are less generous. For instance, in his seminal study of Afghanistan, American anthropologist Louis Dupree commented on several Soviet projects which had failed to fulfill expectations: the Ghori hydroelectric power plant produced less power than planned,[33] while the Ningrahar Valley irrigation project proved to be extremely expensive, for instance.[34] Overall, he concluded, the Soviets "failed to consider adequately the human factor in the developing countries; i.e., the inward-looking, peasant-tribal society. … Soviet planners ignored the difficulties of changing a society (i.e., its values and attitudes) by economic means alone."[35] Dupree was equally critical of American aid projects in Afghanistan.

During the 1980s, nearly all of the very few Western authors who examined Soviet aid to Afghanistan portrayed in the most hostile manner everything the Soviets did and had done, both before and after the invasion. An extreme, but not entirely unrepresentative example was an edited volume published by the American institution Freedom House in 1990. Its editor Rosanne Klass declared that in Afghanistan, "the USSR is following the classic pattern of colonial exploitation, and is doing so with a crudeness seldom seen among other imperialist powers after the nineteenth century; one must look back to the Belgian Congo under Leopold II to find its like."[36] Soviet aid, wrote John F. Shroder Jr. and Abdul Tawab Assifi, was "couched in terminology the Soviets filched from the Marshall Plan and its successors: 'developmental aid,' 'technical assistance,' 'economic assistance,' and similar terms well-suited to the sensibilities of Third World countries. In reality, it has taken the form of the crudest and crassest colonial exploitation."[37]

In writings of this sort, anything done by the Soviets acquired a sinister character. Thus prospecting for and the subsequent mining of hydrocarbons and minerals were depicted not as efforts to aid the Afghan economy, but rather as a strategy to grab Afghanistan's resources at rock-bottom prices. The provision of education and training for Afghans was depicted as an attempt to "indoctrinate." According to Leon B. Poullada, "Soviet programs were devised to win the gratitude of the Afghan public and impress them with Soviet benevolence, so as to lull them into a false sense of security."[38]

The prevailing orthodoxy, which still has some purchase, is that "Soviet-Afghan economic relations were geared to create dependence and to integrate the Afghan economy with the Soviet economy."[39] The theory was that by lending money to Afghanistan to develop industry and infrastructure, the Soviet Union planned to place Afghans in a position of indebtedness. To pay off their debts, they would then be forced to sell their natural resources to the Soviet Union at well below world market prices, as well as to accept the presence of Soviet advisors. Little by little, under the guise of economic assistance, Afghanistan would become trapped in a position of not merely economic dependence, but more importantly, also political subservience.[40] According to Poullada:

A careful analysis of the extensive Soviet economic, military and cultural programs set in motion during the first Daoud regime, 1953–1963, reveals a coherent, integrated, and premeditated plan, disguised as something the Afghans themselves wanted and needed but in fact serving first and foremost Soviet political, economic and strategic interests.

The aim was "the creation of a subversive infrastructure within Afghanistan,"[41] which would eventually lead to the takeover of the country. The invasion of Afghanistan in 1979 was seen as the logical outcome of this process, and the desire to exploit Afghanistan's natural resources was seen as a primary purpose of the Soviet military occupation.

These theories are unfairly negative. As Antony Hyman notes, "The common theme of Afghan nationalists, that the Soviet intervention in their country took place because of Soviet aims to exploit the mineral resources, greatly exaggerates the importance of the economic motives, which were secondary to considerations of Soviet border security, prestige and ideology."[42] Similarly, as we shall see in the chapters that follow, rather than wishing to reduce Afghanistan to a position of dependence, the Soviets actually believed that their assistance would help to eliminate that dependence. Western claims to the contrary are a product of Cold War thinking rather than of objective analysis. The end of the Cold War provides an opportunity to review the subject of Soviet economic and technical assistance free from that era's biases and to produce a more balanced analysis than has hitherto been possible. In addition, advances in our understanding of the processes of international development allow us to examine the issue through new theoretical lenses.

Soviet aid to Afghanistan was substantial, but ultimately unsuccessful. In the pages that follow we aim to understand why.

2

MODELS OF DEVELOPMENT
AND SOVIET THEORIES

Soviet economic and technical assistance failed to produce the economic progress the Afghans needed and the Soviets had hoped for. Poor results were partly a product of the peculiar circumstances of Afghanistan. They were also in part a product of the approach the Soviets adopted. The failure of Soviet economic assistance was not unique to Afghanistan; many other client states failed to prosper despite Soviet help. The failure was also not unique to the Soviets; aid provided by the West both to Afghanistan and to other countries also often proved unsuccessful. In fact, to this day, finding the correct approach to development and foreign assistance has proven to be exceptionally difficult.

To help explain why, this chapter analyses the factors which inhibited economic progress in Afghanistan, as well as the theories and practices of development and foreign assistance that were followed by both the West and the Soviet Union over the past sixty years. The thinking in both Cold War blocs changed over time, moving towards an increasing emphasis on the role of institutions in development and an acknowledgement that development is extremely difficult without institutional reform. However, determining the shape of that reform and how to carry it out is also extremely problematic. Institutions tend to resist change, and institutional reform imposed from outside often fails. The Soviet experience in Afghanistan bears witness to these conclusions.

AIDING AFGHANISTAN

The Situation in Afghanistan Prior to 1953

Development programs in Afghanistan did not suffer from a lack of natural resources. Afghanistan contains over 1,400 mineral deposits, including hydrocarbons, valuable deposits of iron and copper, and precious stones (see Table 1). The most important resource in the context of foreign economic assistance are natural gas deposits in the north of the country, close to the border with the Soviet Union. The Soviets identified some 90 billion cubic meters of proven reserves of natural gas in these areas, and estimated that perhaps another 50 billion cubic meters were present. With their help, natural gas was to become a major source of revenue for Afghan governments in the 1970s and 1980s. The Soviets also identified some 12 million cubic meters of oil, although this is a relatively small amount, about 0.1 per cent of the oil deposits of Kuwait,[1] and was thus unlikely to ever be a significant source of revenue.

Afghanistan also possesses some significant deposits of metals, especially copper and iron. The Aynak copper deposits in Loghar province, about 35 kilometers from Kabul, are possibly the largest in the world, holding up to 12 million tons of high quality copper. The Soviets identified 111 million tons of proven reserves of iron at Hajigak in Bamyan province and estimated that several billion tons still remained to be discovered. In addition, there are minor deposits of gold, chrome, uranium, lead, zinc, and other metals. Other valuable resources include over 70 million tons of coal, marble, barytes, and precious and semi-precious stones, such as emeralds, rubies and lapis lazuli.

While in theory the mining and taxing of these resources could have provided Afghan governments with an independent source of revenue with which to create a strong state, in practice Afghans have lacked the necessary technical know-how. In addition, large-scale resource exploitation has been impossible without the basic infrastructure of roads, railways and electricity, which Afghanistan has lacked. Building this infrastructure is extremely expensive, especially given the mountainous nature of much of Afghanistan, and beyond the means of the Afghan state or private Afghan industries without foreign support. It is not surprising, therefore, that Afghan governments from the 1950s onwards regarded foreign aid (both financial and technical) as essential to the country's economic development.

When Afghanistan began its economic relationship with the Soviet Union in the 1920s, and after 1953 when that relationship began to become much closer, it was, as it still is today, a primarily agricultural soci-

Table 1: Soviet Estimates of Afghan Mineral Resources.[2]

Type of Resource	Location	Estimated Reserves
Natural Gas	Khoja-Gugerdak	58.6 m^3
	Jarquduk	26.8 m^3
	Yatimtak	6.2 m^3
	Juma	21.4 m^3
	Jangali-Kolon	19.9 m^3
	Bashi Kurd	9.6 m^3
	Khoja Bulan	2.5 m^3
Oil	Angot	2.16 million tons
	Ak-Darya	2.01 million tons
	Others	8.2 million tons
Coal	Shabashek	44.4 million tons proven
		29.3 million tons estimated
	Sabzak	9.5 million tons
Iron	Hajigak	111 million tons
Copper	Aynak	8.05 million tons proven
		3.0 million tons estimated
Gold	Zarkashan	6,100 tons
	Samti	7,800 tons
Uranium	Khanneshin	4,150 tons
Barytes	Sangilyan	1.5 million tons
Lapis Lazuri	Sar-e-Sang	206 tons proven
		1295 estimated
Emerald	Darkhenj	95,400 tons
Marble Onyx	Malik-Dukan	760,000 tons

ety. The overwhelming majority of the population lived in rural areas and engaged in subsistence production. There was almost no industrial production, a fragmented internal market, and a poorly developed transport network. Mortality rates were high and levels of education low.

A number of geographic, social, and political factors had led to a lack of economic development. Afghanistan's rugged geography made communications and road-building between parts of the country difficult. Given the almost total absence of paved roads until the 1950s, and the limited scale of road-building thereafter, as well as the absence of railways, there were few opportunities for large-scale internal trade. Such trade as existed was mostly in the form of barter, and "commercial money was virtually unknown outside of the towns."[3] The first Afghan bank only came into being in 1932.[4]

Prior to the Second World War, "Transport of goods was almost always by camel, donkey, or horse, for there were few roads and none for year-round travel. Electricity was nowhere to be found."[5]

Agriculture provided some export opportunities, particularly pelts of kara-kul sheep but also some fruits. Overall, though, cash crops did not account for a significant part of agricultural output. Afghan farms were mostly very small, providing those who worked them with little to sell. As late as 1978, "two-thirds of holdings were smaller than two hectares (five acres), and almost 40 per cent of the landowning households had the equivalent of less than one hectare of good irrigated land."[6] There was a perpetual threat of drought, while the small size of holdings hampered the introduction of modern farming technologies, such as tractors, even if the rural population had sufficient funds to afford them (which, of course, they did not).

Geography had the additional effect of fragmenting the country politically. In a country where nationwide communications were difficult, loyalties remained local. The fact that Afghanistan contains numerous ethnic groups accentuated this problem, depriving Afghans of a strong sense of national unity. The border between Afghanistan and British India (now Pakistan) cut the largest ethnic group, the Pashtuns, in two, with Pashtuns living in both Afghanistan and Pakistan. Pashtun ambitions to reunite in a "greater Pashtunistan" have been a continuous source of tension with Pakistan. Disputes over "Pashtunistan" led to the Afghan-Pakistani border being closed on several occasions in the 1950s and 1960s, impelling Afghan leaders to divert trade to the Soviet Union and to seek Soviet help as a counterbalance to Pakistan.

Throughout the 20th century, Afghanistan also had a relatively weak central government, which lacked the authority to enforce economic reform on a reluctant country even when it wished to do so. With little capacity to raise taxes, the Afghan state had few sources of revenue with which to fund development projects. Land and livestock taxes were not increased for many years, despite inflation, and as a result the volume of taxes gathered from agriculture declined over time.[7] A survey of fifty developing countries undertaken in the 1970s revealed that "only Nepal had a lower tax effort—the ratio of actual tax revenues to estimated taxable capacity—than Afghanistan."[8] This had a debilitating effect on state finances and increased the state's dependence on foreign loans.

Even had the Afghan state had more funds at its disposal, a severe shortage of trained personnel meant that it would have been hard put to use them efficiently. Few Afghans received even basic schooling, and higher education was a rare luxury. The state was reliant on foreign specialists to enact its plans. Yet unfortunately, as knowledgeable as they may have been in their fields, they were generally ignorant of local conditions. Only a massive investment in education could hope to overcome this problem, and then only over a period of many years.

Forces Hindering Modernization

In any case, social and political factors stood in the way of economic reform. Powerful forces within the country actively resisted modernization efforts. According to Antonio Giustozzi, the fundamental problem was that "the tribal character of the aristocracy meant that it was culturally bound to a model of revenue redistribution (geared towards maintaining a retinue and local support) that constrained accumulation."[9] Giustozzi notes that "at least part of the aristocracy viewed the emergence of an industrial bourgeoisie with suspicion or outright hostility."[10] As a result, government "development strategies were meant more as window dressing than as serious efforts to change the structural basis of the country's economy."[11] As we shall see, Soviet economists shared this belief, as it fitted in with their preconceived view that capital accumulation in Third World countries was hindered by outdated social structures. The Soviets therefore concluded that economic progress in Afghanistan was impossible without a profound social and political revolution. When it came, however, the revolution produced a violent backlash, which, far from eliminating the barriers to progress, threw up even more barriers.

In theory, foreign economic and technical assistance should have helped Afghanistan to surmount these barriers. In practice, it may have added to the problem. In his 1995 book *The Fragmentation of Afghanistan*, Barnett Rubin comments that the effect of international aid, both Soviet and Western, was to turn Afghanistan into a "rentier" state which "financed over 40 percent of its expenditures from 'revenue accruing directly from abroad',", in the form of foreign aid and sales of natural gas to the Union of Soviet Socialist Republics.[12] This percentage continued to grow and by the mid1980s was over 60 per cent.[13] Reliance on foreign sources of revenue bypasses the requirement to adequately tax one's citizens, thus creating a divide between people and government and reducing the need for the latter to be accountable to the former.

Rubin's analysis is primarily political, but it has economic ramifications. Paradoxically, the main effect of foreign aid may have been to promote corruption and government inefficiency, thereby reducing the institutional capacity of successive Afghan governments to promote the kind of reform at the lowest levels of society which would have been required to pull the country into the industrial age.

The Mechanics of Economic Growth

These factors represented problems that were specific to Afghanistan. There were also more general obstacles to economic growth which were common to developing countries everywhere in the period after World War II. In brief, both Soviet and Western economists initially viewed the problem of development as one of capital accumulation. Over time, the failures of economic assistance led to a revision of this position and a growing awareness that other factors were also important. Soviet economists determined that in Afghanistan and other developing countries a whole range of social and political barriers stood in the way of progress. In essence, although they used different terminology, the Soviets reached the same position now occupied by most in the West, namely that institutions—the rules of the social game—were the key element. To understand this conclusion, as well as the role and limitations of development assistance, and place the Soviet effort in its correct context, it is necessary to make a diversion into theories of economic growth, with particular reference to the role of institutions.

For most of human history, the world economy expanded only as fast as the population, much in the manner described by Thomas Malthus, who stated in his 1798 *Essay on the Principle of Population* that population grew, on average, to match economic growth.[14] Such an economy provided for little, or no, increase in average incomes. With the industrial revolution, however, the logic of Malthusian growth gave way in some countries to a new process, in which growth in productive capacity by far outstripped increases in population. Accordingly, after 1850 Western Europe and parts of North America experienced unprecedented increases in living standards and declining levels of poverty.

Once a country had passed beyond the Malthusian stage of development, the forces of growth were considered to be the same in both the capitalist and the communist world. So-called "factor accumulation," especially the accumulation of physical capital and, with less emphasis, human capital, was considered the secret to growth.[15] It was believed that developing countries suffered from a failure to accumulate, due to barriers that could be removed by the Western-prescribed reforms or overwhelmed by Soviet-prescribed brute force.[16]

Nobel Prize winner Robert Solow postulated growth models which development experts use to explain differences in levels of development through populations' accumulated savings. Savings financed investment, the building of capital and the concomitant increase in productive capacity. Poorer countries were poor because they had not yet built enough capital. Once they had the opportunity to do so, their living standards and growth rates would converge with those of the industrialized countries.

Convergence follows from the diminishing marginal returns of capital. There is only so much machinery and equipment that workers can use efficiently. More and better tools increase the ability of labor to produce, but each new tool offers less additional output than the one before. The industrialized world had already built a large stock of capital; building more would bring only meager returns, according to this theory. Developing countries, on the other hand, are almost by definition capital-poor. Investment in capital should therefore offer large returns of goods and services to developing societies. Developing countries should, therefore, be a magnet for investment.

Developing Countries' Experiences

Unfortunately, this has not happened. Contrary to the expectations of the conventional growth models, most developing countries have converged only slowly, if at all. Furthermore, capital has tended to flow out of poor countries and to the already capital-rich developed world. Why developing countries consistently failed to converge with developed world incomes, or did so slowly, in spite of ostensibly high returns to capital, was, and is, a mystery.

For most of the second half of the 20th century, advice to developing countries operated on the previously-cited idea that there were barriers preventing the country from taking advantage of high returns to capital. Either poor countries were in a poverty trap in which the lack of capital was itself the problem—the economy could not produce enough to save, and could not save enough to produce—or, in very poor countries, rural families could not send children to school because they could not spare the labor, and they could not spare the labor because they lacked the skills to produce efficiently. Alternatively, problems in the financial system might prevent a country from mobilizing capital. In this case, the root causes might be a lack of trust in society, especially between investors and firms, or insecure property rights. Herman de Soto has argued that a major problem in developing countries is that would-be borrowers have no legal title to the land that they use and live on. Lacking collateral, they cannot raise the funds they need to educate their children or start a business.[17]

Yet another possibility is that there are country-specific factors depressing returns on investment in physical capital and education. One possibility is that required complementarities between investments are lacking. For example, there may not be any point in building a factory if someone else has not built a power plant, and no point in building a power plant if there are no factories to use the electricity. Similarly, there is no point in acquiring skills if the only employment available is low-skilled, but one cannot build a high-skilled industry without a pool of skills to use. Returns from each activity may be high when they are combined, but are low for each one individually, and therefore they attract few investors.

Finally, in industries where scale is important or which take time to master, exposure to the world economy may discourage investment. For example, in a parallel universe Thailand might be a better watch producer than Switzerland. In this universe, though, the Swiss began making watches first. Having mastered the precision techniques required to make high quality watches efficiently, they make better and less expensive watches than any Thailand can produce now. Though they could eventually prove superior, Thai watch producers will not get the chance to hone their craft unless they are willing to incur a long period of losses.

Most advice and aid has been devoted to either removing or leaping over these barriers. In all cases, there was a range of solutions that seemed simple to implement. One cure-all method was to provide the capital directly: give developing countries the resources to invest. If the problem was too few resources at the start, an infusion from outside would be enough to give the economy a "big push" out of the poverty trap. Financial market problems could be similarly overcome by the government's mobilizing savings and allocating capital.

If the trap was caused by too few complementary investments, then it would fall to governments to make those investments. The state could build an apparently uneconomic dam to provide electricity, then, with access to cheap electricity, complementary private investments would justify its construction *post factum*. Developed countries could aid this process by providing capital and also, where developing countries lacked the expertise to build what was needed, building it for them. If they had difficulty operating it, advisors could be sent to help and train the staff.

Soviet economists especially, but many Western ones as well, suggested that lack of development was a function of openness to the world economy. Development has often been considered synonymous with mastering manufacturing industries. These industries were the most productive. They were also capital-intensive, so investment in them furthered capital accumulation. As infant industries, they were often uneconomic, but only until they were of sufficient size and workers had become sufficiently proficient at their tasks. But once mastered, knowledge and skills gained in manufacturing would form the basis for a growing and dynamic economy. As infants, however, they could not compete in world markets with established Western industries.

As a remedy to this last problem, the Soviets in particular, but also many Western economists, advocated substantial government intervention in the manufacturing sector, plus a decoupling of developing countries from the world economy. The Soviets were also particularly keen on the nationalization of key industries, both as an end in itself and as a method of reorienting resources for the greater social good.

Problems of Development

The prescriptions of the 1950s and 1960s led to substantially less progress than development theorists had hoped. Infusions of capital did not generate the expected positive dynamics. Hydroelectric dams did not after all lead to much in the way of factory building, and both dams and the factories that were built operated substantially below capacity. Infant industries remained infants. Insulation from the competitive pressures of the global economy merely encouraged the growth of unproductive industries. The consequences of less, instead of more, efficient production spilled over to the wider economy, hampering growth everywhere.

Perhaps as a result, and contrary to the predictions of standard growth models, factor accumulation explains little of the differences between countries. A study by American economists William Easterly and Ross Levine found that only 40 per cent of growth can be explained by differences in capital accumulation.[18] It also found divergence, not convergence, in incomes across developed and developing countries.

Even countries that did successfully manage to industrialize found their prospects limited when diminishing returns set in. The Soviets themselves found their economy slowing down by the 1960s, although this was obscured for a long time by inflated resource prices and easy international credit. The Asian tigers grew rapidly until the mid 1990s, but growth slowed before their living standards had truly converged to Western levels.

Other developing countries were less successful: in spite of large capital investments and generous support for manufacturing, Latin American economies went sideways from the 1970s, and African economies went almost nowhere after independence. Development was not, or was not only, a question of large dams and heavy industry. In light of experience, therefore, by the 1980s both the West and the Soviets began to re-evaluate their advice.

The soul-searching took two lines. First, there was added emphasis on improving efficiency, for instance through the privatization of government-owned firms. Western economists had by the end of the 1980s reached a "Washington Consensus" (named after the location of the World Bank and the International Monetary Fund).[19] The consensus recommended that governments exercise fiscal restraint and monetary probity along with pri-vatization and an opening of markets. Many Soviet, and later Russian, economists joined this consensus. In both the West and the East, econo-mists thus recommended turning inefficient government-owned firms over to the private sector.

For the most part, economists in both camps also no longer believed in countries isolating themselves from the global marketplace. They realized that most developing countries did not have a large enough market to build industries that relied on economies of scale, and that even those that did could not forgo the opportunities for acquiring the technology and learning afforded by the international market and expect to prosper.

Both the Soviets and Western economists hoped to foster growth in developing countries by better aligning incentives and improving the alloca-tion of resources. Developing countries implemented these prescriptions with varying degrees of enthusiasm and with varying but usually disap-pointing degrees of success. Programs designed to rapidly improve eco-nomic efficiency, so-called "Shock Therapy," in Eastern Europe and the former Soviet Union itself did not prevent large falls in output and incomes. Countries like China and the Asian tigers, on the other hand, had adopted portions of the Washington Consensus but violated others. They grew at astounding rates.

The failure of so many developing countries to thrive despite heeding the advice and accepting the aid offered by the West (and the success of some in spite of ignoring it) has led to yet another re-examination of the prerequisites for growth, this time with an emphasis on political and cultural issues.

Institutions and Economic Growth

In a lecture in 1775, Adam Smith commented that, "Little else is requisite to carry a state to the highest degree of opulence from the lowest barbarism but peace, easy taxes, and a tolerable administration of justice: all the rest being brought about by the natural course of things."[20] Smith's view of the development process emphasizes its institutional underpinnings, but perhaps understates how complex they are and how difficult it is to create them. Many states have struggled to attain and maintain a peaceful concord between the powerful to keep guns in pockets, rapacious hands at bay, and the affairs of the country adjudicated in an even-handed fashion. A lack of one or all of these institutional prerequisites usually shows up in lackluster development.

Economists concerned with development have recognized the importance of institutions, but until recently practical attention has been devoted to the tangible aspects of economic growth. Accumulating capital was much simpler to engineer, and both the Soviets and the West were more comfortable with engineering solutions than with culture and politics. Now, however, the failure of the previous prescriptions proffered by industrialized countries has caused economists to revaluate the centrality of institutions in supporting development. A 21st century consensus has emerged that "institutions rule."[21]

This in turn begs the questions of what institutions are, what they do, and how one acquires them. The Soviets did not have a convincing answer when attempting to create them in Afghanistan in the 1950s, 1960s, 1970s, and 1980s. Neither do economists today. It is clear, in broad strokes, what institutions need to do. But we know too little about the forms they should take in developing countries, and we know even less about how to mould a country's existing institutions to support development.

What Are Institutions and What Do They Do

Rich countries' institutions have evolved over centuries to support high rates of economic growth. Unfortunately, attempts to transplant the growth-supporting aspects of those institutions to other countries have not met with similar success. One major problem is that institutions are poorly understood, as is their connection to the economy.

Institutions, in Nobel Laureate Douglass North's conception, are the rules of a social game.[22] Rules for the economic aspect of the game clarify rights and obligations with respect to resources and how they are transformed and distributed. They consist of both informal norms that develop organically to regulate social interaction, and formal written rules codified by a country's political institutions.

Institutions serve three purposes: to clarify, to constrain, and to sanction. First, they make clear rights and responsibilities. They also provide a predictable way of resolving disputes when there are disagreements over who owns and who owes what. By removing uncertainty, they create a predictable environment for production and exchange.

Second, they constrain agents from undertaking privately profitable but socially destructive activities. There is an ever-present temptation to violate property rights and to renege on contracts. Insecure property rights discourage investment; why build only to have it stolen? Insecure contracts discourage transactions; it is harder to make mutually profitable deals in the absence of trust.

Finally, there are enforcement mechanisms. Violating the rules leads to an appropriate punishment, the credible threat of which encourages economic agents to play fairly. Sanctions may include informal mechanisms, such as shunning, or formally administered fines, imprisonment or limited uses of force. In the absence of such constraints and sanctions life would be, as Thomas Hobbes described it, "solitary, poor, nasty, brutish, and short."[23] Life may be longer and less nasty when the rules are merely inadequate or poorly enforced, but it is still usually poor. Inadequate institutions actively discourage investments in capital and education when they create uncertainty over rights and obligations, and leave disputes to be resolved by open conflict. Good rules, on the other hand, encourage investment in socially beneficial economic activity.

The Structure of Institutions

John Williamson provides a useful schematic for analyzing institutions. He identifies four levels of activity and associated institutions, differentiated by purpose, persistence and origins.[24] At the highest level is culture, followed by political institutions, governance, and finally economic activity.

Customs, traditions and taboos form the first level. They develop spontaneously and are only tangentially entangled with the economy.[25] They are informal guides to citizens' conduct that inform all relationships, including the economic ones. The problem with these types of informal institutions is that they are rarely connected to rational calculation, which often makes them all but impervious to rational argument. It also makes them impenetrable to study by economics, a discipline that has the assumption of rationality at its core. They are also extremely persistent, evolving slowly over hundreds of years. Attempts to change them rapidly have often ended badly. The Soviets underwrote (although they often did not approve of) local Marxist proselytizers' plans to change overnight the customs of rural populations in client states such as Afghanistan, Ethiopia and Mozambique. The result was violent resistance that was supported even by the people whom the reforms were supposed to empower. In part this may have been due to the reforms' poor design and their ham-fisted implementation, but the resistance is also testament to the force of informal institutions.

Second level institutions are the rules that shape the political process. Their study is mainly the realm of political theory, and has thus traditionally been neglected by economists. Political institutions are a mixture of formal and informal rules that govern the interactions of the politically powerful.

One of the primary purposes of political institutions is to define the rights of citizens with respect to those who would infringe upon them, especially the government itself. The commitment to respect and to defend rights, including economic rights, is often codified in written constitutions, or is well known as part of unwritten ones. In most countries, these rules allow for some type of separation of powers between executive, legislative and judicial branches. The independence of the judicial branch is particularly important for defending the citizens' rights and obligations both with respect to government and to each other. The judiciary rules on laws that may have a direct or indirect effect on the value of resources held and developed by individuals.

These institutions are not as persistent as informal institutions, and from time to time they change, either gradually or through revolution. Revolutions are typically costly, however, and are often followed by economically destructive civil wars. Institutions more normally evolve slowly over time, at a pace measured in tens to hundreds of years.

The third level identified by Williamson is commonly referred to as governance. The government acts within the constraints of the second order

Level One
Informal Institutions
Spontaneous: customs, traditions, norms, religion

Level Two
Institutional Environment
Formal rules: property rights, polity, judiciary, bureaucracy

Level Three
Governance
Transaction costs, especially contracts

Level Four
Resource Allocation
Prices and quantities, incentive alignment

Figure 1: Institutional Levels.[26]

institutions to pass the laws, regulations and rules which frame economic activities. These define rights and obligations and resolve disputes when interpretations of them differ.

Governance is frequently about minimizing transaction costs, that is to say the problems associated with making and enforcing contracts. Some contracts are self-enforcing, in the sense that both parties are better off by fulfilling their obligations and thus have no incentive not to. In other cases, there are gains to be had in repudiating a contract after the other side has fulfilled its part, or in violating some of its conditions. These contracts require external enforcement.

It is not always easy to determine whether a party has fulfilled its part of the deal. Contrary to the assumption of many economic models, people do not have perfect information or perfect foresight. They may be rational, but within bounds set by their ability to gather information and to predict an inherently uncertain future. This limits their ability to determine whether their counterparts have fulfilled their obligations, especially when economic conditions change.

One interpretation of third level institutions is that they allow people to economize on information. When unforeseen circumstances arise that test the boundaries of the contracts, courts of law are in place to reinterpret them and peacefully resolve disputes where interpretations differ. When problems arise for which existing laws give no guidance, there are mechanisms to make new laws.

The fourth level of interactions is associated with the day-to-day economic decisions that determine how resources are allocated. These are the interactions that have traditionally occupied Western economic theory. The goal is to make these interactions as efficient as possible in deploying scarce resources. In developed countries, a lot of focus is put on allocating goods and services for consumption. In developing countries, it has been considered particularly important to further the accumulation of capital.

Consequences of Poor Institutions

Institutions are taken for granted when they function well. Developed countries' rules have generally functioned effectively, and so economists have rarely felt the need to model them explicitly. Institutions are most noticeable when they work poorly.[27]

In many countries, problems revolve around rules that are skewed to enhance elites' privileged access to resources. These "privileges" can take many forms. The most noticeable is corruption. The citizens of many countries are familiar with extra payments, informal "taxes" and other charges for "services" that are rendered for a single fairly predictable (tax, user fee) payment in industrialized countries. Many a tourist will remember remitting payments to police officers for imaginary infractions.

It should be noted that not all of these payments need be collected by officials of a government. Organizations like the mafia get their start governing in places and situations where formal rules are weakly enforced. Inner-city gangs in the US, drug cartels in Latin America, and rebel-cum-criminal movements like the Irish Republican Army (IRA) and the Revolutionary Armed Forces of Columbia (FARC) may be poor substitutes for the rule of law, but they do provide a framework for organized extortion where there would otherwise be just wanton destruction. They are even known to dabble in public service provision, as in the case of Hizbullah in Lebanon.

Unfortunately, in general, they provide services neither very cheaply, nor very well. The result is paradoxical, in that even in areas where the official government can collect no revenue, taxes are anything but light. Governments are replaced by large levies on economic activity, which tend to discourage investment and thus growth.

In the absence of other problems, reducing corruption would indeed be an important factor in encouraging development. Corruption is thus one of the most visible targets for international organizations. Many aid programs make combating it a prerequisite for receiving development aid. The problem here is that aid itself can be a major factor in fuelling corruption. As we shall see, this was the case in Afghanistan.

In many countries, however, corruption may not be the most important institutional failure. If it is not, then eliminating it may not improve growth and on occasion can actually make the situation worse. For example, side payments may sometimes allow entrepreneurs to surmount otherwise insurmountable barriers to investment. If corruption eases the way past such hurdles, it may be an important corrective for other institutional failings, rather than a key failure in itself.

It is true that studies have found that corruption is a net negative, and so worth combating.[28] But efforts at reducing the most visible forms of corruption, as worthwhile as they are, will not promote development if other institutions do not support it. In post-Suharto Indonesia, for example, combating corruption may actually have been detrimental to development, at least in the short - term, as familiar, predictable avenues to the law were blocked. The existing system was far from optimal, of course, and other avenues have since developed and have served Indonesia better. Nevertheless, eliminating corruption did not, in and of itself, move Indonesia to a better regime for growth.

More insidious are institutional shortcomings that offer elites more subtle ways to write the rules of the game for their own benefit. By crafting the laws to suit themselves, or by arranging to have the laws selectively enforced, they can extract rents for their private benefit to the detriment of the rest of the economy.

Rents are generated whenever the returns from an activity are greater than the expense and effort it requires. In many countries, control over a scarce and much sought-after resource offers riches far in excess of the costs of extracting it. Oil, in particular, has created greater wealth for many countries than would otherwise be expected at their level of development. Diamonds, minerals and even illicit drugs have a similar effect in many countries around the world.

Resources tend to be a mixed blessing for the countries that have them: they provide enormous wealth, but also incentives to squander it.[29] But even when they are absent, there are other malign ways of rewarding the politically connected. In the absence of naturally occurring rents, governments can create them by interfering in the economy. One of the most popular ways of redistributing resources is to restrict competition, for instance by granting powerful people monopoly powers. Restricting international trade and investment protects monopoly and oligopoly profits from without. Governments can also grant monopoly rights, issue production quotas and the like, to pay off domestic producers.

A less formal but equally effective way to distribute rents is to throw up barriers in front of would-be entrepreneurs. Requiring would-be domestic competitors to spend inordinate amounts of time, effort and money for the privilege of starting a business is a particularly popular way to protect the advantages of established producers. In developed countries, it takes only a handful of days to start a business. In less developed countries it can take over a year to acquire the necessary permits and licenses, and even then the process often requires paying bribes.

Rents can also be created in the interactions between workers and employers. Unions restrict the choices for employers, giving unionized workers the power to ask for a greater share of production, though this can come at the expense of workers outside the union's fold. Many developing countries, such as Argentina and India, suffer from excessively powerful unions, which may slow the pace of change in the industries in question.

Restrictions on labor can also be used to similar effect. One major way is to limit worker mobility. It is more difficult to extract taxes from people who can move out of reach. Some countries, most notably the communist ones, got around this by imposing internal restrictions of movement between cities, and/or professions.

Historically, in rural economies, depriving people of opportunities to move and confining them to the land has been important to preserve the rents of rural landowners. The key institutions here are as much at the cultural and constitutional levels of Williamson's schematic as they are on the level of government, but they cast a long shadow over both governance and resource allocation.

In many cases, some or all of the above-mentioned avenues for extracting and disseminating rents are in use. Interestingly, even in the presence of ample resource rents, elites tend to seek others as well.[30] The Saudi monarchy's oil wealth, for example, has led to an explosion of princes who collectively like to have more easy money than the kingdom's oil reserves can provide. Additional princes can always be placated with a monopoly, a concession or a no-bid contract.

Methods of generating and preserving rents affect the economy in two ways. First, there are static losses from trade forgone. Higher prices associated with monopolies discourage buyers, reducing the amounts produced. Less demand requires less investment in capital. With inadequate institutions, a lack of capital is a symptom of a lack of development, not the cause. Providing more capital will not solve the problem. Second, monopolies tend to be less innovative than firms that must constantly face competitive pressures. Entrepreneurs are typically the most innovative forces in the economy. Putting up barriers to them in favor of less productive cronies severely limits the dynamic potential of the economy.

Reforming Institutions

In Douglass North's conception, institutions develop organically: as much as they shape economic activity, they are also shaped by it. New technologies, new relationships and new activities often require the updating of old rules, and the invention of new ones. Rule changes affect how the economic activity unfolds, which then shapes the future demand for changes in institutions. The process is dynamic, with feedback between institutions and activity, promoting a constant evolution of both.

The quicker and more smoothly social and political institutions respond to new conditions, the more dynamic the economy can be. The problem with many developing countries is that institutions are slow to respond, or do so only at great social cost. Institutional torpor or brittleness hampers the adoption of new technology.

Changes in the demands for governance may lead to changes in political institutions, though not always in a direction that supports growth. Many countries respond to economic setbacks by reinforcing or returning to unfavorable political institutions. Similarly, economic booms can invite changes towards a more liberalized political system, but they can also lead away from political liberalization. The result of either type of change is often weak institutions, which permit and preside over a destructive struggle for resources.

In the wake of perceived failures of orthodox economics to stimulate durable growth in developing and transitional countries, including the former Soviet Union itself, neo-classical economists have been accused of ignoring the importance of institutions.[31] They were concerned with recreating the economic environment of the developed world, but without first creating the rules which make that environment prosper. The most prominent example of this failure is the rapid privatization of industry in Eastern Europe in the mid1990s. The purpose of privatization was to put assets in the hands of profit-hungry entrepreneurs who would then deploy them in the most efficient manner. Instead, in many countries, such as Russia, assets fell into the hands of oligarchs who then used their wealth to gain political influence, and, some argue, to write the country's new rules to preserve their power rather than to benefit the population as a whole.

Equally, much of the assistance given to developing countries concentrated primarily on increasing economic efficiency and underplayed the importance of institutional reforms. This partly reflected a reticence on the part of foreign advisors to tell developing countries how they should govern their countries. But it was also due to a belief that introducing new ways of allocating resources would cause the institutions to change in support of them.

One may argue that both the Western and Soviet approaches to development recognized the importance of institutions, but believed that changing economic relationships would inexorably lead to the desired institutional reforms. There was an implicit belief that the institutions would take care of themselves, perhaps responding to accommodate the investments. In the case of transition economies, newly minted profit-seekers would demand out of self-interest the reforms that would guarantee property rights and enforce contracts.

Institutional Change, Aid, and Development

Why some countries move to a favorable equilibrium and others remain in stagnant ones has produced a volume of literature. Concrete answers remain elusive, however. And because we know so little about how and why institutions change, we have little concrete advice to give on which reforms countries should undertake. For example, privatization may be advocated as a step for creating entrepreneurs who propel development, or not advised for fear of producing oligarchs who impede it.

The increasing emphasis on institutions has typically been associated with attempts to reform institutions from without, rather than from within.

Typically, institutions are associated with a bargain between powerful groups which are loath to upset it. First, they draw their legitimacy from it, and questioning the rules that put them in their place would undermine their own position. Second, the renegotiating process is fraught, often violent, and risks leaving all parties worse off.

Many foreign powers have tried to impose institutions on countries. They have mostly failed, and have found themselves either compromising with, or at the mercy of, existing institutions. When the U.S. occupied Japan, for example, they were committed to deposing Emperor Hirohito, whom they blamed for the war. They finally concluded that Japan would be too difficult to govern were the imperial system demolished, and opted instead to work through Japan's established institutions.

The Soviets supported regimes in countries like Afghanistan, Mozambique and Ethiopia as they tried to rapidly modernize rural institutions. Many of the attempted reforms may have been sensible, and even laudable, at least in principle. In Afghanistan, for instance, the communists enacted reforms that granted land to poor peasants, and undertook measures to liberate women in the countryside. The result, alas, was a massive popular uprising supported even by the very people whom the reforms were supposed to benefit. Soviet cautions were ignored, and the USSR was left as the sole backer of a failed regime. The Soviets were unable to impose institutional changes themselves, and were left at the mercy of their clients.

The current conflicts in Iraq and Afghanistan illustrate the same point. U.S. and U.S.-backed forces helped destroy the governing institutions in both countries (twice in the latter country). Once the Ba'ath Party in Iraq and the Communist Party and then the Taliban in Afghanistan were brought down, chaos ensued as more primitive institutions came to the fore. In the case of Iraq, the U.S. found itself supervising a civil war and being used by both sides to further agendas that were not its own.

The problem for outsiders attempting to influence or impose institutions is that they are playing a game with people who know the rules far better than they do and who have much more at stake. The result is that even well-intentioned reforms can be perverted. Moreover, they can easily provoke resistance. People who stand to lose, or even are unsure whether they stand to win, have an incentive to oppose reforms more vigorously than foreign powers have to impose them. While we may have learned that "institutions rule," we have yet to learn how best to reform them.

Soviet Views of Development and Economic Assistance

Soviet views on development and economic assistance shared many of the ideas mentioned above, albeit with different jargon and some differences in emphasis. In some regards, the Soviets were ahead of their Western counterparts in recognizing the importance of institutions, but they were no better at determining how to change them.

In a quantitative analysis of Soviet economic aid to the non-communist Third World, Charles Dannehl identifies two broad schools of interpretation of Soviet actions, which he refers to as the "strategic" and "interactionist" perspectives. According to the strategic perspective, the overwhelming motivation for the Soviet Union's economic and technical assistance to the Third World was political, namely to further the "expansion of its presence and influence." As a result, "Soviet Third World policy … demonstrated little concern for the developmental assistance needs of LDCs [less developed countries]."[32] Instead, "economic assistance promoted trade dependence by increasing the volume of imports and exports exchanged with the Soviet Union," and "the Soviet Union used this to capture Third World resources and markets, and to ensure the recipient's political compliance."[33]

According to the interactionist perspective, however, the Soviets had a broader range of motivations, including the concept that trade could be mutually beneficial, and their actions did in fact reflect changing ideas of the development needs of Third World countries. As Dannehl says, "According to interactionists, such developmental concerns supplemented but did not supplant the political and trade objectives. In other words, Soviet economic aid activities were driven by a combination of all three objectives."[34]

Having analyzed the patterns of Soviet aid, Dannehl then concludes:

The results obtained … suggest that the political, trade, and developmental objectives more closely conform to the expectations of the interactionist perspective than to those of the strategic perspective. Concerns for the developmental needs of LDCs apparently did affect Soviet economic aid decisions during the period from 1955 to 1989 … Simply put, interpretations of Soviet foreign economic aid activities based on expansionism, influence building, and to a lesser extent, trade benefits, have been inadequate and incorrect. They have failed to account for the diversity of objectives underlying Soviet aid activities … Full understanding of the Soviet economic aid program can only be achieved with a model specifying political, trade, and developmental influences.[35]

As mentioned in the Introduction of this book, Western critics of Soviet economic and technical assistance to Afghanistan charged that the Soviets used aid merely as a tool to reduce Afghanistan to a condition of economic and political dependence. Dannehl's analysis suggests that this is a rather one-sided and inaccurate interpretation of Soviet activity. Certainly, the Soviets did not provide assistance purely out of the goodness of their hearts. Like Western states, they expected to receive some political and economic benefits from the help they provided to others. Nevertheless, the Soviets did not simply ignore the development needs of their clients when deciding what kind of assistance to give, and their assistance was meant to promote economic growth.

In fact, Soviet relations with developing countries prior to the 1980s put a premium on ideology and also on idealism, often at the expense of Moscow's interests. Even in the 1980s, when the Soviet approach became more pragmatic, it nonetheless retained many of its idealistic elements.

The Soviets' economic stake in the Third World was limited, but developing countries held a special place in Marxist-Leninist thought, since Lenin's treatise *Imperialism: The Highest Stage of Capitalism* linked the collapse of colonialism with the end of capitalism. The path followed by developing countries was thus a harbinger of world revolution. For the Soviet Union, intent on cultivating allies for the struggle against the West, fostering success in developing countries would also confirm Marxism-Leninism and vindicate the communist approach to development. Reducing these countries to a state of economic dependence would have been antithetical to the Soviet conception of history and the USSR's place in it.

This does not mean that some degree of dependence did not result from Soviet economic relations with the developing world, but this was more a matter of unintended consequences than deliberate design. Economic assistance was, at least at first, meant to promote national independence in all dimensions, especially economically. With time, it became increasingly clear that this was not happening and that it was necessary to integrate developing countries into the international division of labor. As a result, the focus switched back to the kind of natural resource exploitation that had originally been considered a source of dependence and thus to be avoided. This, however, was a product of economic reality rather than Machiavellian design.

One may conclude, therefore, that even if the Soviets' primary reasons for giving economic and technical assistance to Afghanistan were political, they did genuinely aim to promote Afghan economic development at the same time. Determining precisely how the Soviets imagined they would achieve this objective is difficult since there are few documents on this subject available in the Soviet archives. The archive of the Soviet Ministry of External Trade contains a small number of documents on the related subject of Soviet-Afghan trade, most of which date from the 1970s. There are also a handful of materials concerning economic and technical assistance available online in the virtual archive of the Cold War International History Project. According to Valerii Ivanov, a senior Soviet economic advisor who headed the Permanent Intergovernmental Soviet-Afghan Commission on Economic Cooperation in the late 1980s, most of the relevant papers were never deposited in the state archives and were probably destroyed in the 1990s.[36]

To gain some insight into Soviet thinking, one must therefore rely on the works of Soviet academics who wrote about the development of Third World economies during the years in question. However, the degree to which Soviet academic thinking influenced Soviet government practice is not clear. Academic writing closely followed political orthodoxy, but it would appear that expert opinion did exert some influence on policymakers over the long-term (albeit less so in the short-term).[37] The development of Third World economies was one area of Soviet thought in which a degree of debate and disagreement was permitted. Consequently, these writings provide a window into what the Soviets thought they were doing in providing economic and technical assistance and why they came to believe that it had not brought the desired results.

The academic record shows that the Soviets never wavered in their view of what development would eventually look like, but that their perspective on the optimal path to get there changed over time in response to their largely disappointing experience with developing countries. Finding that favorable political changes in developing countries did not lead to socialism as expected, that Soviet aid did not buy loyalty and that socialist economics did not automatically lead to development, they gradually re-evaluated their initial approach.

Marxist-Leninist doctrine argued that societies needed to first develop a modern, highly-productive industrial base employing a large and increasingly class-conscious working class before they could begin the transition to socialism. Industrialization was required in order to create a proletariat, which in turn would empower a vanguard (i.e. communist) party to make the social and political changes leading to the socialist path. Expanding consumption opportunities was also central to Soviet mythology, even if "really existing socialism" (as it was called in the 1970s) pinched consumption in favor of industrial and military production.[38]

Encouraging industrialization in the Third World was thus seen as serving Soviet interests. The question, therefore, was how to do this. The Soviets shared the Western world's initial obsession with capital accumulation and industrial investment, but at the same time believed that Third World countries had sufficient internal resources to sustain capital accumulation without foreign aid. The problem, as Soviet writers saw it, was that those resources were trapped inside a capitalist division of labor, reactionary domestic institutions, and archaic social structures. Capital that could have been harnessed for industrial development was instead dispersed among a class of people who could not, or would not, direct it to more socially beneficial enterprises. Similarly, technology that could improve agricultural productivity was not adopted for fear that it would change feudal relationships.

Social reforms to break the power of the parasitic and reactionary classes were thus prerequisites for economic development. As A. Sandakov argued, with reference to Africa:

The cause of low accumulation and growth rates in the majority of African states is not so much the absolute lack of capital as the persistence of the socio-economic structure inherited from the colonial past. A significant part of national income rests in the pockets of the landed aristocracy, the trade of the bourgeoisie and other non-laboring classes, and is spent on non-productive purposes. Therefore without breaking the old and creating a new socio-economic structure one cannot productively use the resources held by the parasitical elements.[39]

In this way, the Soviets showed a keen awareness of the importance of institutions from a much earlier stage than their Western counterparts (although using different terminology). What they were not able to do in Afghanistan or elsewhere was to create institutions which were better than the ones they replaced.

In this case, the problem was identified at the first two levels of Williamson's schema and the solution was seen as lying in reform of the second level—political institutions. At first, the emphasis was specifically on communist party institutions. According to the literature of the Stalinist period, only communist parties could lead industrialization. Thus both theory and practice were focused on politics and political institutions, and little attention was given to the mechanics of development.[40] In many cases, the efficacy of socialist economic policies was taken for granted as long as the political prerequisites, consisting essentially of communist-run government, were in place.

Throughout the 1950s, 1960s, and 1970s, most Third World countries, including Afghanistan and the states that gained independence after the Second World War, were run by what the Soviets considered "bourgeois-led" coalitions, often with a nationalist orientation. The Soviet leadership under Stalin viewed them as incapable of rapid development because they did not have communist governments. The Leninist intellectual framework promised that the new states would be "objectively anti-imperialist," but the Soviets had "doubts as to the 'subjective' inclinations and reliability of the nationalists," a position reinforced by the Soviets' experiences with Asian and African nationalists in the 1920s. In particular, the Chinese national-ists' attack on their erstwhile communist allies in 1928 taught the Soviets to be wary of coalitions with nationalist forces.[41] Thus during the Stalinist period the Soviets did not view the "bourgeois" governments of Third World states as reliable allies, and generally refused to deal with pro-socialist nationalist forces, preferring instead to support efforts by local communist parties to foment revolution. This left few possibilities for the provision of economic and technical assistance.

Stalin's death in 1953 and the thaw following Khrushchev's denunciation of Stalin in his "secret speech" of 1956 unleashed a less dogmatic, more critical approach to development issues. In addition, many new states infused with an anti-imperialist and anti-Western nationalism came into being as a result of decolonization. Though most developing countries still did not have communist governments, and in some cases they even repressed local communists, they were nonetheless often sympathetic to the Soviet economic example and impressed with Soviet accomplishments. Many were eager to enact policies that accorded well with the socialist model. In particular, they were keen to break from the world economy and embark on a program of rapid industrialization.[42] This created an opportu-nity that the Soviets were keen to exploit.

Where previously the Soviets had irritated these potentially sympathetic regimes by supporting local communists, they now wished to court them. Stalinist interpretations of Marxist-Leninist doctrine gave Moscow little intellectual scope to do this. To justify the change in policy, therefore, the Soviets of the Khrushchev era conceived the idea of "national democracy," which later morphed into "revolutionary democracy."[43] Later, terms such as "socialist-oriented" also came into use. This innovation gave the Soviets ideological coverage for forming productive relationships with congenial developing countries.[44] It also enabled Soviet academics to move beyond politics and begin thinking about the economics of development.

Marxism's emphasis on the political determinants of development predisposed the Soviets to think of economic growth in terms of institutional evolution. Even as their approach to growth mechanics became more pragmatic, Soviet academics continued to put energy into distinguishing the prospects of different institutional forms. Initially, the idea had been that only the communist party could force the pace of development. Now, the concept of national democracy permitted progressive forces of any class, not just the proletariat, to initiate the process of freeing post-colonial economies from imperialism.[45] What qualified a state as a national democracy was left vague, but such states were typically supposed to be committed to "non-capitalist development": a path permitting countries to proceed from pre-capitalism to socialism without passing through capitalism as the dominant form of production. Non-capitalist development was not socialism, but theorists believed it would create the socio-economic conditions required for socialism just as effectively as capitalism.

Soviet economic theorists of this era considered the obstacles to economic progress facing Third World countries to include: explosive population growth, high illiteracy rates, socio-economic backwardness, lack of internal investment capital, small internal markets and a shortage of qualified specialists.[46] Feudal institutions combined with low quality human capital to thwart agricultural investment. Communal land ownership, A. Sandakov noted in 1970, discouraged peasants from investing in their land[47] (a fascinating observation considering the Soviet Union's record of collectivizing agriculture, but perhaps in accordance with communist thinking about the necessity to pass through several stages of development between feudalism and communism). More generally, "parasitic" small traders and small businesses held the bulk of the capital. There was no way of aggregating it into larger-scale and more socially valuable activities without the state "liquidating" those classes and redirecting it.[48] Feudal institutions thus needed to be smashed for the development process to be successful. In practice, revolutionary action of this sort was rarely possible.

Soviet economists agreed with their Western counterparts that the mechanism by which economies grew was "factor accumulation."[49] Developing countries had to build physical capital, particularly in manufacturing industries, and also improve the quality of their human capital.[50] The basic problem for developing countries was that they lacked much capital to begin with. The most obvious solution was for foreign donors to provide it, and thereby jumpstart the growth process. The general consensus in both the capitalist and communist blocs was that the emphasis should be on heavy industry. This was seen as more beneficial than the primary industries that formed the staple of developing countries' economies. The prices of the developing world's agricultural and resource exports were perceived to be in decline relative to the prices of the developed world's manufactured goods.[51] Dependence on primary exports would thus place newly-independent countries in an increasingly unfavorable position in the international division of labor. Furthermore, countries specializing in resource extraction and other primary industries like agriculture were devoting their energy to activities which had little use for upgraded skills or more complex forms of social organization. Emphasizing these sectors would strengthen the retrograde nature of the country's political and social institutions, limit their human capital development, and thus perpetuate backwardness. Manufacturing industries were required to create the political and social conditions for progressive social reforms.

Industrialization by itself was not sufficient, however, so long as the above-mentioned barriers to progress remained in place. As a solution, the Soviets at first recommended isolating Third World countries from the global economy (a position which they later modified), increasing the size of the state sector, and reforming agriculture. As Sandakov wrote in 1970:

Internal resources will become or should become the main source of accumulation ... the predominant part of the means needed for economic growth could already in the near future be found from internal sources by means of a reorganization of the systems of distribution and by redistribution of national income, i.e. by expropriating the parasitical elements of society, nationalization of foreign property, establishing a state monopoly of foreign trade, cutting the flight of foreign and national capital overseas... the enactment of agrarian reform and other socio-economic reforms.[52]

The Soviets recognized that manufacturing industries in developing countries would start out internationally uncompetitive, as it would take time to master the necessary skills and develop economies of scale. Developing economies thus needed to be isolated from international markets, with cheaper, higher quality imports being severely restricted in the categories that developing countries were trying to nurture. At the same time, Soviet theorists in the 1960s and 1970s believed that economic backwardness was largely a product of the inheritance of the colonial era, and thus "the struggle for real independence inevitably changes after the acquisition of state sovereignty into a struggle for economic liberation, for liquidating the heavy colonial inheritance in economic life."[53]

Together these tenets led the Soviets to believe that developing countries should create a complete "independent" industrial base so that they could fully meet their own needs without the need to trade with capitalist states. In effect, the Soviets were advocating a particular form of import-substitution oriented development that was popular in many developing countries.

By the mid1960s, however, Soviet development economists were increasingly aware that these efforts were not achieving the desired results in economic growth. Consequently, they began to doubt the desirability of promoting an "independent" economy and of import substitution. Many of the industries built behind protectionist barriers had failed to become productive, in many cases because the countries in question were not large enough to realize economies of scale. Developing countries were too small and their mainly rural populations were too poor to buy sufficient quantities of the domestically produced goods. Protecting the domestic market and isolating it from foreign investment cut countries off from competitive pressures and foreign technology; as a result their new industries ran at a loss, and so could not generate the capital required to repay the debts acquired to build them, let alone to re-invest. Countries following the Soviet prescriptions found that they experienced dramatic drops in their economy's traditional strengths while industrial plans went unfulfilled. They were then forced to backtrack and invest in agriculture and natural resources after all. For instance, shortly after embarking on a crash industrialization program, Cuba had to revitalize its sugar industry to repay its Soviet loans and earn hard currency, and effectively had to return to the same position in the international division of labor as it had occupied in the capitalist system. By the mid-1960s Afghanistan was in a similar situation. Soviet economists continued to argue that in theory it was best for a country to possess the full spectrum of industrial enterprises, but they increasingly diluted this conclusion with the remark that only the largest developing countries, such as India and Brazil, could do so in practice.[54]

Consequently, references to the "international division of labor" became more and more common in the Soviet literature, as a growing number of economists argued in favor of greater participation in world trade. This goal in turn required the development of export-oriented industries, which largely meant reverting to the exploitation of natural resources for export. It was hoped that this would generate foreign currency which could be used to pay off loans and invest in further economic development. This evolution was reflected in changes in the pattern of Soviet assistance to Afghanistan.

This rethinking created some problems for Soviet theorists, since their original position had been that relying on exports of natural resources and basic products such as foodstuffs condemned Third World countries to perpetual backwardness. Indeed Soviet economists regularly attacked Western "monopoly capital" on the grounds that it encouraged an international division of labor that reinforced this tendency. The solution was to claim that developing countries could safely trade with the socialist bloc because the "socialist division of labor" differed from the "capitalist division of labor."[55] In theory, the former avoided the exploitative characteristics of the latter. In practice, the primary difference was that socialist countries did not demand payment in hard currency but instead accepted the products of Third World economies directly through barter arrangements.

Another piece of Soviet advice was for the government to exercise greater control over the national economy. In the extreme this meant nationalizing domestic investments alongside foreign ones, while at the more moderate end of the scale it meant the state would channel resources to privately-owned firms that complied with the government's economic priorities. Generally, though, the Soviets considered government ownership an intrinsically good thing and so preferred nationalization to private control. Thus Soviet assistance to Afghanistan, for instance, was nearly all directed to the state sector.

Unfortunately for the Soviets, Third World state-run firms were generally inefficient. In the face of the evidence, the Soviets gradually changed tactics, at least in terms of speed and sequence. They now suggested that developing countries would benefit from cultivating a dynamic private sector that would form the basis of a nationalized economy in the distant future. Some of their more ideologically rigid clients, however, stuck to old-fashioned communist thinking and continued to pin their hopes on expanding the state sector. Afghanistan in the 1980s was a case in point, and it was not until 1987 that the newer thinking concerning the private sector began to take root.

As noted, agriculture was the largest part of developing countries' economies, and much of the capital needed for accumulation would come from the land. Unfortunately, agricultural productivity was usually very low, and so the sector generated little surplus for reinvestment. Soviet economist V.V. Rymalov concluded that, 'the slow rates of growth of developing countries' gross national product is determined above all by the prolonged stagnation in their agriculture.'[56] Large-scale capital accumulation was thus unlikely unless agricultural productivity improved, but this, in the Soviets' view, was impossible under existing circumstances. The Soviets therefore prescribed agrarian reforms, including reforms of land ownership and agricultural taxes, to be accompanied by progressive social reforms. The latter were considered beneficial in their own right, but they were also meant to promote first-level social institutions conducive to agricultural growth. The end result was to be an agricultural sector capable of producing the surplus needed to invest in industry.

The reforms generally involved confiscating wealth from local power elites and reducing their control over the population. Unfortunately, these reforms often generated a backlash not only among the wealthy and powerful who were being dispossessed, but also among the supposed beneficiaries of the reforms. For the developing countries that followed Soviet prescriptions most zealously, such as Afghanistan, the results were politically disastrous. Communists blamed rural rebellions on the reactionary mindset of the peasant class, but given past Soviet practice, the latter could reasonably assume that reforming land ownership was merely a prelude to taking it away through collectivization. In addition, those in authority often mishandled the details of the reform; for instance, land was improperly surveyed, and insufficient funds were provided, while the social reforms often seemed deliberately designed as an urban insult against rural traditions. This was the case not only in Afghanistan, but also in other Marxist-led countries such as Ethiopia and Mozambique.

The Soviets were ambivalent about the provision of economic assistance. They saw it as an obligation on the West, as a form of reparation for colonialism and neo-colonialism, but at the same time viewed the West's aid with suspicion because of its potential to further dependence. For the Soviet Union, not burdened by colonial guilt, economic assistance was problematic because a planned economy was theoretically not meant to produce anything surplus to its own needs. Soviet writers were cognizant that any assistance came at the expense of domestic consumption and investment, while assistance to non-communist countries created tensions with communist allies who coveted it themselves. Because of this, most Soviet assistance took the forms of loans rather than grants, and in theory was to be given with an eye to mutual benefit.

Soviet economists believed that once they were free of capitalism's fetters, Third World countries should have been able to develop successfully without foreign assistance. In practice, the Soviets believed that a number of factors prevented this even if the necessary political and social reforms took place. The existence of these additional restraining factors created a role for foreign assistance. In particular, foreign assistance was required to provide the technology and human expertise needed in a modern economy.

Soviet economic theorists also believed that the Third World could not simply repeat the development experience of advanced industrialized nations in the West because of several fundamental differences between the modern circumstances of the Third World and the conditions faced by Western countries at the time of the Industrial Revolution. One important difference, in the Soviet view, was the legacy of the "scientific-technical revolution." This had created an immeasurably greater demand for scientists and highly qualified workers than during the period of industrialization in the West in the 18th and 19th centuries.[57] Contemporary efforts to industrialize without such workers would lead to the creation of enterprises which absorbed rather than generated investment capital. Along with several other contributing factors, it was believed to create a temptation to focus on low-skill, labor intensive industries, which had the advantage of reducing unemployment in the short - term, but merely perpetuated the backwardness of Third World economies in the long - term.[58]

Soviet economists were firmly of the view that because of the scientific-technical revolution development was impossible without the use of modern technology.[59] Since Third World countries lacked the training to use, let alone invent, this technology, the Soviets considered that "technical assistance of advanced countries to developing countries is an objective necessity for all modern states."[60] This required technology transfers, and with them the provision of technical specialists. That said, Soviet economists complained that Western practice in this area more often than not created a "dependence of national industry on the foreign firm," as the knowledge transfer was generally incomplete, with ultimate ownership and important parts of the process remaining in foreign hands.[61] The Soviet solution to this problem was the provision of "complete" enterprises, which carried out the entire production process from start to finish, with ownership passing into the hands of the aid recipient. Moscow claimed that it transferred to recipients of factory lines complete sets of documentation, including blueprints, patents and licenses.[62] The aim was to eliminate dependence.

Dependence would remain, however, as long as developing countries lacked suitably qualified personnel and had to rely on foreign specialists to run these enterprises. Soviet writings on economic development underlined the lack of "trained cadres," deemed "the most valuable capital that can be accumulated by mankind."[63] According to a 1976 Soviet book on the Third World and scientific and technical progress:

The arrival of foreign engineers, experts, and technical advisers in Asian, African and Latin American countries for a period of time will make it possible to overcome certain objective difficulties. However, the lack of national specialists will permanently cause crisis situations in the process of development, tying the economy and culture to the donor countries of technical aid.[64]

For this reason, the Soviets considered it important for "foreign experts to train local workers and technicians, engineers and scientists,"[65] and did indeed promote the mass training of foreign workers on-site.

This logic provided a justification for the provision of economic and technical assistance, overcoming previous reservations. As G.M. Prokhorov wrote:

The scientific-technical revolution has greatly strengthened the influence of international cooperation and particularly external assistance on the economic and social processes in developing countries ... the countries of Asia, Africa and Latin America ... need to create a national industry and to develop other branches of the economy taking into account modern scientific-technical achievements. Receipt of capital investments, machinery and equipment from external sources, and also the services of foreign specialists, is an objective factor in accelerating the economic growth of young countries.[66]

The Soviets were aware, however, that such assistance could lead to indebtedness and regularly accused Western foreign aid of producing this outcome. They claimed that their assistance was morally and practically superior, first because they accepted payment in kind rather than only hard currency, and second because the terms of Soviet loans were normally very favorable Third World states. It is hard to calculate the exact terms of Soviet trade relations, but when one views how the economies of Soviet client states such as Cuba and North Korea collapsed when their trade with post-communist Russia was put onto a commercial basis, it would appear that the Soviets had good cause to claim that the terms they offered were indeed generally very favorable.

Still, Soviet assistance eventually confronted the same problem as the Soviets had identified with Western aid: even low interest loans had to be paid back. Either the Afghans and others had to repay with goods that could be sold elsewhere for hard currency, and were thus equivalent to payment in hard currency, or they paid with goods that had little value on the international market (and so also little value for the Soviets), in which case accepting them was pure subsidy. To a modern economist, this equivalence is fairly obvious, but it seems not to have occurred to the Soviets. As a result, Soviet assistance led to exactly the same problems of indebtedness as Western assistance. This was especially true because many Soviet projects had low returns and could not produce enough profit to repay even favorable loans.

Soviet economists displayed a keen grasp of the various problems facing Third World countries. Understanding the problems, and having a sincere desire to overcome them, did not, however, translate easily into finding appropriate solutions. Economic and technical assistance did not produce the results the Soviets wanted and ran into many of the same difficulties the West encountered. The Soviets were to become painfully aware of this in Afghanistan.

3

SOVIET ASSISTANCE TO AFGHANISTAN PRIOR TO 1979

First Steps

Soviet economic and technical assistance to Afghanistan dates back to the early 1920s. Following the Second Afghan War of 1878–80, Afghanistan's foreign relations were under the control of the British Empire. After the First World War, the new Afghan King Amanullah wished to re-establish his country's full independence. Soviet leaders similarly wished to gain international recognition of their regime. Mutual interest brought the Soviet and Afghan neighbors together.

On 27 March 1919, the Russian Soviet Federated Socialist Republic (RSFSR), which was the major component of what in 1922 would become the Union of Soviet Socialist Republics (USSR), became the first country in the world to recognize Afghanistan's sovereignty. The two countries exchanged diplomats in May of the same year,[1] and in May 1920 the Afghan government asked the Soviets for military and civilian aid, including a trade treaty, and in due course, on 28 February 1921, a treaty of friendship between Afghanistan and the RSFSR was signed in Moscow. This was the first foreign treaty signed by the Soviet leadership. In it, the Soviets agreed to give Afghanistan financial aid and to provide free transit through Soviet territory for Afghan goods, to permit Afghanistan to break free of its dependence on the British Empire for trade.[2] Following this, the

Afghan government invited Soviet specialists into the country in the mid-1920s, and by 1926 120 of these specialists were working in Kabul.[3] With their assistance, "a telegraph line was constructed between Kushka, Herat, Kandahar, Kabul and Mazar-i-Sharif" and a telegraph office was built in Kabul.[4] Soviet specialists also helped to construct a diesel electrical station and a cotton-processing factory, as well as an electrical station in Herat between 1924 and 1928.[5]

In 1926 Afghanistan and the USSR signed a new treaty of neutrality and non-aggression, and the Soviets promised additional economic assistance. As a result, some forty Afghan pilots undertook flight training in the Soviet Union.[6] On 28 November 1928, the two countries also signed an agreement to establish air links between Tashkent and Kabul.

Relations cooled in the 1930s, in part because of Stalin's attitude towards the developing world, mentioned in the previous chapter, and in part because King Zahir Shah, who ruled Afghanistan from 1933, did not wish to be drawn too close to the Soviet Union. Soviet advisors and technicians left Afghanistan, and the king rejected a Soviet proposal in 1936 to establish Soviet trade agencies in major Afghan cities.[7] Nevertheless, cooperation continued. For instance, the two countries signed a new treaty of friendship and non-aggression in June 1931 as well as agreements in April 1932 to establish postal, telegraph, and communications links. They also signed another agreement in Kabul on 26 May 1938 to work together to fight against agricultural pests and diseases. The latter accord resulted in the Soviet Union providing help to Afghanistan to combat locusts, including delivering pesticides and the apparatus required to use them. Soviet specialists also helped to set up and equip cotton-processing factories, and an agreement was reached in May 1936 to sell Soviet tractors to Afghanistan.[8] In July 1940 the two countries signed a trade treaty, and in the early 1940s a Soviet veterinary station in Kabul trained a group of Afghan livestock specialists.[9]

The Beginnings of Large-Scale Cooperation

Despite these early efforts, large-scale economic cooperation did not begin until the mid-1950s. Following the death of Stalin, a new generation of Soviet leaders emerged who wished to exploit burgeoning national liberation movements and chose to engage more actively with developing countries.[10] Afghanistan was a major beneficiary of this shift in policy, becoming the third largest recipient of Soviet foreign aid after 1955.

This represented a major change for Afghanistan. Immediately after the Second World War, the United States had been the country's largest aid donor. Among other things, the Americans built roads and supported education, but the most significant American aid project was the Helmand Arghandab Valley Authority (HAVA) in the south of Afghanistan. Begun in 1946 and designed to irrigate over half a million acres of land, the HAVA project irrigated only a third of this while absorbing some 20 percent of all government expenditures over more than a decade. Instead of increasing agricultural production, the HAVA actually reduced it, as it caused waterlogging and salination of irrigated fields, "making plots that once held vineyards and orchards suitable only for growing grain."[11] Passing through the Helmand Valley in the mid-1950s, the writer Eric Newby met an Afghan who complained, "It is all salt, the land below the American dam. They did not trouble to find out and now the people will eat *namak* (salt) for ever and ever."[12] By the early 1970s, twenty-five years and tens of millions of dollars after work began, agricultural yields in the Helmand Valley "were below average for Afghanistan and declining."[13] Unsurprisingly, one historian describes the HAVA as "a lesson for what kind of projects should not be undertaken."[14]

The HAVA "caused severe friction between [the Afghan] government and the USA, each blaming the other for disappointments and setbacks," and so encouraged the Afghans to diversify their sources of aid.[15] For both political and economic reasons, Afghan leaders decided to turn to the Soviet Union. The Pashtunistan issue played an important role. As noted in the Introduction, following the creation of Pakistan in 1947, border disputes led to a rapid deterioration of relations between Afghanistan and its new neighbor. Annoyed by Afghan demands, in 1950 the Pakistani government closed its border to Afghan trade for several months. This happened again in 1955, for five months, and for a third time in 1961, for two years.

Following the first closure of the Pakistani border, in summer 1950 Afghanistan signed a trade treaty with the Soviet Union. This "provided for an exchange of agricultural products in return for Soviet petroleum, cotton cloth, sugar and other commodities. In addition, the agreement provided for duty-free transit of Afghan goods over Soviet territory."[16] This enabled Afghanistan to continue exporting its products to markets in the West despite the closure of the Pakistani route, and led the way for what was eventually to be a substantial change in Afghan trade patterns towards the north. Following the trade treaty, Soviet advisors returned to Afghanistan, and between 1951 and 1954 helped the Afghans to build six bulk storage tanks for vehicle gasoline, kerosene and lubricating oil, with a total capacity of 5,000 cubic meters.[17] Subsequently, the Soviets built an oil pipeline linking the two countries and two additional bulk storage tanks, for a total of eight, one each in Kabul, Mazar-i-Sharif, Herat, Kalif, Turgundi, Pul-i-Khumri, Pul-i-Matak, and Qizil Qala.[18] This enabled Afghanistan to stockpile oil for the first time, giving it reserves in the case of subsequent interruption of supplies due to border closures.

In 1953, Mohammed Daoud became prime minister of Afghanistan, a position he held until 1963. At the time, many people throughout the world saw Soviet economic practices as a model of how to turn a backward country into an advanced industrial economy. The supposed success of state-led modernization in other countries, such as Turkey, reinforced the impression that economic planning and state direction were the paths to progress. Daoud's economics minister, General Abdul Male Abdor Rahimzai, was educated in Turkey and was an "admirer of the Kemalist path of development."[19] Daoud himself joined in the prevailing orthodoxy. Turning to the Soviets, the creators of state-led economic planning, was in the spirit of the times.

Political factors provided a final incentive for the Afghans to look north to Moscow. The United States decided to forge a military alliance with Pakistan, and in February 1954 President Eisenhower approved the granting of military aid to Pakistan. Not wishing to antagonize its new ally, in December of the same year Washington refused a similar request for military assistance from Afghanistan.[20] A furious Mohammed Daoud turned to the Soviets for aid instead.

The Soviets were very happy to step up to the plate. In January 1954 the Soviet Union provided US$3.5 million of credit to build two grain silos and a flour mill and bakery in Kabul. After the Americans refused to provide credit for asphalting the roads of Kabul, in October 1954 the Soviets stepped in and provided US$2.1 million for this purpose, which they used to deliver bitumen, road-building machinery, and other equipment, as well as technical assistance (although the actual asphalting was done by Afghans).[21] Fresh from observing how the Americans had turned the Helmand Valley into salt, Eric Newby arrived in Kabul to drive down "great ceremonial avenues, newly asphalted, past Russian steamrollers still ironing out the final bumps,"[22] a telling contrast which was not lost on many Afghans.

In 1955, when the Pakistani-Afghan border closed for the second time, "Moscow promptly provided essential imports such as gasoline and cement to continue construction projects, even including American aid projects."[23] In addition, in June 1955 the Soviet Union signed another treaty with Afghanistan to once again permit free transit of Afghan goods through the USSR and to give preferential tariffs to Afghan exports to the USSR. Sensing an opportunity, in December 1955, the General Secretary of the Communist Party of the Soviet Union, Nikita Khrushchev, and the Chairman of the Soviet Council of Ministers, Nikolai Bulganin, visited Kabul. They announced the granting of US$100 million of Soviet credits to Afghanistan, to be used on projects jointly agreed by the Soviet and Afghan partners. It was at this point that Soviet aid to Afghanistan began in a major way.

Soviet Intentions

Nikita Khrushchev once noted that, "We trade less for economic than for political reasons."[24] Soviet economic interests in Afghanistan were insignificant. As one Soviet trade representative told his Afghan colleagues in 1969, "The Soviet Union does not need to buy any goods in Afghanistan, as we have such goods in large quantities in our own country."[25] The Soviets instead had important political interests in the country: Afghanistan bordered on three Soviet republics, and the Soviet leadership worried about Western, particularly American, expansion into its neighbor. Economic assistance was, above all, meant to buy the Soviets political goodwill in Kabul and influence the Afghans to keep the Americans out. In this sense, Soviet objectives were more defensive than expansionist. Nikita Khrushchev expressed this clearly, saying:

It was clear to us that the Americans were penetrating Afghanistan with the obvious purpose of setting up a military base... The amount of money we spent in gratuitous assistance to Afghanistan is a drop in the ocean compared to the price we would have had to pay in order to counter the threat of an American military base on Afghan territory.[26]

And as one Soviet economic advisor, Valerii Ivanov, said:

You must understand that we never approached the issue from crudely commercial positions, we acted on the basis that this was a neighboring country with which we had had very long relations ... And naturally, as I understand it, from a political point of view we wanted Afghanistan to be closer to us than to anyone else. ... The only strategy was to have friendly relations with this country, because they were our neighbors. And God forbid that there should be some crisis or war there.[27]

Despite all this, economic motivations did play some part in Soviet decisions. As S. Skachkov, chairman of the USSR State Committee for Foreign Economic Relations, put it, Soviet aid to less developed countries "is not charity."[28] According to Bradsher:

After Khrushchev was ousted from power in October 1964 ... Some Soviet economists began to develop an economic, rather than political, rationale for trade and aid... Soviet internal literature came more clearly to reflect the benefits of an international division of labor, which meant attaching aid recipients to the Soviet economy for its own gain... Regardless of whether aid had led to Communist triumphs abroad... it was of benefit in building up the overall economic strength of the Soviet Union.[29]

A 1968 article by Iu.F. Shamrai in the Soviet journal *Narody Azii i Afriki* [*Peoples of Asia and Africa*] expressed this new concern. According to Shamrai:

Now, when socialist countries are undertaking economic reform, and there is a significant growth in the economic cooperation of socialist and developing countries, which is helping to strengthen the independent economies of liberated countries, another aspect of economic cooperation is becoming no less vital: the possibility of using it to raise the effectiveness of production in socialist countries.[30]

Economic cooperation, according to Shamrai, could provide socialist countries with raw materials in short supply in the socialist bloc, and would also promote beneficial international specialization, thereby allowing an "increase in exports from socialist states to developing countries of plants and equipment used to create additional possibilities in those countries for exporting goods which socialist countries are interested in."[31] Due to Soviet economic cooperation with developing countries, wrote V.I. Berezin:

On the one hand, developing countries strengthen their national economy with Soviet help, and on the other hand, the USSR receives in repayment for its credits goods which meet the needs of its national economy. In this way, the spread of economic cooperation helps satisfy the industrial and consumer demand of the Soviet Union.[32]

Stepan Chervonenko, a member of the Supreme Soviet, echoed Shamrai's judgment: aid to less developed countries served Soviet interests, he claimed, because it "stimulates the export of Soviet machinery and equipment, which improves the structure of Soviet exports. The Soviet Union receives from the developing countries in repayment valuable mineral and agricultural raw materials, manufactures and foreign currency."[33]

This combination of objectives had a number of effects on Soviet economic aid. First, although the bulk of Soviet aid came in the form of loans rather than grants, confirming that the Soviets did not view aid as a form of charity, the loans were granted on generous terms. This maximized their political benefits. Typically, the rate of interest on Soviet loans to Afghanistan was 2 or 3 percent, repayable over periods varying from ten to thirty years, which was a lower rate of interest than the Soviets granted most other countries, and lower also than Western loans. Loans were to be repaid in kind through barter arrangements, rather than in hard currency, normally through deliveries to the Soviet Union of goods produced in the factories and farms built with Soviet money. The Soviet Ministry of Foreign Trade believed that this system produced "the greatest economic effect for developing countries, including Afghanistan."[34] The Soviets also proved willing to renegotiate the terms of loans and to defer repayment when this became difficult for the Afghans.

Second, the Soviets were willing, especially in the 1950s, to finance quickly completed, highly visible projects that would maximize the publicity of their efforts. The asphalting of the streets of Kabul is a noteworthy example. One Afghan thus observed in 1969 that, unlike US aid, "the Russian performance was visible and tangible, and many people were directly affected by it."[35]

Third, while in the southern part of Afghanistan they were willing to tolerate American and other Western aid projects, the Soviets sought to monopolize aid provision in the northern part of the country. Thus, "When the US Agency for International Development proposed in 1972 to locate a small project in Baghlan province, the Soviets successfully stalled the project."[36] It is worth noting, however, that in a form of balancing act the Afghans themselves favored the division of their country into Soviet and Western zones of influence and sought to keep their donors to their respective regions as much as possible. Thus the Afghan bank of agricultural development apparently refused all loans to buy Soviet tractors in southern Afghanistan, based on an unofficial division of the country which only permitted British Massey-Ferguson tractors in the south.[37]

In line with their general criticism of Soviet aid projects, many Western Cold War commentators complained that the purpose of Soviet assistance to Afghanistan was "to penetrate the Afghan economy in a manner conducive to the integration of the Afghan economy with the Soviet economy."[38] According to Assifi:

Behind the benevolent terminology, the contracts and agreements signed with the Russians have another face as they are actually implemented. In practice, they are ruthlessly and meticulously manipulated for Soviet purposes. As time goes on and the Soviet economic grip on its beneficiary grows tighter, its dealings are handled in an increasingly domineering fashion. The Soviets' intrusive power grows until they attain a position to invalidate past contracts or demand new ones.[39]

In reality, it was clearly in the Soviet interest to have a prosperous stable neighbor to its south, lest instability from there spread into the Soviet Central Asian republics. Reducing Afghanistan to a condition of economic dependence ran contrary to this interest. Whatever the ultimate political objectives at the highest level, there seems to be little reason to doubt that those tasked with implementing Soviet aid to Afghanistan hoped that it would result in successful economic development. The main aim, claims Valerii Ivanov, was "only the raising, the development of the country."[40] Dependence may have resulted, but it seems more probable that this was an accidental by-product rather than a deliberate aim of policy. As Louis Dupree wrote, "Many foreign observers still believe that the Soviets wish to trap the Afghan economy, but I believe that Soviet patience, their liberal terms for loans, and their occasional extension of payments due belie the hardcore Cold War belief."[41]

Soviet economists did note some problems with their aid, in particular the practice of giving loans rather than grants. Developing countries were "confronting ever greater difficulties in repaying their growing debt,"[42] and "in the end a credit, on whatever favorable conditions it is given, remains a credit and there comes a time when it must be repaid," wrote Iu.F. Shamrai in 1968.[43] States might earn less money through barter agreements than if they sold their produce. Another Soviet economist, V.M. Kollontai also commented that loans encouraged countries to develop export-oriented industries in order to repay their loans, but this took investment funds away from other branches of the economy which might be more productive.[44] "All this means," Shamrai concluded, "that one must find new, more effective means of economic cooperation."[45]

At the same time, the Soviets believed that the practice of giving loans rather than grants, and of linking repayment to the delivery of goods from the factories built with the loans, had advantages for both sides in the exchange. Grants, noted Kollontai, were not as free as they seemed, as they often came with political strings attached. "Exactly for this reason," he continued, "Eastern countries which value their sovereignty often refuse subsidies offered by imperialist states, preferring to receive help in the form of loans, which are not linked with any limitations on their sovereignty."[46]

The Soviet system also supposedly guaranteed the lender deliveries of needed goods while guaranteeing the aid recipient a market for its products. Furthermore, "unlike with other forms of economic aid, the person making the delivery, i.e. this or that socialist state, is interested in the success of the operation, the productivity of the industrial equipment and the high quality of the produce, because of the very character and conditions of the repayment."[47]

Officially, the Soviets and the Afghans jointly determined where to invest the money provided by Soviet loans. For instance, a joint Soviet-Afghan committee decided on projects to be funded by the US$100 million loan granted in 1955. From 1978 onwards a Permanent Soviet-Afghan Committee on Economic Cooperation attached to the Council of Ministers of both countries oversaw business. According to Valerii Ivanov, "Sometimes the Afghans took the initiative, sometimes the Soviet Union." Afghan officials under King Zahir Shah could display considerable initiative in deciding on what projects they wanted funding, claimed Ivanov. Numerous aid projects are described in the Soviet literature as having been undertaken "at the request of the Afghans,"[48] and documents in the archive of the Soviet Ministry of External Trade make it clear that the Afghan government regularly pressed the Soviets to help them develop and expand natural gas production.[49] According to Ivanov, Afghan requests were rarely rejected,[50] although there is some evidence that the Soviets opposed projects which might adversely affect the volume of water in the Amu Darya River, as well as projects to pump natural gas from northern Afghanistan to Kabul.[51]

While Afghan preferences undoubtedly played some part in deciding the allocation of aid, the Soviets were able to influence these preferences substantially, especially in later periods. The Afghan government lacked the technical expertise to make many of the necessary decisions and relied on Soviet specialists for advice. As time went on, this dependence increased, and the Soviets gained more and more influence, especially after the Soviet invasion of Afghanistan in 1979. Nevertheless, the Afghans did not meekly accept all Soviet proposals, and the Soviets sometimes offered various options from which the Afghans could choose. In the case of natural gas exports, for instance, the Soviets proposed two pipeline options crossing the Amu Darya River—one under the water, and one over the water. In this case the Afghans chose the first option as it was cheaper and quicker, and would enable them to start exporting gas and earning revenue quicker. This proved to be a mistake, as the pipelines regularly burst, and the Soviets eventually had to replace the original line with the second option.[52]

Soviet interests and ideas of what Afghanistan needed thus played a significant, and often decisive, role in determining how aid was used. It is alleged, for instance, that the nitric fertilizer plant in Mazar-i-Sharif was built over the objections of the relevant Afghan ministries.[53] One should nevertheless note that foreign aid inevitably involves a degree of negotiation between donor and recipient, and often comes with strings attached. Donors wish to exercise some control over how their aid is used, if only to ensure that it is used appropriately, while in many instances the aid is made conditional on economic and political reform or on contracts being awarded to companies from the donor country. Much of the money provided by the United States for the HAVA ended up in the hands of the American-owned Morrison-Knudsen company. Soviet aid to Afghanistan is notable in that it was given without political conditions and that ownership of the infrastructure created was left in the hands of the Afghans. While Soviet interests and ideas may often have taken precedence over Afghan ones, there is no evidence to suggest that Soviet aid was any worse in this regard than aid provided by Western states.

Afghanistan and the Soviet Model of Development

Intellectual fashion in the 1950s and 1960s favored economic planning and state-led industrialization policies. Viewing the failure of earlier efforts at modernization, Afghan Prime Minister Mohammed Daoud believed "that economic progress required direction by well-conceived plan."[54] Daoud therefore introduced Soviet style five-year plans, the first of which ran from 1956 to 1961. Soviet aid was meant to support the execution of these plans.

As we have seen, Soviet economic theorists, at least initially, shared the Western belief that the development of Third World economies was essentially a problem of capital accumulation.[55] The Soviets differed from the West, however, in believing that the private sector was incapable of accumulating and investing the necessary capital by itself. Instead, they argued that state intervention was necessary. Through a Keynesian-style multiplier effect, the boost to economic growth provided by state investments would in turn stimulate further investments.

This logic applied to Afghanistan. In so far as private capital was available, its owners chose to invest it in land or in banks overseas.[56] The second

Afghan five-year plan (for the period 1962–1967) thus stated that "private enterprise does not possess either the resources or sufficient experience to carry out the important investments required to realize large scale economic growth." The plan therefore laid down that energy and key industries, such as chemicals and cement, would remain the domain of state action.[57]

Soviet economists agreed with this assessment of the need for state intervention. As E.R. Makhmudov wrote:

Pointing to the weakness of the national bourgeoisie, the small size of the proletariat, the absence of qualified technical cadres … and the dissipation of national trading capital, they [the Afghans] made, as it seems to us, a fully justified and correct deduction that the state, which possessed the financial capabilities, needed to interfere in the economic life of the country.[58]

According to Makhmudov, Afghanistan's problems after the Second World War included, "extreme narrowness of the internal market," "lack of qualified workers," "absence of the necessary resource base," and "lack of state funds necessary for financing industry, and the unwillingness of private capital to increase its participation in the sphere of industrial production." The geographic isolation of many parts of the country made it difficult to extract natural resources and transport them. This meant that it was first necessary to create the infrastructure, which in turn required large capital investments. Only the state could do this.[59]

Soviet economic assistance reflected this thinking. In 1958 L.B. Teplinskii described its purpose as follows:

At the heart of Soviet economic aid to Afghanistan, as to other economically underdeveloped countries, is a desire to help the Afghan people create a national industry and to develop their own productive forces so that Afghanistan can in the near future accomplish its own economic plans independently. This explains why Soviet aid to Afghanistan consists mainly of the delivery of complete sets of industrial equipment for fitting out entire enterprises, of constructing these enterprises, and also of sending specialists who train Afghan national cadres.[60]

Teplinskii's use of the word "independently" reflected another concern of the era. Socialist economists believed that the backwardness of less developed states derived from colonial exploitation.[61] According to the article "Financing the economies of the developing countries of Asia," "the struggle for real independence inevitably changes after the acquisition of state sovereignty into a struggle for economic liberation, for liquidating the heavy colonial inheritance in economic life."[62] This meant creating a complete "independent" industrial base so that developing countries could fully meet their own needs, which in turn meant following the Soviet experience in building up large-scale industrial production. Thus, according to the journal *Narody Azii i Afriki*: "From an economic point of view the main task of developing countries consists of carrying out a technical reconstruction of production, of reforming the backward small product economy into large highly mechanized contemporary production, and on this basis liquidating their backwardness."[63]

In Afghanistan's case, it soon became clear that such industrial development could not take place in the face of the almost total absence of critical infrastructure, such as roads and electricity. Funds were, therefore, diverted towards infrastructure projects, in particular road-building and electrical production.[64] Unfortunately, this increased Afghanistan's debt without in the short-term providing sources of funds, especially foreign currency, to pay off that debt.

At the same time, Soviet economists became aware that less developed countries could not advance in isolation from the external economy. As we have seen, this led to reduced emphasis on building an "independent" economy and to greater emphasis on exploiting the advantages of international specialization. Soviet ideology was not completely monolithic, and within the boundaries set by the Communist Party, a degree of debate was possible. From the late 1960s onwards, there appears to have been considerable discussion, and disagreement, among Soviet economists about whether developing countries should focus on their internal market or on creating export-oriented industries. Some argued that the potential of export-oriented development was "overestimated," and that "the widespread use of such a policy could lead to the creation of enclaves in the national economy … and the preservation of developing countries' unfair position in the international market,"[65] but it is clear that, as time went on, supporters of the export approach gained ground.

Underlying this shift was an acknowledgement that most developing countries lacked the resources and internal market of sufficient size to create all the branches of the economy required to operate an "independent" national economy. As S.A. Byliniak wrote in a review of a book discussing inward- and export-oriented industrialization, "there is no doubt that small developing countries (and there are many of them) cannot acquire a complete economic complex, above all because their internal market is too narrow."[66] Consequently, Third World nations required a combination of an "incomplete complex" and participation in the international division of labor.[67]

To justify the fact that they were now advocating what they had previously rejected, Soviet economists argued that the "socialist international division of labor" was qualitatively different from the "capitalist international division of labor." If developing countries became integrated with the former they could avoid the problems of "unequivalent exchange" and dependence, which resulted from participation in the latter. According to Iu.F. Shamrai:

Industrial cooperation aids the formation of mutual complementarities in the economies of socialist and developing countries, based on specialization and the division of labor, and so gives some economic branches of liberated states an entrance into the socialist market, and allows developing countries to form their national economies safe in the knowledge that a series of internal needs will be satisfied with the aid of deliveries from socialist countries.[68]

The failure of industrialization in a number of developing countries also clearly demonstrated that blindly following the Stalinist model of industrialization created more problems than it solved. Two Soviet authors, R.N. Andreasian and L.N. Vinogradova thus commented in 1970 that:

In some countries, where planning derives from ideas of extreme forced industrialization, not reinforced by objective possibilities, one expects an overexertion of effort, the construction of unprofitable enterprises, and the leaping of several stages [of development]. This leads to the exhaustion of financial resources, forgetting the needs of agriculture, inflation, and lower living standards for workers, i.e. in the final analysis, general national crisis.[69]

Put together, these considerations forced a gradual reconsideration of development policy, and with this a gradual change in the focus of Soviet assistance. Thus in 1988, Teplinskii changed his description of the purpose of Soviet aid to reflect this new reality, writing that:

The purpose of the broad and multifaceted economic and technical cooperation of the USSR and Afghanistan was to create a complete national economic complex in the DRA, based on discovering and exploiting the rich natural resources of that country as the base for creating an Afghan national industry and as a stable source of foreign currency for the purpose of economic development, raising agricultural production, improving the living standards of the broad masses of the population and expanding the country's export potential, and to create the corresponding infrastructure for industry and agriculture.[70]

The differences between this description and that of 1958 quoted above make the shift in priority away from economic independence and towards natural resource exploitation and exports clear.

Details of Soviet Aid to Afghanistan, 1955—1978

In January 1956, Afghanistan and the Soviet Union confirmed the details of the US$100 million aid package announced in December of the previous year. In March 1956, a joint Soviet-Afghan team then announced the projects selected for funding: "two hydroelectric plants (Pul-i-Khumri, Naghlu); three automotive maintenance-repair shops (Jangalak, Herat, and Pul-i-Khumri); a road from Qizil Qala to Kabul, including the three-kilometer long Salang Tunnel; an airport at Baghram and improvements to Kabul airport; three irrigation dams with canal systems (Pul-i-Khumri, Jalalabad, Naghlu); a materials-testing laboratory in Kabul; a fertilizer factory; improvement to port facilities at Qizil Qala; and the Alchin bridge north of Kunduz."[71] Thereafter the pace of Soviet-Afghan economic cooperation accelerated, with a succession of other economic and technical agreements between the two countries following that of January 1956 (for a list of these agreements, see Annex II). The third closure of the Pakistani border in 1961 provided additional impetus to this process. The Soviets helped Afghanistan to break the Pakistani economic blockade by airlifting grapes and other foodstuffs to the Soviet Union. This won the Soviet Union considerable political goodwill. By the early 1960s, Afghanistan was moving further and further into the Soviet orbit.

Agriculture

Agriculture provided the great majority of Afghanistan's wealth, with some 80 percent of the population living off the land. In principle, Soviet economists recognized that in developing countries "the main impediment to raising the tempo of growth is the low speed of growth of the central branch of the economy of these countries, namely agriculture."[72] According to R.T. Akhramovich, "Analysis of the economies of developing countries shows that the slow rates of growth of developing countries' gross national product is determined above all by the prolonged stagnation in their agriculture."[73] Soviet economist E.R. Makhmudov commented that, "as the experience of developing countries shows, agricultural backwardness leads to an extremely slow growth of demand for industrial goods, which cannot but have a negative impact on developing industry."[74] Despite this, the Soviets invested far less in agriculture than in industrial infrastructure. This reflected the Soviet obsession with heavy industry as the motor of modernization. Insofar as agriculture benefited from Soviet assistance, it was in the form of large-scale state-run projects, in particular irrigation schemes. A comment on declining cotton production in a 1973 survey of the Afghan economy describes Soviet preferences well:

The most effective way of deciding the problem, guaranteeing the unconditional increase in cotton production would be the creation in the Kochka river valley and the Kunduz-Khanabad region of mechanized cotton state farms, which will permit the use of the newest agricultural machinery, the correct application of mineral fertilizers and agro-technical methods of cotton production.[75]

The preference for irrigation schemes seems odd, given that one Soviet expert commented in 1958 that, "a lack of irrigation is not the fundamental reason for the backwardness of Afghan agriculture. The most serious impediment to its development is large-scale land ownership and small-scale, fragmented land use."[76] However, irrigation projects were another fashion of the times. Dispersed investments in small-scale farms lack the visibility of grandiose irrigation schemes, and do not make use of the technical prowess which industrially-advanced states possess. Within the Soviet Union, the government of Nikita Khrushchev invested heavily in the ill-conceived "Virgin Lands" campaign to irrigate northern Kazakhstan, while the Americans unsuccessfully tried something similar in Afghanistan with the HAVA.

The Soviets completed two major irrigation projects. The first was the Jalalabad irrigation complex, begun in 1962 and finished in 1965. The main canal was 70 km long, with thirty-two smaller canals totaling 200 km. This led to the irrigation of 31,000 hectares of land (24,000 of them previously not in use).[77] Two state farms, Ghaziabad and Hadda, were set up on the new land, and were dedicated to producing goods, especially citrus fruits, which could be exported to the USSR. The farms also sold meat and milk to markets in Jalalabad and Kabul[78] (in the late 1990s Hadda farm would gain some international notoriety as the location of one of Osama bin Laden's training camps). The large size of the state farms, which were said to employ 9,000 people,[79] was supposed to permit mechanization and economies of scale.

The second most important irrigation system was at Sarde on the Jilga River. Work here began in 1964. A dam, 30 meters high and 460 meters long, and a reservoir were completed by 1968, and in 1972 two major canals, 30 and 21 kilometers long, were finished. A total of 17,674 previously unused hectares of land were irrigated and 1,070 previously used hectares were improved.[80]

To further support agriculture, on 16 December 1963 the Soviet Union and Afghanistan signed an agreement for the provision of veterinary aid. Soviet scientists set up veterinary stations and carried out mass vaccinations of cattle.[81] A 1972 Soviet report noted that five Soviet teams had been working for three years combating diseases in the vineyards of Parwan province. The Soviets had also been helping the Afghans combat locusts,[82] and funded and helped to build a nitrogen fertilizer plant at Mazar-i-Sharif to provide fertilizer for Afghan farmers. This was one of the largest industrial enterprises in the country.

The Soviets also tried to mechanize Afghan agriculture. The Jangalak auto-repair workshop, which had been established with Soviet assistance, produced a limited amount of agricultural machinery and materials. In 1971 these included 1,000 ploughs, thirty threshing machines, 10,000 sprinklers, 500 water pumps, and a variety of wheelbarrows, shovels, and picks. More significantly, Soviet tractors began arriving in Afghanistan in the 1950s, and by early 1971 there were about 400 in the country. The Soviet Ministry of External Trade reported that these had proved very popular.[83]

Electrical, Transport, and Urban Infrastructure

Vladimir Lenin famously remarked that communism equaled Soviet power plus electrification. Soviet-style industrialization was impossible without access to electric power. It is not surprising, therefore, that electrical projects were a priority for the Soviets in Afghanistan.

The first Soviet-supported electrical project was the 9,000-kilowatt hydroelectric station built on the Kunduz River in northern Afghanistan between 1958 and 1962 to provide power for the cotton factory and auto-repair workshop in Pul-i-Khumri, a cement factory in nearby Ghori and other industrial enterprises, as well as for the population of the area. In 1968 Soviet engineers laid electrical lines from the Pul-i-Khumri power station to the towns of Baghlan and Kunduz.[84] In 1960 the Soviets began work on two additional hydroelectric power stations, the 11,500 kilowatt Darunta station near Jalalabad, and the larger 100,000 kilowatt Naghlu station, which became the most powerful electrical producer in Afghanistan and provided power for Kabul city. Subsequently, the Soviets also helped to construct a 36,000-kilowatt gas-powered electric station in Mazar-i-Sharif to provide power for the town's fertilizer plant. Together these stations accounted for about 50 percent of all Afghan electrical production throughout the 1960s, 1970s and 1980s.[85] A Soviet-Afghan agreement on economic and technical cooperation signed in February 1975 foresaw the construction of yet another hydroelectric station, to be built at Kelagay on the Kunduz River.[86] The outbreak of civil war in 1978, however, prevented this plan from being put into practice.

The Soviets also paid significant attention to transport infrastructure. Soviet engineers built Kabul International Airport, a port at Qizil Qala (later renamed Shir Khan),[87] and about 1,500 miles of paved roads, most notably linking Herat with Kandahar. This included the construction of a road over the Hindu Kush mountain range, part of which was the famous Salang tunnel. Construction of this road, one of the highest in the world, was a major feat of engineering. Work began in 1958 and was finished in 1964. Thirteen thousand Afghans and 600 Soviet specialists participated in the construction and 2,000 Afghans received on-site training.[88] The completion of the road linked Kabul with the Soviet Union and facilitated both internal trade and the export of Afghan goods to the north. To further facilitate trade, the Soviets also built a short railway line linking Turgundi (Towraghondi) in Badghis province with Serhetabat in the Turkmen Soviet Socialist Republic.

These efforts notwithstanding, throughout the 1970s Soviet trade officials believed that Afghanistan's transport infrastructure remained underdeveloped and that this fact severely limited the prospects for external trade, especially with the Soviet Union. For instance, in 1971 Soviet official V. Anan'ev commented that the main factor preventing Afghanistan from increasing its imports of oil was "the aged transport system along the Amu-Darya river" on both the Soviet and Afghan sides. There were not enough barges, the facilities at the Soviet port of Termez were inadequate, and there was an insufficient volume of oil storage space.[89] In 1969 the Amu Darya froze and then in the spring the waters rose exceptionally high, after which a summer drought reduced the waters to an unusually low level. All this "seriously complicated the transport of oil products."[90] Three years later, another official, A. Borovikov, repeated the complaint: "transport links with Afghanistan along the Amu-Darya river are a real impediment to the further development of economic and trade relations between the two countries," he wrote. Borovikov recommended mechanizing the Afghan port of Hairaton and the railhead at Turgundi.[91] In this regard, the Soviets preferred to develop Hairaton rather than the alternative port of Shir Khan, as the costs of transport to the former were four times less than to the latter.[92] But although plans for the development of Hairaton, including the construction of a bridge across the Amu-Darya, were already being discussed in the 1970s, implementation had to wait until the 1980s.

Due to the lack of railways, the great bulk of Afghanistan's commerce travelled by truck. The Soviets therefore invested in the automobile sector, most notably by creating three auto-repair workshops at Jangalak, Herat and Pul-i-Khumri, each supposedly capable of repairing 1,000 vehicles a year[93] (and in the case of Jangalak also capable of carrying out more general metal-working activities unrelated to the transport sector),[94] although the Herat workshop subsequently lay idle for many years. In July 1976, they also established a trucking company, the Afgano-Sovetskoe Transportno-Ekspeditsi-onnoe Obschestvo (generally referred to as AFSOTR). A joint venture, which was 51 percent Afghan and 49 percent Soviet owned,[95] AFSOTR represented a new form of economic cooperation. Soviet economists were divided as to the benefits of joint ventures with developing countries[96] and perhaps for this reason AFSOTR remained an isolated example.

Finally, the Soviets provided aid in town planning and housing construction. In particular, in 1962 they created the Kabul Housing Combine, which from 1969 began the construction of a modern suburb known as Mikroraion (the Russian word for an urban administrative sub-unit). Consisting of forty Soviet-style five-storey apartment blocks, with 11,000 apartments, Mikroraion had "a 500-seat cinema, a mosque, a restaurant, and a shopping center," as well as a school and a kindergarten.[97] The inhabitants of Mikroraion were generally members of Kabul's growing middle class, consisting of "engineers and teachers, shop owners and truck drivers," among others. Afghans considered living there a "sign of status."[98] Soviet architects also drew up plans for a more general reconstruction of Kabul, but due to the war these were never implemented.[99]

Natural Resources

According to a 1970 article by Soviet authors R.N. Andreasian and L.N. Vinogradova, "there are no conditions in which the industrialization of a weakly developed state can start other than on the basis of at least partial exploitation of national mineral and agricultural resources as the source of accumulation."[100] Andreasian and Vinogradova continue:

The economic potential of the majority of developing countries is so low that they cannot allow themselves to reject mining industry. On the contrary, they should use to the maximum the raw material branches of the economy which have already been created as a primary source of means for economic development... Therefore, the basic direction of economic policy of developing countries consists of using mining industry to the maximum—a dynamic branch and a valuable source of foreign currency—in order to diversify the economy and create the basis for a flexible, developed economic structure.[101]

Thus, according to another Soviet development economist, A.Iu. Shpirt, "one of the most important tasks in the young national states is exploiting their own natural riches to develop extremely backward economies. First of all this means establishing the scale of discovered and potential reserves of natural resources."[102]

To this end, the Soviet Union invested heavily in geological surveying in Afghanistan from the 1950s onwards. To this date, most of what is known about Afghanistan's natural resources derives from these Soviet surveys. Prospecting began in 1957 after an agreement was signed in July of that year for Soviet-Afghan geological cooperation in northern Afghanistan. Under the terms of the agreement the Soviet Union assigned US$15 million of credits for prospecting work.[103] This work continued throughout the 1960s, 1970s, and 1980s. The most important discoveries were the Aynak copper deposits, the Hajigak iron ore deposits, and natural gas fields near Shibirghan in northern Afghanistan in 1961. Efforts to exploit the first two of these floundered due to the war in the 1980s. The Soviets were, however, able to set up natural gas production. A Soviet-Afghan agreement on 17 October 1963 provided for the mining and use of natural gas in northern Afghanistan, and also provided thirty-five million rubles of credits for oil prospecting.[104] Work on facilities proceeded rapidly, and gas production at Shibirghan began in 1967. Soviet engineers also built a 101-kilometre pipeline, able to transmit four billion cubic meters of gas a year, from Shibirghan to the Soviet Union.[105] Thereafter, over 90 percent of Afghan gas was exported to the Soviet Union, most of it piped to the fertilizer plant in the town of Vakhsh in Tajikistan.[106] In 1968, the Soviets also completed an 88-kilometre pipeline from the gas field to Mazar-i-Sharif to provide gas for the power station and fertilizer plant there.[107] In the early 1970s, the Soviets planned to develop oil deposits discovered at Angot in northern Afghanistan and proposed a project to produce 100,000 tons of oil a year.[108] However, nothing came of this project.

Human Capital

"Human development," wrote Soviet author G.M. Prokhorov in 1974, is "the real creator of social wealth."[109] Another author, V.A. Kondrat'ev, agreed, writing that, "the growing role of the human factor is one of the most important features of the socio-economic changes experienced by developing countries... Genuine economic-cultural progress is not possible without the use of modern science and technology, and thus without preparing the corresponding cadres."[110] Prokhorov noted that, "The lack, and in many developing countries absence, of national cadres significantly slows the economic development of these countries."[111] This was the case in Afghanistan, according to L.B. Teplinskii, who wrote that, "one of the most complicated problems in Afghanistan, as in other developing countries, was the severe lack of national cadres, of qualified workers of various specialities. This was a serious impediment to the economic progress of the country."[112]

In March 1956 the Soviet Union and Afghanistan signed an agreement allowing for Soviet specialists to be stationed in Afghanistan in association with economic development projects. Thereafter, Soviet-Afghan agreements, treaties, and protocols on economic and technical assistance generally contained a stipulation that Soviet specialists would be sent to Afghanistan to work on the projects in question and listing their tasks. By the mid-1970s, some 650 Soviet specialists were working in the country.[113] These included 100 working on various water projects, and over 300 at the Mazar-i-Sharif fertilizer plant.[114] They both supervised and carried out construction work, and trained Afghans to take over from them once the facilities were complete. One author noted in 1958 that "to carry out the plan to develop the countryside Afghanistan needs to train 9,600 specialists of various types, including 300 administrators, 600 agronomists, 1,500 doctors and nurses, 1,200 workers for peasant cooperatives, and 6,000 teachers, veterinarians, qualified agricultural workers, etc."[115]

In July 1957 the Soviet Union signed a further agreement with Afghanistan to provide "training of national technical cadres."[116] Soviet specialists trained 500 Afghans while building the bakery in Kabul in 1955 and 190 Afghans in 1960 at the Jangalak auto-repair workshop.[117] Over 2,000 more received training during the construction of the Salang tunnel.[118] Soviet sources claimed that by May 1969 more than 40,000 Afghans had received qualifications in ninety-two specialities.[119]

Most of these qualifications were in basic skills such as the use of industrial equipment. For instance, 250 Afghans were trained during the building of Qizil Qala port as mechanics, excavator users, crane operators, concrete layers, and automobile and tractor drivers.[120] On-site training was by nature fairly limited, being restricted to the narrow set of skills required for a specific job. More advanced education was required to produce the engineers, managers, and other workers needed for a modern economy. Foreign assistance therefore also had to raise the general standards of education in the population. The Soviet preference here was for vocational, practical training. Soviet academics felt that the educational systems in many developing countries had an unhealthy bias towards the humanities.[121] The "excessive intellectualism" associated with the arts produced graduates who only looked for white-collar jobs in the state administration.[122] Many of these ended up unemployed. This not only produced social discontent but also contributed to a dysfunctional "brain drain." The Soviets therefore recommended the building of polytechnic colleges and vocational and technical schools, focused on the development of engineers and other technicians.[123]

Following a 4 March 1960 agreement on cultural exchanges, the Soviets established the Kabul Polytechnic Institute, which accepted its first students in 1967. The 1,500 Afghans at the Polytechnic studied subjects such as mining, communications, town planning, and hydroelectric installations, many of them taught by Soviet professors.[124] The Soviets also established an auto-mechanical technical college in Kabul in 1973 and an oil and mining technical college in Kabul and Mazar-i-Sharif in 1975.[125] In 1977, some 179 Soviets were teaching at these three colleges,[126] which together educated about 2,400 Afghans each year.

The Soviet belief that, in light of the "scientific technical revolution," Third World countries in the long-term had to create their own national scientific establishment, required investment in scientific research and higher education.[127] To this end, and to produce higher-grade specialists in Afghanistan, from 1956 onwards the Soviet Union sent professors to teach at Kabul University.[128] They also accepted Afghans to study in the USSR. By 1979 about 5,000 Afghans had studied in Soviet universities and another 1,600 in Soviet technical colleges.[129] The Soviet Union provided this education free of charge.

Other Investments

The Soviets made investments in a number of miscellaneous other sectors. The first was medical services. During their visit to Kabul in December 1955 Khrushchev and Bulganin announced that the Soviet Union would provide Kabul with a 100-bed hospital. Later the Soviets also provided a maternity center in Kabul and in 1976 they helped to build a 400-bed hospital in the capital.[130]

Another area was meteorology. The Soviets sent meteorological specialists to Afghanistan from the late 1950s onwards. They built several meteorological stations, including one attached to the Meteorological Institute in Kabul, and also twenty-five smaller meteorological posts.[131]

Finally, the Soviets continued to promote Soviet-Afghan trade. The two countries signed a trade agreement based on the "most favored nation" principle on 20 March 1974. A long-term trade agreement followed on 18 June 1976. In part because of these, and in part because of the general shift of Afghan trade towards the Soviet Union prompted by Soviet aid, the volume of trade between the two countries increased from 8.9 million rubles in 1972 to 154 million in 1976.[132]

The Effects of Soviet Assistance

As the account above shows, Soviet aid to Afghanistan was substantial. It did have some positive results, if only purely in terms of physical infrastructure—roads were built, electricity produced, educational institutions established, workers trained and natural gas exported. Soviet writers boasted in 1982 that "over 70 percent of industrial production now comes from state sector enterprises built with the participation of the Soviet Union."[133]

On the surface these were reasonable achievements, and certainly the roads and electric power stations have had a lasting impact on Afghanistan, as they remain key features of the country's economic infrastructure to this day. Nevertheless, the high figures cited by the Soviets were a mark of failure, indicating that Soviet investment had failed to stimulate growth outside of the enterprises the Soviets set up. The private sector, in particular, noticeably failed to make progress.

By the early 1970s Soviet experts were noting that foreign aid had not generated the desired economic progress. According to a 1971 report:

in the past ten years more than 200 million dollars have been spent on providing technical assistance, which is far more per head of population than in any other developing country. Nevertheless, even now Afghanistan cannot carry out an independent program of development, and cannot finance the growing cost of development using only internal income.[134]

The report also commented that "one must also take into account the fact that in the coming years the sums spent on debt repayment will substantially grow. As a result Afghanistan will confront great financial difficulties."[135] Another report similarly remarked that development plans in Afghanistan "could not prevent the growth in unemployment, an increase in the price of necessities, and a lowering of the value of the afghani on world markets, and had not helped resolve the brewing socio-economic problems."[136] The author blamed "the insufficient development of capitalist relations in Afghanistan, the presence of remnants of feudal relations in agriculture and its low productivity."[137]

Economic aid created physical infrastructure but it did not create economic growth. A Soviet expert commented that while in relative terms per capita energy consumption rose faster in Afghanistan in the 1960s than global averages (7.9 percent compared with a global average of 1.9 percent), it started from such a low base that in absolute terms it still fell behind: "this means that if the current tempo is maintained," he concluded, "Afghanistan will never reach the global average."[138]

The cumulative effect of insufficient institutional capacity, poor management, a lack of qualified workers, and investment in products for which there was little demand, was the creation of enterprises that ran at a fraction of their full capacity. A Soviet report on the state of the Afghan economy in 1971 commented that textile factories were working at 70–5 percent of capacity, electro-energy installations at 70 percent, and the Kabul meat factory at only 10 percent. According to the report:

Due to the insufficiently high quality of production, and the lack of demand in the internal and external markets, the canning factory in Kandahar has practically ceased working. The Makhipar hydroelectric station stops for several months of the year. For more than five years the central repair workshop in Herat, equipped with an entire complex of metal-working equipment, has been standing idle.[139]

These problems persisted throughout the 1970s. In 1976 the Soviets noted that the capacity at the Jangalak plant was not being fully exploited:[140] "only 30–40 percent of the capacity of the foundry and of production of vehicle bodies and of spare parts is being used, and in 1974/75 only nine percent of the capacity for repairing engines was used, and in 1975/76 eleven percent." When the Soviets proposed putting their relations with Jangalak on a commercial basis, the workshop's president, Abdul Rakhim Chinzai, declared that in that case "due to financial difficulties," he would not be able to pay "even the sum of one dollar."[141]

Too often, the products created at foreign-built factories reflected the ideas of planners rather than the needs of consumers, and too little attention was paid to the latter's ability to purchase the goods. For instance, efforts to distribute the agricultural equipment created at Jangalak "did not meet success. The majority of peasants do not have the sort of cattle which could be used as draught animals for these agricultural implements," beside which they had no money with which to buy them. Water pumps produced at Jangalak remained unsold and "are accumulating at the Jangalak factory and its stores in provincial centers."[142]

The Kandahar canning factory was a good example of the failings of foreign-sponsored industrial development. Despite having been built in 1962 with "modern equipment," "from the moment it was completed the enterprise has not worked at full capacity for even one year and from 1966 has practically lain idle due to its unprofitability." Its jams and grape and pomegranate juice "were of low quality and found no demand," and were also expensive.[143] In this case, the Czechs rather than the Soviets were responsible for building the factory, but the experience was similar in Soviet-built enterprises.

This pattern repeated itself in the agricultural sector. Large-scale irrigation schemes did not fulfill expectations. As the Soviet Ministry of External Trade noted in 1971, "large irrigation projects ... in which a large amount of resources have been invested, are concentrated in only a few regions of the country, and ... are not providing the necessary economic effect."[144] A few years later, the ministry detailed even more failings: "at many objects which have earlier been brought on line, the irrigated lands are not being satisfactorily used, inventories have not been made, and the irrigation network is not being serviced, and there are delays in giving out land for use." "At Sarde," the report noted, "the question of constructing a pedigree sheep-breeding farm has not been decided, and the lands given to the state seed-growing farm are being poorly used."[145]

Agricultural production stagnated and failed to keep pace with population growth. Although there were small increases in absolute output, per capita food production fell, and it became "very difficult to supply the population with meat." A Polish specialist reported that the calories consumed by many Afghans were "below the most minimal norms."[146] According to Soviet author A.D. Davydov, "By the beginning of the 70s the agrarian situation in the country had become extraordinarily acute."[147] Irrigation schemes did not prevent drought from striking Afghanistan in 1971. This led to a famine in 1972, in which some 8,000 Afghans are believed to have died.[148]

Since agriculture formed the core of the Afghan economy, this had a major impact on overall economic growth. Agricultural backwardness, noted Davydov, "became an ever bigger brake on the development of industry and the expansion of exports."[149] Afghan gross domestic product was 5,062 afghanis per capita in 1961 and declined to Af 5,028 in 1971.[150] By 1978 it had risen to Af 7,370 per capita,[151] but Afghanistan had started from such a low position compared with the rest of the world that even modest increases were not sufficient to keep pace. In the late 1970s, Afghanistan's economy grew by only 1 percent per annum in real terms, and by 1979, annual per capita income was only US$130, leaving the country "one of the poorest in the world."[152]

Human and cultural development remained low as well. By 1978, only 14 percent of children attended school, and the school system remained underfunded—"more than half of school buildings needed repair. There were insufficient textbooks and furniture."[153]

Meanwhile, all of this well-intended foreign aid had left Afghanistan with large debts which had to be repaid. A 1976 Soviet article assessed that Afghanistan, India and Pakistan were the worst placed countries in Asia for repaying foreign loans, as they lacked the means to earn substantial sums from exports. According to the author, V.E. Gankovskii, from 1969 to 1973 Afghanistan was spending on average 20 percent of its income on debt repayments. Gankovskii rated Afghanistan as being capable of repaying only half its debt.[154]

In short, even though Afghanistan received more international aid per capita than any other country in the world between 1953 and 1978,[155] this largesse produced minimal economic progress. Even a Soviet economist could not help but conclude that, "our economic aid to Afghanistan did not promote social and economic progress in the country to the degree which we had anticipated."[156] This pattern repeated itself in other developing countries. As G.M. Prokhorov noted in 1974, "the first steps in industrialization have not so far led to a noticeable improvement in the quality of life of broad layers of the population of developing countries. Moreover, the accelerated rates of industrial construction have increased these countries' technical dependence on the industrially advanced capitalist states, and also increased external debt."[157]

The Causes of Failure

If the Soviet experience is to provide any lessons for the future one must determine why economic and technical assistance failed to promote economic growth. Western and Soviet commentators offered differing explanations, some more plausible than others.

Dependence and Neo-Colonial Exploitation

The least plausible explanation was the one favored by Western analysts in the 1980s, which in essence maintained that Soviet economic and technical assistance was not actually meant to produce economic growth, but rather, as we have seen, to reduce Afghanistan to a condition of economic, and thus eventually political, dependence. This thesis has quite a dominant position in Western analyses and deserves a relatively long rebuttal.

It was the Soviets' involvement in natural resource exploitation that was to prove the most controversial of their aid activities in Afghanistan and the strongest point in favor of the idea that the Soviets were seeking to make Afghanistan a dependent satellite. Anti-Soviet critics regularly cited these activities as evidence that the Soviet Union was endeavoring to gain access to Afghan natural resources at rock-bottom prices. The Soviets, unsurprisingly, portrayed matters rather differently.

The three most significant criticisms of Soviet aid in this area were that (a) the Soviets did not pay fair prices for the raw materials they helped to extract, (b) they limited their investments to extraction and did not assist Afghanistan and other developing countries to create industries which would fully process the extracted materials and (c) almost all of the extracted materials were exported, and very little of the product was assigned to domestic consumption. In short, these criticisms held that extraction industries built with Soviet help were designed to export unfinished materials to the Soviet Union at low prices rather than to help build the local economy.

Ironically, the Soviets (and many socialists in the West) used almost identical language to criticize capitalist aid projects in the Third World. G.V. Gankovskii, for instance, argued in 1976 that:

Imperialist "aid" cannot act as an effective means of solving the problems facing developing countries as it does not strengthen the independence of Asiatic states. The widespread use of western funds attaches the debtors ever more tightly to the international capitalist economy, where they continue to be unequal partners and are subject to exploitation by foreign monopolies. One must also bear in mind that in providing "aid" the creditors are increasing their ability to influence the socio-economic processes in Asian countries.[158]

Specific complaints made by the communist and capitalist blocs against one another were sometimes uncannily similar. For instance, anti-Soviet critics alleged that Soviet geologists wrote two different reports on their finds, "one for use in the USSR and another, pessimistic, one for Afghan consumption... In many cases the results of the Russian geologic reports were not communicated to the Afghan government at all."[159] Supposedly, the Soviets could thus ensure that nobody else could fully exploit what they found. For their part, Soviet authors alleged that "in Asia and Africa, foreign monopolies, relying on the right in concessionary agreements to carry out surveys and extraction of natural resources in vast territories, in practice have prospected in limited areas, and exploited only a small part of declared reserves … [due to] a desire not to allow competitors to exploit rich sources of raw materials."[160] And just as Western authors accused the Soviet Union of paying unfair prices for Afghan goods, Soviet authors argued that capitalist powers maintained a system of "unequivalent exchange" with the developing world. An "important source of funds to finance economic growth," wrote one economist, "is the establishment of just prices in external trade. A cause of unequivalent exchange is the policy of imperialist powers, which is directed at supporting high prices for its exported goods and low prices for imported ones."[161]

Since the Soviet allegations came first, it is not impossible that the language of Western critiques of Soviet aid policy was copied directly from socialist critiques of the West. If both sides in the Cold War were accusing one another of the same thing, it was because their practices were not dissimilar, and the reason they were not dissimilar was that these were the practices believed to make the most economic sense.

Complaints about fair prices in Soviet-Afghan trade stretched back at least to the early 1960s. Afghan merchants told Louis Dupree that during the 1961 Soviet airlift of Afghan grapes and other food products, the Afghans claimed that "the Russians sometimes offered one price in Kabul but actually paid another, lower, price, after receipt of the goods." However,

Dupree also noted that Soviet officials "insisted that the quality of the received items did not meet the agreed specifications, probably the truth." Additional Soviet complaints of damaged or low quality goods were also in many instances "justified."[162]

Far more serious were complaints about the prices paid for Afghan natural gas in the 1970s. Throughout this period the prices received by the Afghans for the gas they exported to the Soviet Union were below world market averages. In addition, the meters that measured how much gas the Soviets received were on the Soviet side of the border, leading to accusations that the Soviets might be cheating the Afghans by claiming that they had received less than they had (though no firm evidence was ever produced to support this allegation).

Certainly, the Soviets paid Afghanistan less for its gas than it paid Afghanistan's neighbor Iran. According to one Western estimate:

prices of US$0.174 and US$0.19 per 1,000 cubic feet of gas were paid to Afghanistan in 1972 and 1973, respectively, while the price paid to Iran was US$0.307 per c.f. for gas that Iran would have flared otherwise. Total losses to Afghanistan (gains to the Soviet Union) for the two years for which data could be obtained were, respectively, US$13.058 million and US$11.363 million based on the reported quantities of export.[163]

The Soviets rejected accusations of unfairness, both in public and in private. For instance, an official in the Ministry of External Trade noted in February 1975 that:

In connection with the fact that the Soviet Union recently raised the price of Iranian natural gas, the Soviet government, without waiting for a request from the Afghan government, took the decision to increase the price of Afghan natural gas from 1 January 1975 to the level of Iranian gas… Comrade Puzanov A.M. underlined that this decision… about raising the price of Afghan gas reflected the policy of the CPSU and the Soviet government to support the measures of the Afghan government in the realm of economics.[164]

In reality, "to the level of Iranian gas" meant 25 percent lower than Iranian gas. This was because, "the calorific value of Afghan gas is 25 percent lower than the calorific value of Iranian gas. Considering that the price of gas is based on the calorific value, the price for Afghan gas, according to us, should be 25 percent lower than that of Iranian gas."[165] Faced with this argument, the Afghan Deputy Prime Minister Dr Mohammed Hassan Shark stated that "the Afghan side has no choice but to agree" to the price offered by the Soviet Union.[166]

A year later, in April 1976, the issue surfaced again, when an Afghan delegation visited the Soviet Union to investigate various issues affecting the price of their gas exports. Among other things the delegation wished to establish firmly the calorific value of Afghan gas, the price paid for Iranian gas and the efficiency of the equipment used to measure Afghan exports.[167] A year after that in April 1977 the Afghan Trade Minister Mohammed Khan Jalallar brought up the subject in conversation with his Soviet counterpart M.R. Kuzmin. According to the record of the meeting, Jalallar told Kuzmin: "We want to receive world-market prices for our gas," and stated that President Daoud planned to raise the issue during his forthcoming summit meeting with the Soviet leadership. This brought a sharp rebuke from Kuzmin, who replied that:

The Soviet Union has twice raised the price for the gas delivered from Afghanistan to the Soviet USSR, and the current price is just and he saw no basis for reviewing it again. As far as the level of world prices for gas is concerned, the decision depends on many factors and there is no single fixed price for gas. The price of gas depends on the geographic position of the partners, the possibilities of transit and delivery of gas, on the participation of the country in building the pipelines, etc. At present, for instance, Holland delivers gas to Italy and the FRG [Federal Republic of Germany] at prices which were agreed earlier and fixed several years ago. You well know, said Comrade Kuzmin, that the Soviet Union receives considerable quantities of gas from Iran at a price which corresponds approximately to that of Afghanistan when you take into account the calorific value of the gas. Considering these matters, Comrade Kuzmin recommended to the minister that he not raise the issue of Afghan gas at the forthcoming summit meeting.[168]

Three points emerge from the discussion over gas prices. First, it confirms what was said earlier about the Soviet view of economic assistance, namely that it was not charity. The Soviets were not going to pay more than they felt something was worth, merely out of some sense of moral obligation to the less well off. Second, the Afghan government felt that the price it received was not high enough. Third, it is clear from the internal Soviet documents that the Soviets felt that their position was strong and that they believed that the price they were offering was fair.

In addition, it is important to note that while it is possible that Afghanistan may not have profited as much from its natural gas as it could have, this was one Soviet project which could with some fairness be deemed a success, as it did turn a profit. Indeed it supplied the Afghan state with some 34 percent of its revenue by the early 1980s,[169] putting money into the hands of the Afghan state at a rate which more than compensated for the debts accrued in starting production.

There is some superficial evidence to support another complaint—that the Soviets only supported the initial extraction of raw materials while refusing to support further working of the materials within Afghanistan—but deeper analysis suggests again that desires to reduce Afghanistan to colonial dependence did not lie behind this strategy. Economic realism provides a simpler and more accurate explanation.

At the heart of this complaint lie Soviet plans for the Aynak copper and Hajigak iron ore reserves. One anti-Soviet commentator, Abdul Assifi, argued that "the Russians wanted a total monopoly of Haji Gak's iron ore." The Soviets, according to Assifi, believed that "only the mining of the ore should be done in Afghanistan. The ore would then be transported to the Soviet Union, to the area of its coke and electric power sources, and the production of iron and steel would be done entirely in the Soviet Union."[170] In this way, the Soviets were supposedly trying to keep Afghan industrial development at a low level and to reduce the country to a simple supplier of unprocessed materials. Assifi further commented that "Soviet proposals for Ainak copper were remarkably similar to those for Haji Gak iron ore: only the mining of the ore and its concentrates was to be in Afghanistan. The concentrate would then be shipped into the Soviet Union, where it would be smelted and refined."[171] In this way, "the Russian hand of assistance was extended not to aid but to subjugate the Afghan people."[172]

In line with early Soviet thinking about the need for developing countries to break free of colonial exploitation and build an independent national economy, Soviet writers stressed that it was desirable for developing countries to do as much of the processing of raw materials themselves as possible. As Iu.F. Shamrai noted in 1968, "it is more profitable to export goods which are highly processed than those which are little processed."[173] This belief was, however, tempered with a growing realism, as well as a growing acknowledgement of the benefits of the international division of labor. A 1970 article showed this clearly. On the one hand, the authors claimed that:

It is still possible to use the export branches of the raw material sector as the base on which to accomplish industrialization... The key to solving this problem lies in vertical diversification of mining industry, which means the creation of a specific form of mining complex which carries out the subsequent working of the mined material right up to the final product or semi-finished product, with the simultaneous construction of the corresponding enterprises which supply the mining industry with the necessary components.[174]

On the other hand, they noted that in practice this was not always possible, for:

the creation of enterprises which work the raw materials up to the semi-finished products or even final products, requires a contingent of highly qualified workers and a general increase in the productivity of labor in the given country... In practice, only a few, more developed countries (India, Brazil, Pakistan), can realistically create the entire complex of contemporary heavy industry and receive from this the necessary economic effect.[175]

Another Soviet economist, A.Iu. Shpirt, agreed. "In many cases," he wrote, "the small size of the internal market and the lack of resources renders ineffective the construction of large contemporary enterprises for extracting and processing raw materials in order to serve the needs of one country."[176] Soviet authors thus concluded that it would be incorrect to blame colonial exploitation for the fact that so little processing of raw materials was done in developing countries. Rather, "the main cause of this lies in technological-economic factors, which favor only initial working of the metal on site and then extracting the metal from it in the region where it will be used."[177]

Afghanistan was certainly not among the limited group of developing countries such as India, Brazil and Pakistan, which could "realistically create the entire complex of contemporary heavy industry." Not only did it lack qualified personnel, but it also lacked the necessary infrastructure. Creating the roads and electrical power needed simply to extract iron and copper from Afghanistan would be expensive enough. Creating the even greater infrastructure required for the complete processing of raw materials would have required a level of investment beyond the limited abilities of the often cash-strapped Soviet Union. There was a good reason why both capitalist and communist states largely limited themselves to raw material extraction in the Third World, and so ended up accusing one another of the same crime of colonial exploitation: it was the practice which seemed to make the best economic sense given the resources available.

The same applies to the third complaint made against the Soviets—that they only provided funds for the export of raw materials, while denying aid to projects designed to promote local consumption, thus depriving Third World states, including Afghanistan, of the use of their own resources. The fact that only a small fragment of Afghanistan's natural gas was used domestically, while over 90 percent was exported to the Soviet Union, was cited as alleged proof of the Soviets' malign intent. Supposedly, when the Afghan Ministry of Mines proposed construction of a gas pipeline from Shibirghan to Kabul to power an electric station, a Soviet engineer in the Ministry of Planning immediately summoned the Afghan official who had drafted the proposal, and "called him on the carpet."[178] The Soviets, it seems, were not interested in helping Afghanistan, merely in taking its natural resources.

In fact, many Soviet economists agreed with Shpirt that, "to achieve economic independence, progressive elements in the developing countries consider that exploitation of natural resources must be directed not only to increasing exports, but also to guaranteeing the local needs of national industry and transport."[179] In principle, therefore, the Soviets were not averse to promoting some domestic consumption of raw materials. In Afghanistan's case, however, there were serious practical considerations militating against this. Afghan natural gas deposits are all located in the north of the country. From there, production could be easily linked to the Soviet gas pipe network through the construction of relatively short new pipelines, so providing a market for Afghan gas after a relatively small investment. By contrast, linking the gas fields to the major Afghan cities was much more difficult. As Valerii Ivanov noted, "there was an idea to build a gas pipeline to Kabul, but this was a costly idea because it is necessary to cross the mountains, and additional stations are needed to raise the pressure. And that is very expensive."[180]

In short, it is not necessary to resort to complaints of communist scheming to explain the Soviets' behavior. Simple issues of cost provide a much clearer explanation. The Soviets found deposits of many materials other than gas, copper and iron, such as precious stones (e.g. lapis lazuli), but never made any effort to export any of them to the Soviet Union: "We always had an imbalance of trade with Afghanistan," protested Ivanov in a 2008 interview, "All this talk that we stole their natural wealth... how did we steal it? ... Who built the majority of economic sites there?"[181] The Soviets' trade with Afghanistan was tiny compared with the scale of the overall Soviet economy, noted Ivanov. "From 1955 to 1979," comments Leslie Dienes, "Soviet planners channeled perhaps 400 times more money into their domestic mineral resources than into those of Afghanistan." Afghan production was "negligible."[182] Economically, Afghanistan was not of great importance to the Soviet Union.

It is a mistake to view Soviet-Afghan relations solely through the prism of the 1979 invasion and occupation of Afghanistan. Although the Soviet share of Afghan trade increased during the 1970s, the government of Mohammed Daoud proved very capable of pursuing an independent foreign policy line, balancing both East and West. Prior to Daoud's overthrow in 1978 the number of Soviet advisors in Afghanistan was in decline, as other countries, most notably India, were gaining influence. In 1974, for instance, Daoud replaced between 300 and 400 Soviet advisors with Indians.[183] In addition, at the same time as the volume of trade increased, the Afghan balance of trade with the Soviet Union improved throughout the 1970s.[184] This does not suggest that the relationship was becoming more one-sided.

The Quality of Soviet Assistance

Another explanation for the failure of Soviet assistance lies in the allegedly poor quality of Soviet work. This was a matter of some concern. For instance, the natural gas pipelines built under the Amu-Darya River to transport Afghan gas to the Soviet Union regularly burst, cutting the flow of gas, and causing the Soviets to expend additional resources repairing them. The pipes burst three times in the course of 1971 alone.[185] Western sources claimed that, "Soviet machinery and materials used—in natural gas exploration and exploitation for example—did not have the efficiency and productivity of their Western counterparts."[186] Analysts stated that "the Soviet-made drilling rigs sold to Afghanistan under the economic assistance agreements were clumsy and very much outmoded… Thus… it cost Afghanistan more in return for a relatively smaller amount of services and production."[187]

According to Louis Dupree, the Pul-i-Khumri hydroelectrical plant, built with Soviet aid, "was developed without adequate information about annual and seasonal water fluctuation." As a result, the plant produced only 2,000 kilowatt-hours rather than the planned 9,000, and at peak periods could not meet the demand from local factories.[188] Dupree also noted that water, sewage and electrical facilities in the homes built by the Kabul Housing Complex were irregular, and that the Jalalabad irrigation complex was plagued with problems, causing costs to rise substantially. The Salang tunnel similarly faced problems with "seasonal melting and freezing [which] has produced many cracks in the concrete."[189] Given that the Soviet Union was not noted for high quality produce, many of the complaints were probably valid.

Opinions varied as to the quality of Soviet specialists. One advantage the Soviets possessed over Westerners was a Central Asian population which had at least some degree of cultural and linguistic affinity with Afghans.

Central Asian companies and specialists took a leading role in many Soviet aid projects. For instance, the Central Asian section of the Soviet hydro-energy company "*Gidroenergoproekt*" participated in building the Pul-i-Khumri hydroelectric station. The Ministry of Water Resources of the Uzbek Soviet Socialist Republic provided most of the supplies for irrigation projects, and the Central Asian institute "*Sredazgiprovodkhlopok*" acted as project manager.[190]

The adaptability of Soviet advisors made a favorable impression in some circles. French author Pierre Metge, for instance, commented that Afghans were impressed by the "discretion and frugality of Soviet experts."[191] Another Western observer, Eden Naby, also noted this frugality, writing that:

Soviet advisers in Afghanistan have expended more effort in learning about the country and people than have most Western advisers. The Soviets have adhered to modest living conditions in the country, thus projecting an image of equality rather than superiority to Afghans. They have not had Afghan servants, nor have they had access to social elites, and are thus forced into contacts with their co-workers and with the middle classes. Because they have not acted or been treated as elites, they have had to learn the Persian language at least to a degree that would allow them to live and function in Afghanistan. In fact, many Russian and other Soviet advisers over the years have lived very much the way that Peace Corps volunteers have lived. While this has not necessarily made them popular, it has provided many of them with a deeper understanding of the country, the people, and their problems.[192]

The noted American anthropologist Louis Dupree had a somewhat different view. While he commented negatively about the tendency of American specialists to "live mainly in what I call the 'covered wagon complex',," and contrasted this with the Soviets in Kabul who "often cram five or six families into a house where one American family would live,"[193] he nevertheless complained that "few Russian technicians speak fluent Farsi or Pashto, nor do they mingle unrecognized in the Afghan population, in spite of myths to the contrary … Soviet blue collar workers live more clannish lives and fraternize less with Afghans than do American technicians." Outside Kabul, he said they often lived in considerable luxury.[194]

The quality of training and education provided by the Soviets may not always have been of a high standard. According to J. Bruce Amstutz, "Afghan returnees from the USSR found their new skills compared unfavorably to those who received education in North America and Western Europe."[195] Nevertheless, Amstutz admitted that "not all Soviet projects were of low quality … On balance, Afghans believed that Soviet trade and economic aid were beneficial."[196] Soviet-built roads, for instance, were considered to be very good,[197] a fact still remarked on by some visitors today.[198]

In fact, Soviet aid seems to have had some advantages. In particular, Soviet projects often cost less than those of other countries, and the Soviets proved to be adept at completing their projects speedily. As Nake Kamrany wrote in a 1969 comparison of American and Soviet aid in Afghanistan:

Speed in the completion of the projects has been another impressive feature of the Soviet aid program and undertakings in Afghanistan. While Afghan officials have been frustrated a number of times with some European and American undertakings by delays and interruptions, the Soviet Union has demonstrated that it could finish similar projects in less than half the time.[199]

Overall, it seems fair to conclude that there were some problems in the quality of Soviet aid, but given that similar problems accompanied the aid provided by other countries, most notably the American-sponsored HAVA, there seems no reason to suppose that Soviet aid was less efficient than that of others. The key to the Soviet failure needs to be found elsewhere.

Failings of the State-Industrial Model

A more satisfactory explanation lies in the nature of the state-centered industrial model favored by Soviet experts. This suffered from significant flaws, including: insufficient institutional capacity to carry out efficient economic planning; poor management; a lack of qualified personnel; the production of low quality goods; and the production of goods for which there was little, or no, demand.

One Soviet commentator noted that state industrial enterprises were "unprofitable,"[200] while a Western observer claimed that the state farms established on the Jalalabad irrigation complex "perennially operated at a large loss."[201] A survey of the Afghan economy produced by the Soviet Ministry of External Trade boasted that in 1976 and 1977, "all objects of Soviet-Afghan cooperation were working profitably," producing an overall profit of over two million afghanis (See Annex III),[202] but in fact over 80 percent of the touted profits came from the production of natural gas. Other enterprises generated very little income. Furthermore, although the ministry's report does not specify this, it seems probable that the profits it refers to were operating profits, that is to say that they were not taking into account the costs involved in creating the enterprise or the payment of interest on the debts. Unfortunately, the financial data at our disposal refers only to the overall amounts spent by the Soviets, and not the amounts spent on any individual enterprise. It is not possible, therefore, to calculate in individual cases whether the operating profits were sufficient to repay the costs of construction, including interest payments. But it seems almost certain that with the exception of natural gas production, this would not have been the case. If the purpose of these enterprises was to bolster the accumulation of capital that could be reinvested to stimulate further accumulation and thus boost economic growth, they failed. They were drains on national resources and left the state with large debts which had to be repaid.

During the 1970s the Soviets regularly complained about the lack of Afghan planning and management capacity. A report on the state of the Afghan economy in 1971, for instance, commented on the "absence in the country as a whole and also in ministries and institutions of statistical accounting."[203] A report in 1976 similarly noted that "the absence of reliable statistical data ... hinders the making of any sort of scientifically-based development plans and any control of their fulfillment. Existing accounts are ... incomplete, unsystematic, and of doubtful reliability."[204] The report noted that numerous Afghan ministries shared control of state enterprises, and "the necessary apparatus of industrial management and the corresponding cadres of trained specialists were lacking."[205] A similar report a year later echoed these complaints:

The correct organization of the industrial management of the state sector should guarantee the uninterrupted and planned development both of individual enterprises and of all branches of industry. The management structure which exists in the country does not permit this... unified and qualified leadership cannot be guaranteed in these circumstances.[206]

The basic problem, therefore, was that the Afghans and the Soviets were attempting to produce progress through economic planning in a country that lacked the institutional capacity to plan in an even remotely efficient manner.

There were also significant problems with the management of individual enterprises. According to a Soviet report:

A review of the state of industry and agriculture in the third five-year plan reveals serious deficiencies and weaknesses in the leadership both of the state apparatus as a whole and of individual ministries and institutions, which do not take responsibility for the results of the work undertaken by enterprises under them. These deficiencies are particularly noticeable in the leadership of enterprises of the state sector: here there is neither sufficient responsibility nor any interest in improving the economic results of their work.[207]

Soviet analysts were extremely critical of the performance of enterprises in the state sector in Afghanistan. "One must note their low effectiveness as a whole," commented one Soviet survey, "in many enterprises internal economic planning is absent, one cannot observe financial discipline, and they have not worked out a mechanism for their relations with the state budget nor a mechanism for paying their own way without a subsidy (i.e. self-financing)."[208]

A lack of qualified personnel at lower levels matched that at the management level. Despite efforts to train Afghan workers, the Soviets regularly complained of insufficient qualified personnel. A report written in September 1971 complained that the Jangalak workshop had had "significant difficulties" in producing agricultural goods, due to "the lack of qualified cadres in the factory."[209] Similarly, a 1972 report on the automobile service industry in Afghanistan noted "workers' complete indifference to timeliness, the quality of repair and the service of automobiles,"[210] while in 1973 a Soviet official blamed the slow pace of road construction in part on "the low qualifications of workers."[211] While the Soviets claimed to be training some 2,500 Afghans a year by the late 1970s, the problem was that personnel often left the jobs for which the Soviets had trained them: "Part of them join the army and don't come back, part of them go abroad, and part of them join the private sector."[212] There were also regular complaints that Afghans misused Soviet machinery. They were said to take Soviet trucks "along mountain roads and through the desert without observing the rules and recommended instructions for their use" (although this was hardly their fault as the instructions came only in Russian and English).[213] Similarly, the Afghans allegedly misused specially-equipped Gorkovskii Avtomobil'nyi Zavod (GAZ) trucks the Soviets provided to help eliminate locusts. According to a 1972 report, "as a result of clumsy use of the machines on different work than that intended, the apparatus is almost completely out of operation, and the trucks require major repairs."[214]

The goods produced by state factories were often over-priced, of poor quality, or simply of a sort for which there was no demand. For instance, due to a lack of the correct metals, the ploughs made by the Jangalak workshop could not be used on hard or stony soil.[215]

In large part these failings were an inevitable product of socialist economic institutions. As noted in the previous chapter, fourth level institutions aim to make economic interactions as efficient as possible in deploying scarce resources. In capitalist economies, the institutions of the market serve this purpose. In socialist economies, it falls to state planners to determine how scarce resources should be allocated. Even in countries as advanced as the Soviet Union, obtaining sufficient information about economic requirements to do so efficiently proved ultimately to be impossible. As a result, resources were invested in producing goods for which there was insufficient demand, while at the same time state ownership of the means of production too often removed incentives to produce goods of high quality.

Bad as they were in the Soviet Union, these problems were even greater in developing countries such as Afghanistan. The severe lack of economic data and planning and management capacity meant that the Soviet model could not even repeat the limited success it had had in its country of origin. This experience shows very clearly how institutions cannot easily be transferred wholesale from one country to another and must adapt to the circumstances of individual countries.

Soviet Assessments

Interestingly, as the magnitude of the failure in developing countries became clear, many Soviet economists came to similar conclusions. Yet they were not willing to entirely abandon the industrial model. Instead they found barriers to it in the form of first and second level institutions, the elimination of which they hoped would enable the preferred model to eventually be enacted.

Following Lenin himself, Marxist-Leninist theorists were regularly willing to bend ideology to meet political desires and realities, within certain limits. Already by the late 1960s, and increasingly throughout the 1970s, it was clear that the economies of the Soviet Union's Third World clients, including Afghanistan, were not developing as had been hoped. Theory then adapted to the new reality as Soviet economists sought to explain why this was so and to devise new strategies for accelerating the spluttering economic progress.

From the mid-1970s they began to caution the Third World against over-zealous copying of the Soviet experience of industrialization. Economic planning could not guarantee growth, warned one article in 1975: while generally beneficial, often "plans turn out to be unrealistic, are not fulfilled, or are subject to large changes."[216] Similarly, if carried out in the wrong conditions, nationalization could be counterproductive.[217] In a 1974 article, R.N. Andreasian went so far as to warn that the "non-capitalist path of development" might not be suitable for many countries. It had worked in the cases of Mongolia and the Soviet Central Asian republics because they were part of, or, in the case of Mongolia, highly influenced by, a larger country in which the proletariat governed. This allowed them to skip several stages of development and advance to socialism. This condition did not exist in developing countries, and they should not blindly follow the non-capitalist path to development.[218] Echoing this in 1975, another Soviet author, A.I. Dinkevich, argued that, "models of economic development … cannot be identical for all developing countries. As is well known, third world countries differ significantly in terms of territory and population, natural resources, transport, the size of the internal market, etc."[219]

Numerous Soviet articles observed that economic growth rates in Third World countries were declining. The gap between the developed and developing worlds was increasing.[220] This forced Soviet economists to reconsider, at least in part, their previous belief that development was a simple problem of capital accumulation. As L.A. Zevin commented in 1977, "The process of development in the majority of liberated countries is being achieved primarily by extensive means"[221] (i.e. by increasing capital inputs). But although levels of capital accumulation in Third World countries varied substantially,[222] overall they were approaching those of the developed world. This meant that "for many countries of the Third World possibilities for development along this line are already almost exhausted."[223] And according to P.I. Pol'shikov, "if in capitalist countries an increase in capital investment is accompanied by a corresponding increase in production, in African countries there is no direct dependence of growth in gross domestic product on increasing the norm of accumulation."[224]

Growth rates remained poor even in countries with large amounts of physical and financial capital. Algeria, for instance, gained independence in possession of substantial physical capital, but struggled economically thereafter. A Soviet economist concluded that, "the rates of Algeria's economic growth [were] held back not so much by the possibilities of accumulation as by the lack of national cadres and of experience of economic construction, of running the planning system, directing the economy, and so on."[225] Similarly, another Soviet writer, A. Sandakov, noted that, "in oil producing countries in the Near East, where incomes from oil provide a sound financial base, we do not observe more rapid economic growth than in other developing countries."[226]

The Soviets also observed that invested capital did not multiply itself in the manner that Keynesian economic theory suggested it should. Investments in the state sector did not produce growth in the private sector. Sounding remarkably like an early Soviet version of Margaret Thatcher, L.I. Reisner wrote in the Soviet journal *Narody Azii i Afriki* in 1969, that:

The influence of Keynes' multiplier is smaller in underdeveloped countries than in developed ones. It is clear in the first case that the impulse from state investments, financed through budget deficits, does not pass automatically into other sectors of the economy… This means that in weakly integrated, multi-structure economies, the multiplier hardly exists at all.[227]

The sole product of Keynesian policies, argued Reisner, was inflation. Put together, all this meant that a development strategy based on capital accumulation and the multiplier theory was not likely to succeed.

This proved to be the case in Afghanistan. As noted in the previous chapter, early development economists hoped to overcome the difficulties of complementarities by building infrastructure which would justify its construction *post factum* by boosting other sectors of the economy. Problems with the quality of Soviet aid might not have mattered very much had the investments in industry and infrastructure done this, but they did not. For instance, although Afghanistan acquired a road network, and with this the beginnings of a national market, the network was small given the size of the country and, according to the Soviets, "remained inadequate."[228] Furthermore, "there were inadequate feeders off the main routes." As a result, "the development of a national market bypassed many of the local or regional market centers."[229] By themselves roads did not produce major increases in commerce, while at the same time they produced no revenue to repay the debt acquired in building them. This, the Soviets eventually realized, was a common problem with aid to developing countries: "The need to create industrial complexes from scratch in developing countries requires correspondingly large investments in passive elements of basic capital with low capital returns … This is one, if not the most important, factor explaining the tendency for the rate of growth in liberated countries to decline."[230]

One reason why infrastructure investments did not stimulate economic growth was that such growth was impossible unless more money was put into the pockets of the rural poor who made up 90 percent of the population, but development aid did little to help the rural population. As one Western commentator puts it, "the economic benefits of this transformation [brought about by economic aid] were not spread around the rural population, accruing instead to traders and transport entrepreneurs."[231] By sucking up resources which could more usefully have been directed elsewhere, irrigation projects may even have done more harm than good.

Looking back at these failures, Soviet economist E.R. Makhmudov concluded that the key to economic development lay in the agricultural sector: "As the experience of developing countries shows, agricultural backwardness leads to an extremely slow growth of demand for industrial goods, which cannot but have a negative impact on developing industry."[232] The development of Afghan industry remained dependent on the primary sector of the economy—agriculture—and problems in the agricultural sector had an impact on industry. Thus poor harvests led to rising prices and lower demand for industrial goods from 1963/4 to 1967/8.[233] Another author, R.T. Akhramovich, agreed. In Afghanistan, he wrote, "the failure to resolve the agrarian question continues to limit entrepreneurial possibilities, especially for the lower levels of the national bourgeoisie."[234]

This analysis reflected a growing realization that investments in industry and basic infrastructure would not by themselves bring economic growth. Rather, they merely created industrialized enclaves, cut off from the rest of the economy. R.N. Andreasian and L.N. Vinogradova described this process with regard to mining industries in developing countries:

States with economic monocultures typically create export branches which are very weakly linked to the background of the traditional economy which provides the means of living to the bulk of the population. In mining industry countries enclaves are formed… In these countries infrastructure is developed to secure the needs of the mining industry. It creates the impression of a highly industrialized country. Nevertheless, the mining regions have little or no link with the rest of the economy of the country; connections between branches and regions are weak or entirely absent… mining industry exerts a weak influence on demand in the country… In this way, the influence of the mining sector in forming the economic structure of the young countries of Asia, Africa and Latin America is limited.[235]

Makhmudov echoed this complaint. In the specific case of Afghanistan, it was clear that:

The problem of industrialization could not be solved only by creating contemporary manufacturing factories. In the conditions of a traditional society they were alien organisms, enclaves, having practically no link with the existing system of traditional economic links… Thus, the first step of industrialization showed the necessity of a holistic approach to solving the problem, i.e. carrying out structural reforms in the entire economic and social system.[236]

Instead of emphasizing the creation of industrial infrastructure, especially transport, energy and irrigation, policy "should have sought to change both the quantity and quality of consumer demand."[237]

Soviet economists increasingly stressed that successful development depended not just on the quantity of capital accumulated, but more importantly on how the accumulated capital was used.[238] The latter in turn depended on a large variety of factors, not all of which were purely economic: "Internal possibilities for accumulation are not limited only to the presence of financial resources," wrote A. Sandakov, "They also depend on the social and economic structures … on the organization, structure and level of production, the effectiveness of capital investment, the level of labor productivity, etc."[239] "Economic growth experiences the influence of political, social, historical, cultural, and other factors, which interact with economic ones," agreed A.I. Dinkevich. "Consequently," he continued, "economic growth … is the result of the interaction of a multi-level complex of various factors, the function of all the activity of society—economics, politics, science, culture, etc."[240] Neglect of these other factors meant that foreign aid had not produced positive results. G.M. Prokhorov wrote:

As the experience of international economic relations shows, the flow of resources from outside and the use of the technical experience of foreign specialists does not always help economic growth and promote the interests of the countries who need aid… to turn external aid into a real factor of development one must above all actively help the most rational and effective use of developing countries' own natural, financial and human resources.[241]

In short, some years before their Western counterparts, Soviet economists had come to the conclusion that "institutions rule."

Above all, Soviet writers concluded that economic progress was impossible without far-reaching reform of first and second level institutions, i.e., without massive changes in social and political systems. Given the Marxist dictum that economics drove social and political processes, the Soviets now somewhat surprisingly argued the inverse—that social and political systems affected economic processes. Thus in a discussion of capital accumulation in Africa, A. Sandakov argued that:

If all African countries distributed their resources in the best way, they would not need external aid on a large scale… The cause of low accumulation and growth rates in the majority of African states is not so much the absolute lack of capital as the persistence of the socio-economic structure inherited from the colonial past. A significant part of national income rests in the pockets of the landed aristocracy, the trade of the bourgeoisie and other non-laboring classes, and is spent on non-productive purposes. Therefore without breaking the old and creating a new socio-economic structure one cannot productively use the resources held by the parasitical elements.[242]

P.I. Pol'shikov agreed: "The low level of accumulation in African countries is determined by the entire socio-economic structure ... a significant part of the surplus product ... is simply not assigned to increasing capital investment, but is spent on non-productive accumulation or for a variety of types of speculation."[243] The low productivity of agriculture was blamed on "feudal landlords," who "were not very interested in introducing better agricultural technology, or employing chemical fertilizers, as they rent out all the land and receive good profits without additional expenses."[244] In Soviet eyes, therefore, progress was impossible without fundamental reform of landholdings. As a 1976 Soviet survey of the Afghan economy put it, "raising agricultural production is impossible without changes in the system of land use itself."[245]

This fits in with Antonio Giustozzi's analysis cited in the previous chapter, that "the tribal character of the aristocracy meant that it was culturally bound to a model of revenue redistribution (geared towards maintaining a retinue and local support) that constrained accumulation."[246] It would appear, therefore, that the Soviet analysis of the fundamental institutional problem was not inaccurate.

During the 1990s, many of the discussions concerning the transition of communist economies to free market economies focused on the order in which reforms should be carried out. The Soviets faced a similar problem, since, in their eyes, the "parasitical" elements held political power and resisted efforts to reform the socio-economic structure. This meant that first level institutions could not be altered unless second level institutions were altered beforehand. Progress, therefore, required that the parasitical elements first be swept from power. This logic meant that by the late 1960s, and increasingly through the 1970s, Soviet theorists had come to the conclusion which their Western counterparts would not reach until the 1980s—that development was more a political than an economic problem, dependent on the enactment of democratic reform (although the Soviet definition of "democratic" was very different from the Western one). As a 1968 article put it: "Corruption is a real obstacle in the way of improving the effectiveness of the state sector and the taxation system in the majority of developing countries... A broad democratization of all political life and economic direction is the only real method capable of curbing the embez-zlement of public funds."[247] Sandakov agreed: "The experience of liberated countries shows that … only eliminating reactionary elements from power, and the democratization of state power, open the road to solving the prob-lems of developing the national economy."[248]

This logic applied to Afghanistan, which can be seen as a classic case of the problems mentioned in the previous chapter of rent-seeking and of elites skewing the rules of the game to enhance their access to privileged resources. According to an American report, infrastructure projects "were unable to spur rapid growth in the agricultural and industrial sectors by themselves,"[249] because:

The traditionally wealthy and powerful landowning and trading interests had previ-ously seen a threat in the growth of a new group of industrialists and had supported those who advocated the dominance of government enterprise. The tariff policy had militated against local industry because custom duties had taxed intermediate goods to be assembled by local private industry more heavily than the imported finished goods sold by the traders… By the 1960s, therefore, private investors had become primarily interested in real estate and bazaar banking.[250]

Makhmudov made a similar observation. Despite the investments in infrastructure, "The owners of private capital continued to be very cautious about investing in the sphere of production."[251] The Soviet experience made it "all the more obvious that mobilizing private national and international capital was insufficient for the achievement of economic progress."[252]

A major problem was that increases in absolute agricultural production in Afghanistan had come almost entirely through increases in the volume of cultivated land rather than through improvements in agricultural tech-niques.[253] As nearly all of the land which could be cultivated was now cul-tivated, further expansion of this type was impossible. Raising agricultural production thus required new intensive methods, which were considered barely possible given that 5 percent of the population supposedly owned 50 percent of the land and in most cases was not interested in reinvesting its profits in agriculture.[254] Afghanistan's economic situation could not improve until agriculture was reformed, but agricultural reform was blocked by the landowning interests: "because of the large land- and livestock-owners almost none of the government's proposed laws for agrarian reform were passed by Parliament."[255] The Soviets complained that a land law intro-duced by Mohammed Daoud in 1961 was shelved after his overthrow in 1963,[256] and that the parliament subsequently blocked all efforts in the

1960s to increase land and livestock taxes and to improve their collection, going so far as to vote down the budget for 1965/6. "For four years," complained V.V. Basov, "various parliamentary commissions have discussed the possibility of increasing the land tax and the livestock tax, but each time the interests of large land and livestock owners have prevailed, and a decision of the question has been frozen."[257] Eventually, in May 1969, parliament in principle approved tax increases, but in practice postponed them until corresponding land laws should be passed.[258] Afghanistan had to wait until 1975 for a law on land reform. However, this largely remained a dead letter. According to Davydov, "over the next two years not one of the law's clauses was enacted even to the smallest degree."[259] Thus although Soviet officials originally welcomed the land reform, they very rapidly came to the conclusion that "the question of land use in Afghanistan is not being decided consistently and finally to the benefit of the majority of the people."[260]

Foreign aid contributed to this problem. Inflows of money had the effect of turning Afghanistan into a "weak rentier state," depriving the ruling classes of the incentives to reform the existing system. Some Soviet authors were aware of this problem: "The exceptional role of external aid in financing the development of this country over the past decade," wrote E. Urazova and L. Teplinskii, "has created a situation in which not only are internal sources not being used in full measure, but also, as practice has shown, even the external aid itself cannot be used in full measure and in the most effective manner."[261] As so often, though, practice ignored theory. Rather than conclude that aid was counterproductive, the Soviets concluded that if they reformed the political institutions, the aid would then become productive. As Makhmudov commented:

Afghan society wasn't ready for such [economic] reforms. As a result all government efforts to raise the efficiency of manufacturing industry failed to produce the expected results... Thus the experience of Afghan industrialization showed that resolving this problem required not only the corresponding national technical and financial resources, but also complete fundamental reforms, that in the conditions of a developing state, where the pre-capitalist classes and social forces retain a strong position, industrialization is not only a socio-economic, but also a political, problem, for its preconditions demand fundamental changes in the traditional system of societal relations.[262]

Determining that the primary problem was political was an important step forward. Unfortunately, the method chosen to resolve the political problem proved to be massively counterproductive. As we have seen, aid projects in Afghanistan produced industrial "enclaves" isolated from the rural economy. Because of this, one of the by-products of Afghanistan's limited economic development was the creation of a small urban class, which was culturally separated from the rural masses. As Gilles Dorronsoro writes, "Afghanistan's development strategy only reinforced the distinctions between regions and social groups... [and] led to ever greater contrasts between the ways of life and the aspirations of the urban and rural population."[263] In April 1978 a segment of the urban minority came to power. Following the logic that only fundamental social and political reform could remove the logjams blocking Afghanistan's economic development, it set about enacting a social revolution to sweep away the traditional conservative culture it held in contempt. The result was counter-revolution. The subsequent war then wreaked terrible economic destruction and destroyed what small economic progress foreign aid had hitherto achieved.

4

SOVIET ASSISTANCE TO AFGHANISTAN

1979–86

Introduction

In 1973, Mohammed Daoud overthrew King Zahir Shah and proclaimed himself president of Afghanistan. His rule lasted only five years. In April 1978 the Afghan army in turn overthrew Daoud and put into power the communist-oriented Peoples' Democratic Party of Afghanistan (PDPA). With this a new era in Afghanistan's history began.

The PDPA had few roots in Afghan society and little support outside the major cities. Divided into two factions—Khalq and Parcham ("Masses" and "Banner" respectively)—its members often seemed to spend as much time fighting one another as fighting common enemies. Once in power the PDPA chose to enact a dogmatic program of radical social and economic reform, which revealed its lack of understanding of the balance of forces in Afghan society. In doing so it hoped to sweep away what it viewed as the institutional barriers to Afghanistan's progress. Instead, it provoked violent counter-revolution and eventually Soviet military intervention. The Soviets responded with military support and increased economic and technical assistance, but this could not prevent a massive collapse in Afghanistan's economy.

Within a few weeks of assuming power, the PDPA had already alienated broad swathes of the Afghan population. In a sense the PDPA was more rigidly communist than the Communist Party of the Soviet Union. This was especially true during the first eighteen months of PDPA rule under the presidencies of Nur Mohammed Taraki and Hafizullah Amin, the latter of whom the Soviets overthrew when they invaded in December 1979. While Soviet economists warned Third World countries against blindly copying the Soviet experience, and cautioned that overly rapid transformation could be counterproductive, the PDPA determined to embark upon a rapid course of enforced modernization, creating enemies every step of the way. Before long, large parts of the country were in rebellion. Most notably, in March 1979 the population of the city of Herat rose up in revolt and the military garrison mutinied. The government regained control of the city only with the greatest difficulty.

The government's initial attitude to private industry was representative of its ideological zeal. As the Afghan trade minister M.Kh. Jalallar admitted to the Soviets in August 1980:

Until December of last year [i.e. until the Soviet invasion and the overthrow of Amin], many unjust measures were undertaken with regard to the private sector. Among them were forced requisitions from merchants. If any merchant "voluntarily" gave a sum which was less than that given by other merchants, they declared him an enemy of the state. Unjust measures against merchants led to a reduction in their activity. The number of specialists in the state sector also fell.[1]

A significant factor in undermining support for the new regime was its program of land reform. As we have seen, Soviet economists had come to believe that the main impediment to economic progress in the Third World was low agricultural productivity, and that in the case of Afghanistan the cause of this lay in the system of land ownership. Significant economic progress was thus, in theory, dependent on the enactment of radical land reform. The PDPA took this advice to heart and hoped that land reform would bring the support of the rural poor who made up the majority of the country's population. They were soon to be disabused of this notion.

Decrees issued in 1978 limited the size of landholdings and confiscated any above the limit without compensation. They also eliminated peasants' debts. State credit and agricultural organizations were then meant to provide farmers with credit, equipment and fertilizers on favorable terms.[2] Here, though, the government ran into a basic problem of institutional capacity. It simply lacked the means to make good on its promises of aid. Deprived of their traditional sources of credit and supplies, but lacking any alternative provision from the government, the farmers could not buy the seeds and materials they needed.[3] Agricultural output suffered, and farmers proved receptive to the appeals of counter-revolutionary forces. Far from removing barriers to economic progress, this attempt at land reform made matters worse.

Before long much of the Afghan countryside was in open rebellion, a situation worsened by infighting within the PDPA and by the repressive measures used by government forces. The April Revolution simply substituted one set of institutional problems for another, as the new government proved to be catastrophically incompetent. Soviet leaders were well aware of this, and spent much of the next decade trying to restrain the excessive zeal of their Afghan clients. They were, however, in a bind. It is often said that if you owe the bank US$1,000 dollars, the bank controls you, but if you owe the bank a billion dollars, you control the bank. The Soviet-Afghan relationship was rather like the latter. The Soviets had invested so much in Afghanistan in the 1980s, especially in the form of political capital, that for many years they could not bring themselves to abandon their Afghan ally, however badly that ally behaved. Because the leaders of the PDPA knew this, the incentives to change their behavior were small. Afghanistan experienced the same phenomenon as many other Third World countries: the steady flow of aid reduced incentives for good governance and thus reinforced institutional barriers to progress. Only when the Soviets made it clear that they really were going to leave Afghanistan, and soon, did this situation begin to change even slightly.

Soviet Aid Prior to the Invasion

The April 1978 coup had taken the Soviet Union by surprise. Nevertheless, it moved rapidly to take advantage of the situation and establish friendly relations with the new regime. Wishing to support a government that declared itself to be ideologically pro-Soviet, the USSR agreed to expand economic and technical assistance. The major product of this was a new treaty of friendship signed by Leonid Brezhnev and the Afghan President Nur Mohammed in Moscow in December 1978. Article 2 of the treaty stated that:

The High Contracting Parties shall make efforts to strengthen and broaden mutually beneficial economic, scientific and technical cooperation between them. With these aims in view, they shall develop and deepen co-operation in the fields of industry, transport and communications, agriculture, the use of natural resources, development of the power-generating industry and in other branches of the economy, to give each other assistance in the training of national personnel and in planning the development of the national economy.[4]

Article 3 further obliged the contracting parties to "promote the development of co-operation and exchange of experience in the fields of science, culture, art, literature, education, health services, the press, radio, television, cinema, tourism, sports, and other fields."[5] Details, however, had to wait until several agreements on economic and technical cooperation were signed throughout 1979.

The Soviet Union and the Democratic Republic of Afghanistan signed the first of these on 1 March 1979. The Soviets agreed to help exploit the Aynak copper reserves, and the two parties agreed to cooperate in building an oil refinery, exploiting oil deposits at Angot, Akdaria and Kashgari, building an electrical transmission line from the Soviet border in the region of Shir Khan to Kunduz, renovating Kabul airport, and building six smaller airports. To these ends the Soviet Union agreed to provide 200 million rubles of credit (US$250 million at the official exchange rate) for the work at Aynak and 70 million rubles of credit (US$87.5 million) for the other projects, both loans being repayable at 2 percent interest per annum. The agreement stipulated that Soviet specialists were to be sent to Afghanistan to assist in the projects, and that the USSR would receive Afghan citizens for technical training in appropriate Soviet enterprises and institutions.[6]

Two more agreements followed in 1979: one signed on 30 August in which the Soviet Union agreed to establish seven machine-tractor stations in Afghanistan, to equip them, and to send specialists to help set them up and train Afghans in the use of the equipment;[7] and one signed on 30 October for "economic and technical cooperation in preparing Afghan national cadres." In the latter, the Soviets agreed to create five educational centers to train qualified workers in Afghanistan, to accept up to 350 Afghans every year for technical training in Soviet institutions, and to dispatch up to 115 Soviet professional-technical education specialists for three-year postings working in Afghan professional educational institutions.[8]

The Soviets were clearly not anticipating having to operate in a dangerous security environment and Soviet aid was set to continue on much the same lines as before. The Soviet invasion of Afghanistan in December 1979 put an end to this false assumption.

The Soviet Invasion and Aid Policy

As the Afghan government lost control of the country during 1978 and 1979 in the face of mounting rebellion, it repeatedly called upon the Soviet Union to give military assistance. Time after time, the Soviets refused. In early 1979, for instance, the Soviet Politburo debated sending troops to Afghanistan several times and each time categorically rejected the idea. Politburo member Andrei Kirilenko pointed out that Soviet troops would have to fight the mass of the Afghan people.[9] KGB chief Iurii Andropov argued that Afghanistan was not ready for socialism—it was deeply religious and economically backward—and that the revolution there should not, therefore, be supported, as it could only be maintained by means of bayonets. Foreign Minister Andrei Gromyko agreed: the army should not enter Afghanistan, he said, as the Soviets would be portrayed as aggressors and would have to fight the entire Afghan people.[10]

Despite this, on 12 December 1979, a small group within the Soviet Politburo consisting of Andropov, Gromyko, Defence Minister Dmitrii Yazov, and Communist Party of the Soviet Union (CPSU) General Secretary Leonid Brezhnev issued an order for the Soviet Army to invade Afghanistan in order to crush the rebellion and support the PDPA government.[11] On 25 December, the Soviet Army crossed the border and rapidly occupied the major Afghan population centers. Soviet leaders anticipated that the military campaign would be short and that Soviet troops would return home within months. In reality they stayed there for almost ten years.

What made the Soviet leadership change its mind and go against its own prescient objections is not clear. One Western suggestion was that the Soviets' primary motive was economic: that they wished to seize control of Afghan natural resources, and that the Soviet invasion was the logical culmination of a decades' long strategy designed to bring Afghanistan entirely under Soviet economic control. American author John Shroder, for instance, claimed that "Soviet policy, in general, is motivated by a desire to control resources… The invasion of Afghanistan should be seen in this light,"[12] while Abdul Assifi commented that "Whatever their other geopolitical motives in trying to seize Afghanistan, not least is the crude exploitation of its mineral and other natural resources."[13] However, as another commentator noted, "there is not enough evidence to substantiate this claim, and it certainly could not rank high among the key motives for the Soviet invasion."[14] In fact, Politburo discussions of whether to intervene did not discuss economic issues at all, except to suggest providing additional economic assistance as a means of support short of a military invasion.[15] From the point of view of subsequent Soviet economic and technical assistance in the 1980s this was important, as it meant that the purpose of this aid was primarily political rather than economic—to shore up the Afghan government rather to pursue Soviet economic advantage—and the form it took followed this imperative.

As the Soviets at first did not expect to remain in Afghanistan for a long time, they did not give a high priority to economic and technical assistance. Once the Soviets realized that they would have to stay longer, they initially put most of their hopes on finding a military solution. It took some time for the understanding to sink in that a broader range of measures, including economic ones, were required to defeat the insurgency and put the government on a stable footing. According to Valerii Ivanov, "For about the first two years, nobody paid attention to the economy, but then they understood that the economy is the basis of everything, including military operations."[16] Eventually, therefore, the tempo of Soviet economic and technical assistance to Afghanistan increased.

Throughout most of the 1980s, Soviet aid priorities remained remarkably similar to those before the war insofar as they were focused on infrastructure, natural resource extraction, and state-owned industry, with some additional investment in agriculture and education. This continued unaltered until 1987.

The ruling PDPA had a somewhat dogmatic communist attitude to economic development, regarding the state sector as being the primary motor of progress. As E.R. Makhmudov noted, "After the April revolution a course was taken to carry out core socio-economic transformations by strengthening the state sector, especially in key branches of the economy."[17] As a result, "state control in manufacturing eventually reached 80 [percent], in the construction sector—90 [percent], and in transportation—60 [percent]."[18] The new Afghan government placed an even higher priority on industrial development at the expense of agriculture than its predecessors. According to a U.S. study, after the revolution the government "allocated proportionally smaller amounts to the [agricultural] sector than had any previous government. In the 1982 plan, agriculture received just 10 percent of the allocations, even though agriculture provided nearly two-thirds of GDP."[19] The Afghans had great hopes for natural resource exploitation, and throughout the 1980s pressed the Soviets to develop the Aynak copper mines (Soviet efforts to do so were thwarted by the poor security situation).[20] To some degree, therefore, the direction of Soviet assistance during the war merely reflected the Afghan government's desires.

The Afghans were perhaps less subordinate to the Soviets than is commonly assumed. From December 1978 a Permanent Intergovernmental Commission on Economic Cooperation (with transport and planning subcommittees), attached to the Councils of Ministers of both countries, coordinated work between the governments in this area.[21] Valerii Ivanov, who eventually became the commission's secretary, claimed that the Soviets accepted "eighty-five to ninety [percent]" of Afghan proposals.[22] Given Soviet practice elsewhere, this may well be true.

As Marshall Goldman noted in a commentary on Soviet aid policy, the Soviets were often "too eager to please and find it hard to say no," even when they knew their clients' suggestions were poor ones (although they did summon up the courage to say no on occasion, as witnessed by the rejection of the Shibirghan-Kabul pipeline plan mentioned in the previous chapter).[23]

Having said that, the Soviets had ways of subtly influencing Afghan ideas of what should be done. As time went on and Afghan ministries came increasingly under the sway of a growing number of Soviet advisors, what appeared to be Afghan proposals were often, in fact, Soviet ones planted into the minds of the Afghans. As Ivanov explained:

The Afghans studied with our people at our Gubkin Institute [the Gubkin Russian State University of Oil and Gas], they graduated, went home, worked together, and sitting together said, "Aha, here they've discovered a new gas deposit, we should build a pipeline to guarantee export." And so, a paper or a note was written, or a proposal was made in the Ministry of Mines and Industry. And this Ministry then turned to the leadership of the Soviet Union and said, "We believe that we must do this and this." But in essence, this was our proposal, which came from our specialists, who worked in Afghanistan.[24]

It would appear that as new ideas gained ground they did not so much supplant old ones as come to coexist with them. Asked what model the Soviets used to determine their aid policies, Valerii Ivanov claimed that, "There was no model."[25] This was slightly disingenuous in that the Soviet emphasis on the state sector clearly reflected a certain dominant mode of thought, but in a sense it was also accurate: there was no single master plan determining the pattern of Soviet aid. Although Soviet academics had long since abandoned the concept of the "independent national economy" in favor of the integration of developing countries into the international division of labor—and although in Afghanistan's case the increasing emphasis in the late 1960s and 1970s on exports of natural resources showed that this shift in thought had some effect on practice—the older idea had evidently been sufficiently powerful that it still held many Soviets in its grip. Thus Telegrafnoe Agenstvo Sovetskogo Soiuza (Telegraph Agency of the Soviet Union) (TASS) reported in March 1983 that, "The Soviet Union sincerely strives to help the developing states build up truly independent national economies. This is why the USSR renders assistance to its economic partners in the development of the state sector, in the first place."[26] It took overwhelming evidence of failure as well as the advent of new leadership in both the Soviet Union and Afghanistan to force a change in direction, and even then this would prove to be only partial. Old ways died hard.

Details of Soviet Aid to Afghanistan, 1979–1986

Financing for Soviet projects was provided by the 270 million rubles of credit promised in the agreement of March 1979, as well as an additional 200 million rubles of credit provided by a further agreement signed on 24 December 1978 and another 168 million rubles provided by a third agreement signed on 27 February 1985. The latter two were to be repaid over the welve years after the money was used, with an interest rate of 3 percent per annum (see Annex IV). These agreements, as well as various protocols stipulating how the funds were to be used, invariably used the same terminology, namely that:

The Government of the Republic of Afghanistan will pay off the credits … and the listed percentages by deliveries to the USSR of natural gas, citrus fruits, and other Afghan goods … the exchange of rubles into American dollars will be carried out according to the exchange rate of the State Bank of the USSR on the day preceding the payment.[27]

Again, this represented a continuation of previous Soviet practice.

The receipt of further loans increased Afghanistan's already substantial foreign debt. As noted in the previous chapter, the Soviets were well aware of Afghanistan's indebtedness and the problems this caused and it was in their interest to prevent their client from becoming insolvent. It is, therefore, perhaps a little curious that they persisted so long in providing aid in the form of loans rather than grants. This may have been inertia—simply the way things were done. However, the Soviets proved flexible when demanding repayment and several times rescheduled Afghanistan's loan agreements. In July 1983, for instance, the Permanent Intergovernmental Commission for Economic Cooperation reached agreement to reschedule payments on Soviet credits.[28] Further agreements on postponing debt repayments followed in April 1986, July 1987, February 1988, January 1989, February 1990, and April 1991. Overall, the Soviets postponed repayment of some 1.8 billion rubles (see Annex V). It does not seem to be the case that any development projects were cancelled or delayed due to lack of funds. Security problems were instead the primary cause of delays or cancellations.

Agriculture

According to a US study:

When the People's Democratic Party of Afghanistan came to power in April 1978, it inherited one of the poorest countries in the world. Afghanistan was still at a very early stage of development. Traditional activities in agriculture still dominated an economy in which many people lived right at the subsistence level.[29]

In a post-war review, the Soviet General Staff noted that at the time of the invasion, "Industrialization of the country was just beginning … Over 85 [percent] of the population of Afghanistan was involved in agriculture… Afghanistan's agriculture was only capable of providing the minimum necessary food and resources for the local economy."[30] Boosting agricultural production was absolutely essential for the overall development of the economy.

The Soviets claimed to be providing "substantial aid" to Afghan agriculture. According to *Pravda*:

Soviet tractors, combines and other agricultural equipment are operating on Afghan fields. Mineral fertilizers and seeds are delivered from the USSR to the DRA. Soviet specialists render the Afghan peasants aid in animal husbandry and veterinary services, the protection of plants against pests and diseases, and the repair and modernization of irrigation systems and installations.[31]

This was true, but agriculture received less funding than other sectors of the economy, and investment remained largely tied to a mechanical-industrial model, with continuing support for the state sector rather than large-scale aid to individual farmers. As one pro-Soviet Indian author noted, "ever since the Saur [April] Revolution there has been a regular rise in the state sector in agriculture. Its total output has gone up one and half times when compared to 1978–79."[32] Private agriculture, meanwhile, suffered considerably throughout the 1980s.

Irrigation projects remained a priority for both the Afghan and Soviet governments. According to *Moscow News*:

Arkadii Vasilenko, as a major Soviet expert on irrigation in the early 1980s, put all his weight behind convincing the republic to radically change its attitude toward irrigation. In 1982, the Revolutionary Council adopted an important decree on water, making it henceforth an asset of the people. Soon after, the Ministry of Irrigation was formed. Local water agencies were set up in the provinces. The ministry sent hundreds of young people to the USSR to learn their trade there. Study courses and technical schools appeared in Kabul. A large-scale reconstruction work of old irrigation networks, general repair of peasants' water ditches, and designing and building of big irrigation complexes have been launched.[33]

In reality, the big irrigation complexes remained a higher priority than the "general repair of peasants' ditches," many of which were destroyed in the fighting which ravaged the Afghan countryside. Soviet specialists continued working on the existing Jalalabad and Sarde irrigation systems, developed plans to construct a third system using water from the Kochka River and began preliminary work building a dam at Kosh-Tepe.[34] In October 1984 the Afghan Ministry of Irrigation and the Soviet agricultural export organization *Selkhozpromexport* signed a contract for the delivery of equipment and materials "to fulfill a plan to irrigate Afghan pastures."[35] However, probably because of the security situation, the Kochka River system never advanced far beyond the production of technical plans and some preliminary work.[36]

The Soviets tried to promote the mechanization of agriculture through the seven machine-tractor stations (MTS) established in accordance with the 1979 agreement. MTSs were an invention of Stalin-era collectivization, and are sometimes seen as a means by which the Soviet government established control of the countryside, by regulating who had access to the limited supply of agricultural machinery. They essentially provided a pool of agricultural equipment which was loaned to farms. Given that most Afghan farmers were too poor to afford such machinery themselves and their plots of land were in any case too small to justify the expense of purchasing it, MTSs in theory provided them with an opportunity to access equipment such as tractors for short periods of time to plough fields and collect harvests. Under the 1979 agreement, the Soviets were to have established all seven MTSs by the end of 1982,[37] but they failed to meet this schedule. A 1982 report in the magazine "*Za Rubezhom* (Abroad)" stated that four MTSs were already in operation, one each in Balkh, Jowzjan, Kabul, and

Baghlan provinces. According to "*Za Rubezhom*," the Jowzjan MTS had twenty-eight tractors, twelve combine harvesters, and other equipment.[38] Only one more MTS was finished by the end of 1987. In January 1988 TASS reported that five MTSs were working and another two were under construction.[39] Only in October 1988 did TASS state that all seven stations were functioning.[40]

MTS equipment was provided under the terms of the credit agreements between the Soviet Union and Afghanistan, and was thus not free. *Pravda* claimed in October 1980 that "2,000 tractors made in the USSR are being used in Afghan agriculture,"[41] but many of these probably dated from before the revolution. Thereafter the Soviet Union delivered hundreds more, including 1,200 in the period 1979 to 1982[42] and an additional 200 which the USSR agreed to supply on a long-term soft-credit basis in April 1986.[43] Western sources note that perhaps as a result of this, "tractor use by Afghan peasants increased significantly during the war."[44] The head of the Jowzjan MTS, for instance, claimed in 1982 to "have collected the harvest from 1,900 hectares with our machines, and ploughed more than a thousand hectares."[45] Overall, though, this represented only a small fraction of Afghanistan's land and was insufficient to reverse the decline in production brought about by the war.

The largest input of Soviet aid in the area of agriculture came with an agreement signed on 21 September 1982. In this, the USSR agreed to help Afghanistan to build six soil laboratories in Kabul, Mazar-i-Sharif, Jalalabad, Kunduz, Herat, and Kandahar, three seed control laboratories in Kabul, Kunduz, and Herat provinces, and five cotton seed laboratories in Kabul, Kunduz, Balkh, Herat and Helmand provinces; to reconstruct the artificial insemination station and its six affiliates in Balkh, Baghlan, Ghazni, Jalalabad and Herat provinces; to create mobile veterinary points in border posts at Turkham, Khost and Spin Boldak; to create a bird incubator station in Balkh province; to create an agricultural technical college for up to 750 students on the base of the existing professional technical college in Kandahar; to send Soviet specialists to assist in all these projects; and to accept Afghan students into the USSR for training in corresponding enterprises in order to be able to work in these new institutions. The Soviet Union assigned 200 million rubles in credit for these purposes.[46] This plan was never completed in full: the Soviets finished only three of the six soil laboratories, one of the three seed control laboratories, two of the five cotton seed laboratories, and three of the six artificial insemination stations; the bird incubator station project was cancelled (see Annexes I & VI).

The Soviets also continued work they had undertaken before the revolution "helping Afghanistan to combat agricultural pests and various livestock diseases and to organize a veterinary service."[47] To this end, in January 1984, the Soviets agreed to supply Afghanistan with pesticides and to establish a laboratory to help combat agricultural pests.[48] How much ordinary farmers benefitted from these measures is not clear.

The Soviets did not entirely overlook private farmers, even if they came relatively far down the list of priorities. Throughout the 1980s the Soviets provided seed and fertilizer free of charge. In 1983–84, for instance, the Soviet Union delivered 112,000 tons of chemical fertilizer and 13,000 tons of wheat seed to Afghanistan.[49] Similarly, the Soviets delivered 40,000 tons of chemical fertilizer free of charge in spring 1986.[50] The Afghan government tried to encourage cotton production, hoping this would provide a taxable form of income as well as boost the textile industry. The Soviet Union helped by providing cotton seed, enabling the government to distribute 2,000 tons of seed in 1986 (compared with only 65–80 tons annually in the 1970s).[51]

To give farmers a market for their products, encourage light industrial production, and satisfy consumer demand, the Soviets also invested in related industries. Results of these investments included: another bakery in Kabul, with a capacity of 65 tons of bread products a day, completed in 1981; a mill in Pul-i-Khumri with a production capacity of 60 tons a day, finished in 1982; and a factory for processing citrus fruits and olives in Jalalabad, completed in 1984.[52] The Soviets also built new woolen and cotton factories in Kandahar, as well as another textile factory in Herat, and expanded the existing Balkh textile factory. A Soviet reference book declared that "textile industry has received the most significant development in Afghanistan in the sphere of factory production."[53]

Electrical, Transport, and Urban Infrastructure

The urban population grew significantly during the 1980s as a result of war-related depopulation of the countryside, thus increasing demand for electricity in the cities. The development of a new industrial zone in Kabul furthered this trend in the capital city.[54] At the same time, rebel attacks damaged many power lines, causing power shortages. For instance, the rebels destroyed the power lines bringing electricity from the American-built Kajaki dam to Kandahar city. Iurii Sal'nikov, a Soviet civilian advisor in Kandahar, thus noted that "the city is without electrical supply and lives now entirely on diesel generator stations. They need a lot of fuel, which automobile tanker columns bring from the Soviet Union over a distance of 700 kilometers."[55] This had seriously negative effects on industrial production (in Kandahar's case severely restricting capacity at the new textile factories). Consequently, electrical infrastructure received a high priority in Soviet aid plans.

As a first step, the Soviets upgraded the existing power stations at Mazar-i-Sharif to increase output by a third (from thirty-six to forty-eight megawatts).[56] This, however, was not sufficient to meet increased demand. In 1982, therefore, the Soviets and Afghans signed an agreement under which the former agreed to help the latter construct a 490-kilometer power line linking the Soviet Union with Kabul.[57] Nothing was done about this until 1986, when the Afghan Ministry of Energy and the Soviet company *Tekhnopromeksport* signed a series of contracts to construct three power lines linking the electrical grid of the Soviet Central Asian republics with cities in northern Afghanistan, from where the lines were eventually meant to extend south to the Afghan capital. The two sides also signed contracts to carry out a feasibility study for building a new hydroelectric cascade at Sarobi (known as Sarobi-2, Sarobi-1 being an earlier German-built cascade), and to draw up plans for a fourth power line.[58] Work on two of the lines began almost immediately and was completed by the end of the following year, resulting in two 220-kilowatt lines running from the Soviet border to Kunduz and to Mazar-i-Sharif. The final stage, extending the power lines to Kabul, never happened (at least not until 2009, when it was finally completed by Uzbek engineers).

Transport infrastructure also received considerable attention. Rebel forces destroyed on average forty-five trucks a month,[59] and damaged or destroyed numerous roads and bridges. Meanwhile, heavy military traffic added to wear and tear. According to a 1984 report: "Afghanistan's highways and roads are increasingly hazardous … Their physical condition has deteriorated dramatically; bridges have been destroyed and left unrepaired… there is also the increasing risk of getting caught in a crossfire… As a result, the amount of non-military travel and transport in Afghanistan decreased significantly in 1984."[60] This greatly complicated internal commerce. According to one Soviet author, rebel attacks:

led to the destruction of communications within and between branches of industry. Industrial enterprises have begun to experience difficulties with the supplies of fuel, electricity, raw materials, spare parts, and the sale of produce.[61] Consequently, in 1983 the Afghan Prime Minister Sultan Ali Keshtmand commented that "transport is our main economic bottleneck."[62]

Afghanistan had few good roads for a country of its size. As a Soviet reference book noted: "The lack of good roads still in the recent past complicated the economic development of certain regions which are linked with other parts of the country only by caravan routes."[63] Despite this, the Afghan government and the Soviets put very little effort in this period into building new roads. The 1982 economic plan, for instance, called for only 47 kilometers of new roads.[64] Instead they focused on repairing and upgrading existing infrastructure and on supplying and maintaining the state trucking fleet.

In 1985, for instance, the Soviets modernized Kabul airport[65] and in 1987 they reconstructed the railway station at Turgundi.[66] They also upgraded transport links between the Soviet Union and northern Afghanistan. This work served military as well as civilian purposes, but the plans for these projects dated back to several years before the invasion and had their origins in a desire to enhance trade. As noted in the previous chapter, the Soviets considered the lack of port capacity to be a major impediment to Soviet-Afghan trade. In 1978, the Soviet Ministry of External Trade noted that:

Due to the unsatisfactory mechanization of Afghan ports, an insufficiency of dockers, and a lack of storage buildings and platforms for storing loads there were serious difficulties in 1977 in carrying out loading and unloading work in the Afghan ports of Hairaton and Shir Khan and at the railway station in Turgundi. The Soviet port of Termez is literally stuffed with loads for Afghanistan (31,000 tons).[67]

The solution was the development of the Afghan port of Hairaton. In 1980, the Soviets resolved to provide containers, cranes, and machinery for unloading, to increase the concreted area of the port and to construct new storage spaces. These measures were meant to double the port's capacity.[68] Progress in implementing the plan was slow. In 1982 the Soviets constructed a transhipment base on the Afghan bank of the Amu Darya near Hairaton.[69] Later in the decade, they also remedied other perceived deficiencies of the port, building a facility for unloading special loads in 1986 and three concrete platforms for storing containers in 1987.

Another important feature of the plan was the construction of a bridge designed to permit transportation of 800,000 tons of cargo a year[70] across the Amu-Darya River, linking the towns of Termez in Uzbekistan and

Hairaton in Afghanistan.[71] The planning of the bridge had a long history. The Afghans had supported the concept in the early 1970s, seeing it as a cheaper means of ensuring oil deliveries from the Soviet Union than the construction of an oil pipeline.[72] The Soviets gave the technical plans for the bridge to the Afghans in 1976,[73] but although the Afghans agreed to the plans, by 1978 they had grown cold to the idea, considering it too expensive.[74] The Soviets, however, remained keen, and following the 1979 invasion hurried to complete the project, finally opening the "Friendship Bridge" in May 1982.

Significant efforts went into repairing existing roads. Engineer forces of the Soviet Army regularly repaired war-damaged roads and bridges, although this work could barely keep pace with the damage caused by overuse of the highways by military traffic, meaning that the army's contribution to maintaining transport infrastructure was neutral at best.[75] More significantly, in 1985 the Soviet Union undertook to repair the Hairaton-Kabul highway over which most traffic from the Soviet Union travelled and which therefore constituted Afghanistan's main economic artery.[76] By the end of 1986 Soviet engineers had completed reconstruction of all road installations on the Hairaton-Kabul highway. This included the Salang tunnel, in which the Soviets "improved the ventilation and power supply, installed automation in signaling systems and telephone and television communications, and built new technical installations." This "made it possible to triple the tunnel's capacity."[77]

The main Soviet solution to Afghanistan's transport crisis was to supply hundreds of Soviet-built trucks. These went to state-owned enterprises and to the joint Afghan-Soviet transport company the Afgano-Sovetskoe Transportno-Ekspeditsionnoe Obschestvo (AFSOTR). By 1986 the Afghan government had created ten state trucking enterprises with a total of about 3,500 trucks.[78] AFSOTR alone possessed 743 Soviet heavy trucks and employed 2,500 workers and drivers,[79] as well as fifty Soviet specialists.[80] Because of all this, the state's share of the Afghan truck fleet grew from 12.4 percent to 40.7 percent in the period 1978/9–1986/7.[81]

The Soviets built several repair shops to service these trucks. In 1983 they completed the first of what by 1985 would be three service stations in Kabul, each able to service 300 Kamaz trucks a year,[82] and in 1984 they built another service station for Kamaz trucks in Hairaton.[83] The Soviets also upgraded the Jangalak auto-repair shop, allegedly increasing output by 22 percent by 1985,[84] and in 1987 set up within the Jangalak complex the first metal casting shop in Afghanistan.[85] Soviet specialists continued to work at Jangalak while Afghan workers were sent from there to train in the Soviet Union.[86]

By the mid-1980s the population of Kabul had risen substantially, to about one and a half million. This put great pressure on housing and other facilities within the capital. "The housing situation," said the newspaper *Novoe Vremia* in December 1981, "is difficult—it is simply bad."[87] In an effort to cope with the problem, from 1981–2 the Soviets expanded the capacity of the Kabul Housing Combine.[88] Soviet architects drew up a new plan for the reconstruction of the capital city in 1979. Among other things this envisioned the building of a new *mikroraion* on Bibi-Mahru hill in eastern Kabul, which was to consist of 50 four- and five-storey apartment blocks housing around 90–100,000 residents.[89] Beyond an Olympic-size swimming pool, it does not seem as if much progress was made in enacting the plan, but the Housing Combine did manage to complete some projects, such as the construction of a giant boiler-house to supply much of Kabul with hot water.[90]

Natural Resources

The Soviets continued to show considerable interest in natural resource exploitation during the 1980s. As a result, the Soviet and Afghan governments signed a series of agreements promising cooperation in this field. These included the previously mentioned March 1979 agreement to develop copper deposits at Aynak as well as oil deposits at Angot, Akdaria and Kashgari; a 1983 agreement to extend Soviet assistance in geological surveying for five years;[91] an August 1985 agreement on cooperation in the gas industry, to include further prospecting for gas from 1986 to 1990; to build a gas purification plant at Mazar-i-Sharif; to repair and improve existing pipelines and install 50 kilometers of looping on the Afghanistan-USSR pipeline; and to work on the compressor station at Jarkaduk.[92]

At the time of the Soviet invasion, Afghanistan was producing about 220 million cubic feet of natural gas a day. Due to the depletion of existing reserves this was down from a peak of 275 million cubic feet in the mid-1970s. To boost production, work began in 1977 on a new gas field and purification plant at Jarkaduk, also in northern Afghanistan. Work was completed and production began in May 1980.[93] The new gas field was expected to produce two billion cubic meters of natural gas annually, as well as 15,000 tons of gas condensate, thereby nearly doubling national production to a little under 400 million cubic feet a day.[94] In 1984 Soviet prospectors discovered two more new gas fields at Bashikor and Jangal in Jowzjan province, and in 1985 TASS reported further exploration work, stating that "In the past few months, 10 gas wells were drilled with the participation of Soviet specialists and boring work has begun on another four."[95] However, full-scale production at the new sites never commenced.

Projects completed after the opening of the Jarkaduk gas fieldconsist of the 50 kilometers of pipeline looping mentioned above,[96] the construction of a compressor station at the Khodzha-Gugerdag gas field,[97] an expansion of the oil storage facility at Hairaton to 5,000 cubic meters of capacity and the construction of two new oil storage facilities at Mazar-i-Sharif and Logar, of 12,000 cubic meters and 27,000 cubic meters volume respectively.[98]

Following a 1979 agreement in which the USSR agreed to help Afghanistan develop oil fields,[99] the Soviets surveyed for oil and by late 1984 were reported as having discovered seven new fields. Preliminary work was said to have begun in the Sar-e Pul region of Jowzjan province,[100] but as with the new gas fields, full-scale production never commenced.

The story with mineral deposits was very similar. According to an American report, "By 1985 Soviet surveys had revealed potentially useful deposits of asbestos, nickel, mercury, lead, zinc, bauxite, lithium, and rubies."[101] The Soviets also set up a laboratory for the analysis of minerals in Kabul in 1986 to assist with survey work.[102] Very little was done, however, to exploit what was found. The poor security situation prevented the Soviets from carrying out their promised plan to create a copper mining and enrichment plant at Aynak,[103] and although preliminary work began on the iron deposits at Hadjigak in 1983, production never began there either.[104] Thus, as Bradsher has noted, despite claims that the Soviets invaded Afghanistan in order to seize its natural resources, in fact "Moscow made no significant effort to tap them."[105]

Communications & Media

Telephone, radio, television and newspapers were important new areas of Soviet investment after the 1979 invasion. Despite claims that "By the end of March 1986, 180 telephone exchanges and radio stations have started operating,"[106] it would appear that radio and satellite communications received far more attention than telephone systems. The war not only put many of the latter out of action but also made it almost impossible to repair them. As one Soviet author noted, "Counterrevolutionary bands have destroyed practically all 17,000 kilometers of wire communications which existed in Afghanistan prior to the revolution. An insignificant part has been rebuilt, but Kabul's basic link with the provinces, and of the provinces among themselves, is radio, for which 234 radio stations have been built."[107]

The first major communications project constructed with Soviet help was a 1,000-kilowatt medium-wave radio broadcasting station, for which the Central Committee of the CPSU approved ten million rubles of credit in 1980, repayable at 3 to 4 percent annual interest over ten years. Originally destined to be built in Kandahar, this was moved to Kabul at the request of the Afghan government.[108] Thereafter the Soviets helped to build a multi-channel communications line from Mazar-i-Sharif to Hairaton in 1982[109] and in the same year they helped to build a satellite communications station which, according to *Pravda*, "ensures reception and transmission of color and monochrome television programs, radio programs, and telephone communications."[110] The Soviets subsequently helped to build television stations and rebroadcast stations in various major cities. For instance, *Izvestiia* reported the opening of a television station in Herat in November 1984,[111] and Iurii Sal'nikov, who worked in Kandahar in the mid-1980s, noted in his diary that "In Kandahar a rebroadcast station was recently set up, and one can now watch television broadcasts from Kabul."[112] Mazar-i-Sharif, Nangarhar, Ghazni, Paktia, Farah, and Badakshan provinces were also reported to have received new radio and television stations using the new satellite system, and as a further step, "in September 1986, Kabul Radio announced that the USSR would help set up twenty television stations as part of a nationwide network."[113]

These projects reflected the importance Moscow placed on fighting the ideological struggle in Afghanistan. This was an early priority of Soviet leaders after the December 1979 invasion. In February 1980 the Central Committee of the CPSU passed a resolution ordering Soviet organizations to provide support to the Afghan mass media. The Soviet mass media, the Central Committee instructed:

Are to continue work to explain the actions of the Soviet Union directed at defending the national sovereignty and territorial integrity of Afghanistan, the good neighborly relations of friendship and cooperation between the peoples of the Soviet Union and Afghanistan, and unmask the anti-Soviet, anti-Afghan policy unleashed by imperialist circles and the Peking hegemonists.[114]

Among the specific measures the Central Committee ordered were the following: the Soviets were to accept a group of Afghan television specialists into the USSR for internships and to send three Soviet specialists to Afghanistan for two months to help increase broadcasts in Dari and Pashto; TASS was to provide aid to its Afghan equivalent, the Bakhtar News Agency, rebroadcasting its programs to Arab and European countries, giving Bakhtar twenty teletype machines, sending a specialist to Bakhtar for six months, receiving six Bakhtar workers on internships in Moscow, and sending five specialists to Afghanistan to train personnel; the State Committee on Printing was to send specialists to Kabul to help production and to improve the qualification of Afghan printers; the Ministry of Higher Education was to accept twenty Afghan students and train them to work in newspapers, radio and television; editorial workers from Soviet newspapers were to go to Afghanistan to help their Afghan counterparts; and two Soviet teachers were to teach in Kabul University's journalism faculty.[115]

Human Capital

The instructions above to send specialists and receive Afghans for training were very similar to those found in almost every Soviet-Afghan agreement on economic cooperation. The Soviets continued to place a strong emphasis on the development of human capital. This included support for education from elementary school through to university as well as professional and technical training. Unlike economic development projects, which the Afghans had to pay for using Soviet credits, the Soviets provided this educational assistance free of charge.

At the time of the 1978 April Revolution, the great bulk of Afghanistan's population was still illiterate. Only 14 percent of the population went to school.[116] The PDPA regime placed great hopes on education as a modernizing force. Perhaps in response, rebel forces deliberately targeted schools and teachers. According to the official Afghan press, there were only 4,185 schools in the country at the time of the revolution; over 2,000 schools of these were destroyed after 1978.[117] Others still had to close. By 1983, only 860 schools were still open and by 1986 some 2,000 teachers had been killed.[118] Iurii Sal'nikov noted that in Kandahar province, "Before the war there were 190 schools in the cities and the villages. There was no shortage of teachers… Now only 34 schools are open in the province, 26 of them in the provincial center and only eight in rural areas."[119]

Soviet organizations undertook a number of measures to try to reverse this decline. The Soviet Army, for instance, claimed to have built or repaired around 100 schools during its ten-year stay in Afghanistan.[120] In addition, soon after the April Revolution, education specialists came from Soviet Central Asia to help reform the Afghan school and university curricula. They introduced new textbooks for both primary and secondary schools, which supplanted the older versions produced in the United States, and replaced them with modified versions of Soviet books. By 1982, sixteen such textbooks had appeared.[121] Another significant change was the introduction of school education in languages other than Dari and Pashto. Previously, Afghan children were only educated in these two languages. Hoping to win the support of other nationalities, and at the behest of Soviet advisors who drew on experience with the nationalities question, the PDPA introduced schooling in Uzbek, Turkmen, Baluch and Nuristani.[122] The problem was that there were no curricula or textbooks in these languages. Soviet linguists stepped in and rapidly translated and adapted existing Soviet texts to fill the gap. According to Eden Naby:

The Nuristani language, never before written, appeared in print only some months after the 1978 coup. Soviet advisers who were questioned about the speed with which an alphabet had been adapted to the language replied that they had been working on the problem for many years. In the same way, the development of school books in ethnic languages appears to have been anticipated before the coup. By the fall of 1978, Soviet Uzbek advisers were busy adapting Soviet grade books to Afghan needs. In six months, the first Uzbek reader for Afghan Uzbeks was ready for publication. It followed closely the format of Soviet books.[123]

Soviet involvement in primary and secondary education led to some complaints that a deliberate campaign of "indoctrination" was underway to "Sovietize" Afghan youth. American author Jeri Laber wrote in 1980 that "Afghan children who live in cities under Soviet control are being subjected to a Soviet-style education aimed at creating a new, communist Afghan."[124] Programs that brought young Afghans to the Soviet Union for varying lengths of stay were seen as further evidence of this. Among the instructions given by the CPSU Central Committee in 1980 was an order to the young communist league (the Komsomol) and the Soviet health ministry to provide "sanitary holidays" for young Afghans.[125] This meant bringing them to Komsomol and Pioneer summer camps (Pioneers being younger than Komsomols and somewhat akin to compulsory boy scouts). No reliable figures exist for how many Afghan children attended these camps, which were primarily in Uzbekistan and Tajikistan. The British Foreign and Common-wealth Office estimated the amount as about 3,000 children aged ten to fourteen each year,[126] while an American diplomat in 1982 put the number at 1,200, "most aged 10 to 12."[127] Another estimate of about 11,000 during the period from 1980 to 1988 is probably not far off the mark.[128]

More controversial still was a project announced in 1984 to provide long-term education for Afghan war orphans in the Soviet Union. The first batch of 870 children, aged between seven and ten, departed Afghanistan in November of that year. They were meant to study in the Soviet Union for ten years and then return home.[129] Anti-Soviet commentators claimed that these children were subjected to intense communist indoctrination. One such commentator, Jeri Laber, stated:

When older children are sent to the USSR to attend school for short periods the Soviet authorities take account of their religious upbringing. They are usually sent to Soviet Central Asia, where they are taught by teachers who know their language and religions… With orphans, however, the approach is direct. "The curriculum … is different," according to Professor Amin, "based completely on the communist way of teaching."[130]

How far the negative claims about Soviet education were true and how far they were simply anti-Soviet rumor and propaganda is impossible to tell.

In any case, primary and secondary education were not the Soviets' priority. Far more important from their point of view was training the future leaders and technicians of Afghanistan. As *Pravda* noted in 1984, "The success of the cause depends to a large degree on the preparedness of cadres."[131] To this end, a Soviet-Afghan protocol of 30 October 1979 on "economic and technical cooperation in the preparation of Afghan national cadres" committed the Soviet Union to send "up to 115 specialists in pro-fessional-technical education for a period of up to 3 years for work in professional technical education in the DRA [Democratic Republic of Afghanistan]."[132]

Soon after, in December 1980, the Soviets and Afghans signed a second protocol on assistance in the preparation of national cadres. In this, the USSR agreed to accept various quantities of workers and leaders into the USSR from the ministries of water resources and energy, agriculture and land reform, and mines, as well as agricultural and light industry specialists, state farm and cooperative workers and trainee drivers to take courses and internships of between fifteen days and six months. The Soviets also prom-ised to send eighty-five socio-economic, technical, and language teachers to

Afghanistan, provide equipment for a chemical laboratory at Kabul University, help publish 150 textbooks in Dari and Pashto and build a boarding school in Kabul.[133] This aid was free of charge.

Following these agreements, the 1980s witnessed a large increase of Afghan workers and students studying in the Soviet Union. Figures cited by Afghan and Soviet sources varied: in 1983 the Afghan minister of higher education claimed that 12,000 Afghan students were in the USSR[134] (compared with 1,500 in 1978/79),[135] while in September 1984 *Moscow News* was reporting that "7,500 Afghan young people now study in the Soviet Union,"[136] and by 1987 the new President of Afghanistan, Najibullah, was citing a figure of "more than 10,000 Afghan students in the Soviet Union."[137] An academic source claimed that about 60,000 Afghans studied in the USSR from 1980 to 1984, including party members, military personnel, police, and intelligence personnel, as well as "200 musicians and others from Afghan radio, television and films; 669 mullahs, elders and personnel from the Ministry of Islamic Affairs; 569 tribal figures and personnel from the Ministry of Tribes and Nationalities; and 900 more identified simply as 'workers'."[138] Put together, these would suggest a probable total of about 10,000 at any one time. Most of these probably received training in technical subjects, especially engineering, in colleges in Central Asia, although some went elsewhere.[139] An analysis of PhD dissertations submitted by Afghan students in the USSR suggests that higher-level students were oriented more towards the social sciences (economics and political science) and history.[140]

The Soviets also helped to educate and train tens of thousands of Afghans within Afghanistan. TASS claimed in July 1988 that "over 100,000 Afghan workers, technicians, and engineering-technical specialists have been trained,"[141] a total which does not seem improbable. Technical training was once again the priority. In accordance with the agreements mentioned above, Soviet teachers continued to teach at existing institutions such as the Kabul Polytechnic Institute and the Mazar-i-Sharif mining college. Meanwhile, the Soviet Union helped to construct new colleges and educated Afghans in their workplaces. New educational institutions built with Soviet help included "eight vocational colleges to train specialists for various branches of the national economy."[142] According to the terms of a Soviet-Afghan agreement of 1985, the Soviets also agreed to create by 1990 a further ten professional technical institutes and one industrial-pedagogical technical college, to educate up to 4,000 students and also send Soviet specialists to work in these institutes.[143] However, it does not seem that this was done.

Soviet advisors and teachers also played an important role in the Ministry of Education and at Kabul University. In 1982, it was estimated that "no fewer than 140 Soviet specialists and 105 Russian language teachers taught at the university and Kabul technical colleges."[144]

In addition, acknowledging the grave shortage of qualified personnel within the ruling PDPA, the Soviet Academy of Sciences helped to establish an Institute of Social Sciences for the Central Committee of the PDPA.[145] This, combined with the training given to personnel from various ministries mentioned above, represented an attempt to carry out what in modern parlance is called "capacity building"—an attempt to increase the capacity of state institutions by improving the quality of the personnel within them.

Provision of Specialists

After the 1979 invasion the number of advisors attached to state institutions, such as the ministries, media, and military and intelligence apparatus increased substantially. TASS stated in February 1982 that there were Soviet specialists working at fifty joint Soviet-Afghan enterprises, where they "share their experience with Afghan workers."[146] There were, for instance, 190 Soviet specialists working at the nitrogen fertilizer plant in Mazar-i-Sharif alongside 2,500 Afghans,[147] and more than fifty working for the Ministry of Irrigation.[148] Lack of qualified Afghan personnel meant that Soviet advisers "were placed in key positions throughout the government to direct the planning of projects and their implementation,"[149] so that "every ministry and department had its own set of advisers from its Soviet counterpart."[150] Some Western estimates put the number of Soviet advisors as high as 10,000,[151] but Soviet sources put it as between 2,500 and 3,000, which seems a more likely number.[152]

Money was a major motivation for many specialists, as they were paid much more than in the Soviet Union and could gain access to Western consumer goods which found their way into Afghanistan from Pakistan.[153] Still, many seem to have sincerely believed in what they were doing. This was especially true of the approximately one-third of advisors who came from Soviet Central Asia. Some of these appear to have looked at Afghanistan and thought, "There but for the grace of Lenin go I." In their minds, Afghanistan represented what their own republics would have looked like had it not been for the benefits of Soviet power, and they wished to spread those benefits to the Afghan people. As one Uzbek later said: "We felt we were bringing freedom and democracy to Afghanistan, especially to women. We felt we were liberating them from their miserable past."[154]

Unlike their twenty-first century Western counterparts, Soviet civilians working in Afghanistan brought their wives and families with them and lived in ordinary houses and apartments, not in fortified compounds, although "people always carried their personal weapons and every apartment block had an armed guard."[155] "I would freely get in my car and drive around alone," says Valerii Ivanov.[156] However, this was only possible in the towns, and mainly Kabul; the situation was worse elsewhere. Braithwaite records that, "In Jalalabad women were not allowed to go on the streets without an armed escort,"[157] while Iurii Sal'nikov described walking around downtown Kandahar "with a machine gun on my shoulder and two pistols on my belt."[158] Outside the cities, even this was impossible. As Ivanov also says, "Generally security was guaranteed in the towns, but everywhere outside the towns, as today, there might be mujahideen, or might not. Nobody would risk people, why do so?"[159] As time went on, Kabul also became increasingly insecure, and by 1986 Soviet civilians were not allowed downtown without armed escorts even in the Afghan capital, although this did not apparently stop some of them from doing so anyway.[160]

The areas where the Soviets lived were thus tightly guarded, as were the families when they left these areas. As an Afghan shopkeeper in Kabul told a Western journalist:

We always know when Russian families are coming to do shopping. It begins with the arrival of two Russian trucks full of soldiers who take up positions along the street with their fingers on the trigger. The limousines full of Soviet husbands and wives arrive. The husbands never let the wives out of their sight. As if at a given signal, everyone seems to have completed their purchases and the whole convoy sets off again for Mikrorayon.[161]

Despite these precautions, Soviet civilians were not safe from danger. Iurii Sal'nikov recorded being blown into the corridor by the explosion of a shell which landed just 10 to 15 meters from his home in Kandahar. Although Sal'nikov was only slightly injured, his colleague Grisha Semchenko was badly wounded in the right foot. This was the second time Semchenko had been wounded in Afghanistan.[162] Similarly, in Kabul "a rocket hit a wall and destroyed the living room of three nurses living together in a Microrayon apartment,"[163] while Soviet doctor Alla Alekseevna

Tsybaneva recounted in the newspaper *Sovetskaia Rossiia* how she was caught up in a firefight when rebel fighters seized the building next to the clinic in which she worked in Kabul.[164]

These Soviets survived. Others were not so lucky. Several Soviet civilian specialists were killed by insurgents in the years after the April Revolution. Valerii Ivanov calculates the number at not more than three or four,[165] but this is certainly an underestimation. In March 1979, an uprising in the city of Herat resulted in the deaths of a Soviet trade representative, Iurii Bogdanov, who was murdered by an Afghan mob, and of a Soviet oil expert, who was "killed by a stray bullet."[166] Another Soviet specialist supposedly disappeared while fleeing the city. It is said that when his colleagues found his body, it had been "sliced open, disemboweled, and stuffed with straw."[167] Despite some claims that up to 100 Soviet citizens were killed in the Herat uprising, these (and a Soviet military officer, Major Nikolai Biziukov) appear to have been the only victims of that particular event, although others were killed elsewhere on other occasions. These included the Soviet geologist E.R. Okhrimiuk, who was abducted in a "daring daylight raid"[168] in Kabul in August 1981 and then murdered after attempts to negotiate a ransom or a prisoner exchange failed;[169] a woman professor killed when a bomb exploded in the dining room of Kabul University in 1983;[170] a scientific assistant at the polytechnic institute, Aleksei Muratov, who was shot in Kabul;[171] a Soviet specialist killed when rebels seized a group working at the grain elevator in Mazar-i-Sharif (the others who were captured were later rescued by Soviet forces);[172] and the bookkeeper at the Russian trade office and his wife, Evgenii and Nina Konovalov, who were killed by a tank shell when Kabul fell to the rebels in August 1992.[173]

Because of these dangers, after the Herat uprising Soviet specialists were forbidden to drive into the countryside on their own. Specialists continued working in most major cities, but not Herat, to which they never returned.[174]

Assessment of Soviet Aid

Soviet and pro-Soviet propaganda lauded the economic progress made in Afghanistan following the April Revolution and Soviet military intervention. In a typical example, a pro-Soviet Indian author claimed in 1987 that:

During the five years 1981–1986 the national income rose by 11 per cent and it was now more than what obtained in 1978–79. Much of this increase in national income was contributed by the joint and state sectors. Production rose by 47 per cent in these sectors during 1980–81 and 1985–86.[175]

A 1986 *Pravda* report echoed this, stating that, "industrial output as a whole has increased by one fourth. The output of electricity, natural gas, cement and nitric fertilizers is greater than before the revolution. … Gross agricultural output has increased. … Afghanistan's foreign trade turnover has increased from 740 million dollars in 1977 to 1.6 billion dollars in 1985."[176] The Soviets claimed credit for these alleged achievements. According to one Soviet author, L.B. Teplinskii:

After the April revolution more than 50 projects were completed with Soviet assistance … Enterprises, constructed with Soviet economic assistance accounted in 1987 for more than 60 percent of factory production, provided 100 percent of gas production, the production of items for home building, nitric fertilizers, and 60 percent of energy.[177]

In truth, Soviet-built enterprises only made up such high percentages of industrial production for the simple reason that Soviet aid enabled them to keep going while the rest of the economy disintegrated. The war in Afghanistan brought economic catastrophe to the country. Between 1978 and 1982, "per capita gross national product fell from an already low Af7,370 to Af6,852 … the countryside was reverting to a subsistence agricultural economy."[178] Inflation "soared … food prices … rose by over 500 percent between 1979 and 1984."[179] By 1986, the annual inflation rate had reached somewhere between 600 and 1,000 percent.[180] Afghan Prime Minister Sultan Ali Keshtmand said in 1983 that, "The counterrevolutionary bands sent from abroad have destroyed 50 percent of the country's schools, more than 50 percent of our hospitals, 14 percent of the state's transportation vehicles, 75 percent of all communications lines, and a number of hydroelectric and thermal electric stations."[181] *Pravda* also noted the economic damage in a 1982 article, stating that:

Counter-revolutionary gangs have more than once destroyed citrus crops and stolen livestock from units of the Jalalabad complex. They have blown up a gas pipeline which supplies the Mazar-i-Sharif nitrogen fertilizer plant with raw materials. They have set fire to machines and Niva combine harvesters supplied to the machine and tractor station, have attacked other civilian installations and have attempted to cut communications.[182]

The war overshadowed everything else; in the midst of the fighting, economic progress was impossible. The war damaged existing infrastructure and hampered new projects. While the Soviets carefully guarded all the installations that they had built and were able to keep them operating throughout the 1980s, the war made the situation too dangerous for many new projects to make progress. As a result, in July 1980, November 1983 and November 1985, the Soviet and Afghan governments officially agreed to suspend work on thirty-seven projects, including:

the construction of the Kosh-Tepe canal, of the Chashman-Shafa, Kelegai and Kochka dams, of six aerodromes, of the Shibirghan-Herat highway and part of the Kunduz-Keshm road, of cotton and textile enterprises, of a bread factory and mill in Herat, of an electrical transmission line from the Naghlu power station to Jalalabad, of the Aynak mining enrichment combine, of an oil refinery and oil fields, and the carrying out of cartographic and other work.[183]

(See Annex VI for a complete list of cancelled projects.)

Agriculture

Agriculture was hit particularly hard. The PDPA's policy of land reform, combined with its institutional incapacity to provide promised goods such as credits, seeds and fertilizers to farmers, had played a large part in provoking rebellion against its rule. This rebellion brought enormous damage to Afghanistan's countryside. Thus agricultural collapse had its roots in institutional and political failings for which no amount of aid could compensate.

Despite government claims of rising agricultural production, the opposite was the case. Due to fighting, by 1985, "over half the labor force in the countryside has disappeared… corn acreage dropped by two-thirds, barley by half, rice by 80 [percent], and cotton by 85 [percent]."[184] Approximately 15,000 villages were estimated to have been destroyed or damaged. In addition, the agricultural crisis caused serious shortages of basic supplies in the major cities. As a result, the Soviet Union had to resort to feeding Afghanistan, delivering 200,000 tons of wheat a year by the mid-1980s.[185]

This reduced incomes and demand and had a knock-on effect on related industries, such as textiles and food products. Textile output was said to have fallen by 50 percent between 1978 and 1982, sugar production by 97 percent, and vegetable oil production by 73 percent.[186] Rebel attacks, the flight of trained personnel and problems with the supply of electricity compounded this problem. After defecting in December 1981, Ali Shah Qayumi, formerly chief administrator of Afghanistan's largest textile mill at Bagram, said that only 1,800 of the original 4,000 workforce remained: "Of the factory's original fleet of 33 trucks, nine were burnt by the resistance and two captured… The mill has been attacked three times, causing considerable damage and heavy losses."[187]

One cause of the drop in agricultural production was the excessive force used by the Soviet Army in its fight against rebel forces. Western observers regularly accused the Soviets of deliberately seeking to depopulate the countryside in order to deprive the rebels of the support of the local population.[188] In large part, though, Soviet tactics were simply a product of ignorance—Soviet commanders did not know any better. As General A.A. Liakhovskii later wrote, "Although the theoretical military training of officers in general was high, it was oriented to traditional forms of fighting battles, without considering the specifics of local conditions and the methods of partisan war, the study of which had not had sufficient attention."[189] It took many years for Soviet commanders to realize that traditional methods were counterproductive. In the meantime, they acted in the only way they knew when facing resistance, that is by using maximum force. The result was widespread destruction of fields, orchards and local irrigation systems, as well as the flight of farmers and their families from the land.

The Soviets were not the only ones responsible for economic destruction. The rebels also waged war on the countryside in a form of economic warfare. Iurii Sal'nikov commented that the Arghandab district near the city of Kandahar was "fertile, but the bandits do not allow the peasants to carry out agricultural work. As soon as a group of peasants appears in the fields, they start to shoot them."[190] The incapacity of the Afghan state and the Soviet army to provide basic security thus played an important role in ensuring economic failure. Sal'nikov noted the consequences: "Littered with mines, shells, bullets, smashed by aerial bombardment … the green zone around Kandahar no longer feeds the city with grapes, apricots, pomegranates, tomatoes, and potatoes. The farmer is afraid to work his plot."[191]

Soviet economic and technical assistance could not halt the agricultural decline. Irrigation projects made little difference, and in any case little progress was made in irrigating new land. The planned Kochka irrigation system was an early casualty of war, being cancelled in 1980. Even the land irrigated as a result of previous projects was not being fully exploited, as peasants fled the countryside. Thus Gorbachev complained in 1988 that "11,000 hectares of irrigated land are not being worked."[192]

Even though tractor use did increase during the war, the hopes placed in mechanization projects were not fulfilled. Rebel groups targeted the MTSs.

For instance, the head of the Jowzjan MTS told the Soviet newspaper *Za Rubezhom* in 1982 that, "In the past two months counter-revolutionary bands have killed five MTS workers, burnt six vehicles and two tractors and seized part of the equipment."[193] This was not the only problem. The MTS strategy ran into human problems, namely that the Afghans distrusted the stations. Thus in 1980 *Za Rubezhom* quoted a "Comrade Iosuf" from the Balkh province MTS who said: "Not all the province's peasants at once appreciated the role of the MTS,"[194] while in 1982 the head of Jowzjan MTS told the same newspaper that, "The peasants did not trust the MTS at first."[195] As shown also by the problems with land reform, a failure to understand the rural Afghan mentality plagued agricultural policy.

Efforts to help individual farmers by distributing seeds and fertilizers also ran in to difficulties. Sal'nikov noted that the Soviets took care always to act through Afghan government agencies. This is in accord with the thinking of many modern development practitioners who feel that if state legitimacy is to increase, the state itself must take control of aid programs, rather than have the aid distributed by foreigners. The problem was that the Afghan state could not be trusted to deliver the aid to those for whom the Soviets intended it.

Iurii Sal'nikov described the problem well. In the first place, local Afghan officials were often incompetent. According to Sal'nikov:

The government is trying to help the peasant, but it is not easy to do this. In order to sow the land, and then harvest it, one has to inform the municipality that one will be working in the fields at such and such a location, at such and such a time, on such and such a day. In this event the peasant will be safe, they will not bomb that place. But these declarations often get lost in the bureaucratic swamp. If they start work without the declaration, then people start shooting, but if they make the declaration, then people start shooting anyway, because the declaration was given to one set of people, but others are doing the shooting.[196]

In the second place, officials were often corrupt. Visiting Panjwai district in Kandahar province, Sal'nikov wrote:

The bandits do not allow the peasants to go to the district chief to get mineral fertilizer. The feudal lord takes the fertilizer from the agricultural directorate, which is in Kandahar city, and uses it on his own land. Peasants with little land have to buy fertilizer on the black market at 1,200 afghanis a bag.[197]

This sort of behavior was a widespread problem. According to Sal'nikov:

The directorate's job is to distribute mineral fertilizers in five provinces in the south of the country… They get the fertilizer from Herat by truck… The governor has a commission which assigns fertilizer to the peasants. But in practice it works like this: the boss of the area orders somebody to give it out. Here a bag of fertilizer (50 kilograms) costs a peasant 400 afghanis, but on the black market it is 1,200 afghanis. As a result most of the mineral fertilizer falls into the hands of traders. And the farmers walk around the government institutions for a day or two, or even a week, then spit and go away with nothing. There is an order of the Revolutionary Council not to give any person more than 30 bags of fertilizer, this being quite enough… But the provincial leader personally writes an order to the boss of the supply depot to give, for instance, 300 bags to one person. They give out a particularly large amount of fertilizer in Spin Boldak. In fact, the lands there are in the third category, there are almost no landholders, only herdsmen. In addition, Spin Boldak is next to the Pakistani border. I have seen an order by one leading personality to give the Spin Boldak tradesman Rasul, son of Mohammed, 1,000 bags of fertilizer. Another resident of Spin Boldak, Hadji Akhtar Mohammed, received 300 bags, although he owns no land… they sell the bags on the black market at three times the official price, i.e. at 1,200 afghanis a bag. Ask oneself how the ordinary farmer can respect the representatives of the national government if they allow such injustice.[198]

Corruption of this sort was endemic. As President Najibullah admitted in 1987, Soviet aid was "not being justly distributed … hoarding and bribery have been transformed into a source of wealth for individuals."[199] However, it was precisely the existence of Soviet aid which created so many opportunities for corruption. As Sal'nikov said, "Of course there is corruption. Many want to grab something in difficult times. All the more so when valuable goods are passing through their hands."[200] The Soviets were, therefore, in something of a catch-22 situation: their Afghan allies could not survive without their aid, but their aid contributed to the corruption and incompetence which made their allies so hated.

Electrical, Transport and Urban Infrastructure

One can observe a similar picture in other sectors of the economy. The Afghan and Soviet governments claimed that electrical production increased in the early 1980s,[201] but this seems unlikely given the damage done to power stations and transmission lines. According to Soviet author M.N. Khodzhaev: "The undeclared war caused significant loss to the electrical energy sector."[202] The two new power lines from the Soviet Union did alleviate the situation to some degree, but only in the north of the country. Elsewhere there were major power shortages. Kandahar, for instance, relied entirely on oil-powered generators due to damage to the line bringing power from the Kajaki dam.[203] The situation was a little better in Kabul, but electrical generation could not keep pace with the growing size of the city. By the end of the decade, a Soviet analyst reckoned that one central district of Kabul city alone suffered from "a deficit in electrical energy of about 250 million kilowatt hours," which was expected to grow before long to a deficit of 500 million. "Due to a lack of generating power," the author continued, "the overload of transformer stations and distribution networks, in winter electric use in Kabul is limited to 80 megawatts or less."[204] As a result there were "frequent blackouts" and poorer parts of the city received only "four to five hours power per week."[205]

Efforts to solve this situation largely failed. Plans for a new 60-megawatt hydroelectric dam at Kelagay on the Kunduz River[206] were among those cancelled in 1980. In 1987, Soviet troops under Colonel Anatolii Kozin made a major attempt to repair the power line from the Kajaki dam to Kandahar using materials brought from Alma-Ata. It was hoped that this would provide power to the two Soviet-built textile factories in Kandahar, which had not been fully functioning due to the lack of electrical supply. This, wrote General Varennikov, "would have been an enormous contribution to the development of Afghanistan's economy, and, consequently, to improving the life of the people."[207] The effort failed, due to repeated sabotage of the steel-concrete supports of the power lines. The Soviets were in a chicken-and-egg situation. Improving the security situation relied on economic development; but economic development proved impossible given the security situation. Only a political resolution offered a means out of the impasse, but that depended on the Soviet Army withdrawing. (Although, of course, if the Soviet Army withdrew, the regime was likely to fall, and civil war ensue, creating even more economic havoc! There were no easy solutions to Afghanistan's problems.)

Transport also suffered. Again this was not merely because of rebel attacks but also because of the government's ham-fisted policies. In a study of the Afghan transport sector, Soviet economist E.R. Makhmudov commented that the decision to focus resources on the state-trucking sector was forced on the government by the manner in which it alienated the private truck owners. Private Afghan trucking companies "sabotaged the transport of state loads, and took their vehicles out of the country. This was to no small degree helped by President Amin's policies of unsubstantiated accusations and persecutions of large entrepreneurs."[208] Once again, therefore, politics proved to be the crucial element in provoking economic collapse.

Natural Resources

Natural gas was possibly the lone sector that maintained production levels throughout the 1980s. This reflected the importance the Afghans and Soviets assigned to it, although, as we have seen, hopes of doubling production were not fulfilled. This was in part due to sabotage. Although the gas fields themselves were well protected by the Soviet Army, the pipelines were vulnerable to attack. By the end of 1983, the pipeline linking the Afghan gas fields with the Soviet Union had been cut "at least three times, and possibly as often as seven."[209]

Despite these problems, Afghanistan benefitted from rising world gas prices during the early 1980s. With further reference to complaints that the Soviets underpaid for Afghan gas, it is worth noting that in a 1988 memorandum detailing Soviet expenditures in Afghanistan, the Soviet State Planning Committee listed expenditures of seventy million rubles for 1986 and sixty-five million for 1987 as "Aid through preferential prices for Afghan goods delivered to the USSR." These goods included natural gas,[210] indicating that the Soviets believed that they were making a loss on purchases of Afghan gas. This might be because the Soviets agreed to a succession of increases in the price of Afghan gas after the April Revolution, rising from US$83.37 per cubic meter in February 1979 to US$111.45 in 1981/2 and US$117.83 in 1982/3.[211] Western critics complained that the amount paid in the last two years was still "comparable to the lower end of the scale for world markets"[212] (which may not have been unfair given the relatively poor quality of Afghan gas). Afghan officials claimed that "The price of the gas we export to the Soviet Union is higher than the world export price,"[213] and by the late 1980s the Soviets were claiming that the price they paid was "1.5 to two times higher than the price of gas on the world markets."[214] A 1986 memorandum of the Ministry of External Trade commented that, "In our opinion, the prices in Soviet-Afghan trade are favorable to the Afghans. In several cases these prices have a political tinge. The prices for Afghan natural gas, which are now above world prices, are especially favorable for the Afghan side."[215] It seems that the Soviets certainly believed this to be true.

The result of the higher prices was that although the volume of gas production leveled off after the Jarkuduk field came on line in 1980, the amount of money Afghanistan received increased substantially. This meant that, "By 1982 natural gas contributed 44 percent of all government revenues, compared with 17 percent in 1978."[216] Natural gas production thus continued to be the one sector built with Soviet aid that could be deemed a definite success.

By contrast, other projects for natural resource extraction were being derailed. Plans for exploiting oil fields and the Aynak copper mines were among those cancelled. Security was once again the primary problem. Although *Pravda* claimed in 1982 that "Joint work by Soviet and Afghan geologists has produced very favorable results … natural gas, oil, and many solid mineral deposits have been discovered,"[217] prospecting proved difficult, and exploiting discoveries was almost impossible. In 1981, as previously noted, the rebels captured and killed the chief Soviet geologist in Afghanistan, E.R. Okhrimiuk.[218] In papers found on him, Okhrimiuk had written that "the present situation excludes geological work without dependable protection by Soviet troops." He noted twenty-six attacks on the Aynak copper mine project between July 1980 and July 1981, and "cited 40 instances of destruction of Soviet drilling sites, trucks, and technical equipment. Damage inflicted to mining plants and equipment in Kabul province was estimated at Afghanis 108.4 million (US$2 million)."[219] In short, significant progress in natural resource exploitation was impossible as long as the war continued, and the investments made were to no avail.

Human Capital

Again and again, the Soviets found that human factors frustrated their attempts to improve the situation in Afghanistan. The large investments made in education, training and the provision of specialists failed to make an important difference and in some cases were counterproductive. This was to prove absolutely crucial.

Soviet contributions to primary and secondary education could not make up for the damage caused by the war. The 100 schools the Soviet Army claimed to have built could not compare with the 2,000 destroyed by the rebels.[220] While the government could claim some success in enhancing educational opportunities for girls—the enrolment rates rose from 8 percent to 14 percent from 1975 to 1985—overall, the number of Afghan children in schools fell precipitously—male enrolment fell in the same time period from 44 to 27 percent.[221]

Meanwhile, there were numerous criticisms of the new curricula and textbooks brought in by the Soviets. The fact that textbooks had been rapidly translated and adapted from Soviet Central Asian examples led to complaints that they contained "irrelevant examples" unsuited to Afghan pupils. Allegedly, there were also many translation errors, possibly a result of the haste with which they were prepared.[222]

The project to educate Afghan orphans in the Soviet Union backfired spectacularly, at least in political terms. Far from winning the Soviets good-will for their humanitarian gesture, the scheme led to accusations that the Soviets were kidnapping and mistreating children and became a prime piece of anti-Soviet propaganda. Reports claimed that "hundreds of children have been taken from their homes by agents of the secret police or seized on the streets. Parents have been arrested for refusing to let their children go."[223] Anti-Soviet sources claimed that some of the children were orphans but others "were more or less rounded up from poor neighborhoods or from schools in Kabul and sent without the knowledge or consent of their parents."[224] Rumors abounded of mistreatment in the USSR both in this program and at the Soviet summer camps. A former Kabul teacher said:

They were sending seventh and eighth grade students to the Soviet Union. When they came back, they were weak, worn out. I asked them why. They say, "They were taking us by bus and forcing us to work in a garden and wash carpets. We were forced to work a lot in Russia."[225]

As a result, "During 1984–86, this program created considerable resentment and fear in Kabul."[226]

In fact, the Soviet leadership seems to have genuinely regarded its program as a humanitarian gesture, to the extent that the Central Committee of the CPSU cited it in a memorandum for party members in 1988, saying that "The Soviet people hold the fate of the Afghan people close to their hearts. A symbol of this is the care given to hundreds of Afghan children—war orphans, who have found warmth and shelter on our land. They receive education and professional training from us and return home as good specialists."[227] Whether or not those who went to the Soviet Union were really orphans or were abducted by the Afghan police cannot be confirmed: there seems little reason to doubt that the Soviets intended the former, but the Afghans tasked with finding the orphans may have chosen to cut corners and do things their way.

Higher education also suffered in the 1980s, despite, and perhaps to some extent because of, Soviet involvement. Afghan defectors stated that Soviet advisors sought to eliminate "unscientific" elements from the university curriculum, such as the history of Islamic art, and simultaneously introduced new subjects such as dialectical materialism.[228] Changes of this sort led to some absurdly paranoid charges such as that "The science and engineering divisions of Kabul University … are now reliably reported to have been transformed into a terrorist training center."[229] However untrue this was, Soviet innovations, like the "irrelevant examples" in textbooks, reveal a startling degree of cultural blindness. Too often Soviet advisors sought to make Afghans adopt a Soviet model which simply did not fit Afghan circumstances.

It is also not clear how much Afghan students benefitted from education in the Soviet Union. Many certainly profited, but President Najibullah complained in 1987 that "a majority … are weak in their studies."[230] Soviet education could also turn out students who were inflexibly doctrinaire. Iuii Sal'nikov observed this phenomenon in an Afghan journalist named Matiullah who had just returned from studying Marxist-Leninist philosophy in the Soviet Union: "He acts just like he learnt in the institute: he divides people into friends and enemies. But society contains a large layer of people who are wavering, unsteady, hiding, or waiting to see who wins."[231] More education did not necessarily translate into more competent national cadres.

The brutal behavior of the Afghan regime made matters worse. After the 1978 coup, supporters of the Parcham faction within the PDPA set about purging members of the Khalq faction. As a result, before long, the Ministry of Education "did not have many qualified Afghan educators. In part because of this vacuum, Soviet advisers in the Education Ministry took over *de facto* management."[232] This process repeated itself in educational and cultural institutions, with hundreds of trained personnel being arrested or losing their jobs. Many of those who survived chose to flee rather than be next in line. As a result, by 1984 the number of professors at Kabul University had fallen from 750 to 432.[233]

The Soviet effort to improve Afghanistan's human capital thus ran afoul of a regime determined to eliminate independent thinking, proving once again the central role of politics in determining the success of development programs. University professors were not the only ones to suffer from the PDPA's repressive policies. Anybody with an education was vulnerable (even if they were loyal to the regime, given the infighting between Parcham and Khalq). According to one estimate, by 1985 "ninety [percent] of Afghans with higher education from non-communist universities had been killed, imprisoned, or scattered into exile."[234] This led to a shortage of trained personnel in numerous branches of life: civil servants, professors, teachers, doctors and engineers, among others. The Soviets trained replacements, only to see them flee the country as well. As Soviet author L.B. Aristova wrote, "Because of the exodus of doctors abroad the number of doctors in the country has not grown, even though the Kabul medical institute graduates 150–200 doctors a year."[235] And according to a Western report:

Since 1978, most of Afghanistan's doctors have been arrested, killed, or pressured into leaving the country... of 1,200 physicians in Afghanistan before 1978, only 200 now remain... General Naik Mohammed Azizi, former head physician of the Military Medical School in Kabul, who defected in early 1983, said that two-thirds of military doctors had left the country since 1978 and that of twenty military doctors trained in the Soviet Union in the previous two years, eight were in Pakistan, three were in West Germany, and three had been killed.[236]

Even when people stayed in the country and avoided arrest or death, they rarely left the major cities, especially Kabul. For instance, in 1987, "80 [percent] of Afghan physicians were still working in Kabul."[237] Simply put, while the Soviets may have trained tens of thousands of Afghans, this did not guarantee an appropriate supply of qualified personnel anywhere outside of the capital. The result of all this was that "many enterprises came to a virtual stop, government administration barely functioned, and services like medical care became scarce."[238]

To make matters worse, the quality of those who remained was often poor, especially in government and party institutions. The Soviets continually complained about the incompetence and corruption of Afghan officials. Iurii Sal'nikov, for instance, commented of Afghan officials in Kandahar that:

Party and state institutions are manned by a number of well educated people who enjoy authority among the population. But newly arrived cadres are often talentless and at times untrustworthy. Getting any kind of thing from them is difficult. It is even more difficult to extract information, as they are afraid. They reply, "all is well, there are no problems." They are not in control of the situation and exert no influence over the townspeople.[239]

As we have already seen, corruption was endemic. Soviet Defence Minister Marshal Sokolov complained that Afghan officials stole millions of rubles of Soviet aid: "It all stayed with the elite," he said, "In the villages there is no kerosene, no matches, nothing."[240] "Try giving the money to the Afghan government and of course it will disappear" said Valerii Ivanov.[241] Ivanov drew a distinction between aid provided with Soviet credits for major development projects and other aid. Very little of the former disappeared due to corruption, but this was not the case with the latter. "If you are talking about credits for deliveries and equipment, then almost 100 percent was used for the designated purpose," Ivanov claimed: "The only instance I am aware of was when we were building the Polytechnic Institute [in the 1960s] and the president of the institute said, 'There is some steel, and I'm building a house, give me 300 kilograms'."[242]

There was a simple reason for this. The Soviet credits always remained in Soviet hands, and the Soviets deducted the relevant sums from them when they delivered equipment. Furthermore, Soviet specialists delivered the equipment and supervised its installation. Theft was difficult. This was not true with aid which was distributed through the Afghan government, such as the agricultural assistance mentioned above. For instance, one Soviet advisor claimed that "four hundred trucks of Soviet relief supplies were once diverted to markets in the Pakistani tribal territories under the cover of claims that they had been attacked by 'counterrevolutionaries'"; the proceeds, he said, were divided among members of the PDPA Politburo.[243]

In order to boost the Afghan government's revenue, the Soviet Union delivered consumer goods to Kabul, some free of charge and some paid for by credit, which the government then sold to Afghan citizens, so bringing cash into its coffers (see Annex VII for details). The Soviet Ministry of External Trade optimistically considered that these deliveries "help the government of the [Democratic Republic of Afghanistan] DRA decide tasks such as providing the country with goods and bringing additional revenues into the state budget. In the end, this aid strengthens the DRA's economic position. The experience of previous years confirms this."[244] In reality, corruption bedevilled the operation. "Of course part of these goods disappeared," said Ivanov, "We could not control the budget and people took what they wanted from the budget."[245] At a meeting of Soviet and Afghan officials in February 1985, the head of the Soviet directorate of trade with Asian countries, M.A. Kiselev, demanded to know what was happening with these goods. According to the record of the meeting:

Comrade Samandari [the deputy Afghan minister of finance] noted that originally the Afghan side had problems with this issue. No stock taking was arranged of the receipt and sale of the goods, no special accounts were opened into which the sums received from the sale of the consumer goods should be placed. In addition, not all the organizations involved in the sale of the goods in question handed over the money received in a timely manner or in full.[246]

Samandari claimed that the majority of the goods received were sold rapidly. The exception was vodka. In response, the Soviets pointed out that they had expressed doubts about the expediency of sending vodka to Afghanistan, but the Afghans had insisted.[247]

Samandari also claimed that the Afghan government had taken measures to overcome the problems he had identified. If so, they do not appear to have been very effective. In 1987, Mikhail Gorbachev complained to Najibullah that this type of aid was being misused. "Information is coming to us," said Gorbachev, "that the aid is not reaching the people." Najibullah admitted this, though he claimed that losses were only 2 percent. Gorbachev told Najibullah to keep these funds in his hands: "If the fund is administered by a bureaucrat," the Soviet leader warned, "then it will all trickle into the hands of his relatives, through clan and family ties. In a word, it will end up with those who handle its distribution."[248] This warning appears to have been entirely accurate.[249]

The Provision of Specialists

The provision of Soviet advisors and technical specialists was meant to help compensate for this appalling lack of human capacity within the Afghan government and economy. Unfortunately, the quality of Soviet advisors was not always high and, even when it was, the very fact of their presence often had a negative rather than a positive effect on the performance of their Afghan colleagues.

According to Gilles Dorronsoro, "Most Afghans who were in contact with the occupiers stress 'the superiority complex' of the Soviets in their dealings with the Afghans."[250] Soviet Foreign Minister Eduard Shevardnadze acknowledged this in a 1986 Politburo meeting. "Our comrades, both here and there in Afghanistan," said Shevardnadze, "can't get used to the idea that we are dealing with a sovereign country."[251] General Varennikov also complained that many advisors "were disastrously lacking in knowledge of oriental affairs," a complaint echoed by a Soviet writer who noted that advisors "were not always carefully selected and trained with a view to specific features of [Afghanistan], its customs, culture, and the people's lifestyle. Sometimes our specialists unthinkingly endeavor to transfer artificially to Afghan soil Soviet experience."[252] General Gareev similarly complained that:

There were various people among the advisers, including some who worked hard. It was not so much the fault as the misfortune of our civilian advisers in Afghanistan, especially those from the party, that they were typical products of our cadre system, trained to be loyal executors, capable only of putting into life the line that the party had given them.[253]

There were also some accusations of corruption. For instance, the Chairman of the Supreme Court of Tajikistan, Rajabov, took responsibility for supervising the Afghan Ministry of Justice, but was then arrested "for smuggling gold from Afghanistan."[254] One former Soviet advisor also "claimed that the wife of one Soviet ambassador directed a large black market operation."[255] The Central Committee of the CPSU admitted the problem, stating in 1988:

We must criticize some aspects of our apparatus' activity in Afghanistan. It did a lot to help strengthen the PDPA and the national power. But often our people, acting with the best intention, tried to export onto Afghan soil approaches to which we were accustomed, pushed the Afghans into copying us. This did not help the situation, it and it bred a dependent mood among the Afghan leaders of that time in their relations with the Soviet Union both in the conduct of military operations and in the economic sphere.[256]

This was true. While the Soviets were correct to identify the institutional shortfalls of the Afghan government and its members as fundamental to the failure of economic development, the way they went about correcting this was flawed. As Anton Oleinik notes:

There is a growing consensus among actors involved in the process of "catch-up" modernization that institutions matter… Nevertheless, modern institutions—laws, norms and habits as well as mechanisms of their enforcement—do not emerge "from scratch" … The more dissimilar and incompatible institutions are, the less chances of successfully adopting new institutions … repeated failures of institutional transfers in Afghanistan can be attributed to the lack of elective affinity between traditional institutions … and new exported institutions.[257]

By unthinkingly bringing in Soviet methods (as, for instance, in the reforms of the Afghan education system mentioned above), Soviet advisors repeated this mistake. As Nabi Nisdaq notes:

The massive number of advisors who they had placed from the office of the president down to the smallest department were expected to rectify the cultural traits of the Afghans; namely distrust in central authority, jealousy and resentment amongst the ethnic groups and local and cultural divisions on linguistic, ethnic and religious bases. They never appreciated that the Afghan state, though it might seem to Russians as corrupt and inefficient, nonetheless somehow worked for a developing country like Afghanistan… The system was not totally unfamiliar even to those who lived in rural areas. This system did not need thousands of advisors or armies of soldiers to make it function… [As a result of the advisory system] the Afghans became more and more suspicious and hostile and their hatred intensified both against the Soviets and their Afghan allies.[258]

The Central Committee was also right to note that advisors created a culture of dependence. Najibullah complained of Soviet advisors' "petty interference."[259] The advisors so permeated every aspect of decision-making that they sapped Afghan initiative. The Afghans' attitude appears to have been, "You came here for this, you do the work."[260] General Boris Gromov, the last commander of Soviet military forces in Afghanistan, commented that Afghan officials "mainly adopted a parasitic position. Through their entire demeanor and behavior the Afghan leaders let us understand that we should do all for them." As a result, General Varennikov said that "some advisers often found it easier to do things themselves than to get their Afghan colleagues to fulfill the task set."[261] Soviet Deputy Foreign Minister Iulii M. Vorontsov told the Politburo in 1986, "Many members of the PDPA leadership are without initiative, they are accustomed to waiting for the recommendations of our advisers and have in this way become incompetent."[262]

Freed from responsibility for their jobs, too many Afghan officials instead devoted their time to political infighting and personal wealth creation. Paradoxically, the Soviets found that their notional control of the Afghan state did not enable them to control the behavior of their clients. Efforts to restrain the excessive revolutionary zeal and brutality of the regime failed. As Barnett Rubin writes:

Soviet penetration of the Afghan state apparatus did not enable Moscow simply to issue orders that would be followed. The experience of Soviet advisers in Afghanistan seems to have been at least as frustrating as that of American advisers in Vietnam. Not only did the PDPA leaders involve Soviet advisers in their factional conflicts, but the growing divisions within the Soviet party and state reinforced Afghan factionalism.[263]

At the heart of the problem was the fact that the Soviets had committed so much to the defense of the Afghan regime that they could not bring themselves to abandon it, and thus had to put up with whatever it did. Afghan officials were aware of this and exploited it. As Anton Minkov writes, "until the very end, the Kabul regime did not believe that their Soviet allies would ever withdraw their patronage."[264] Thus, as Halliday and Tanin say, "The knowledge of the Soviet commitment, with whatever reserve, served to make the PDPA more, not less, independent and even reckless. It encouraged extremism, intransigence and factionalism."[265] They therefore conclude:

The greatest problem the Soviet advisers and officials had with the Afghan regime, and in particular with the top officials of the PDPA, was the refusal of the latter to follow the advice which Moscow was giving them. The overall picture given over the period from 1978 to 1989 is of constant disputes between Soviet and Afghan officials, and of persistent obstruction, overt and covert, by the latter of the policies that Moscow was advocating. The story of Soviet-Afghan relations throughout this period is therefore one of the inability of the Soviet leadership, despite Kabul's reliance on its economic and military support, successfully to impress its policies on the PDPA leadership.[266]

The experience of Soviet advisors in Afghanistan constitutes a stark lesson in the difficulties and dangers of "capacity building." In her book *Dead Aid*, Dambisa Moyo expresses the modern belief that "Good governance trumps all."[267] "The cornerstone of development is an economically responsible and accountable government," writes Moyo, "Yet, it remains clear that, by providing funds, aid agencies (inadvertently?) prop up corrupt governments," and so undermine development.[268] Soviet economic and technical assistance to Afghanistan after the April Revolution of 1978 failed to deliver economic progress largely because the quality of Afghan governance (third level institutions or those concerned with governance, according to Williamson's scheme) was appalling low, producing war, in the context of which economic progress was impossible. Worse, the provision of aid coupled with Afghan officials' near certainty that nothing they did would cause the flow of aid to be cut off encouraged the negative behavior which caused so many of Afghanistan's problems.

Soviet economic and technical assistance did achieve its goal in one important way. Its aim was always primarily political rather than economic, and throughout the 1980s it kept its sponsored Afghan regime afloat. Insofar as any economic activity continued, it was largely in sectors which received Soviet assistance. In addition, "by 1988, 75 [percent] of state revenue came from establishments and projects built with Soviet assistance,"[269] most notably natural gas production. Thus the Afghan commerce minister was quite right to remark in 1988 that, "We have the enormous amount of Soviet economic aid to thank for the fact that we have been able to survive at all."[270]

Economically, however, Soviet assistance was not able to prevent almost total collapse. As we have seen, Soviet economists had previously come to the conclusion that the development of Third World countries, including Afghanistan, was more a political than an economic problem. Their experience in Afghanistan proved them right. At the heart of the economic collapse lay a series of disastrous political decisions made by the Afghan and Soviet governments alike. Only radical changes in political direction could possibly turn things around. The 1985 promotion of Mikhail Gorbachev to the position of General Secretary of the CPSU set such changes in motion.

5

SOVIET ASSISTANCE TO AFGHANISTAN

1987–91

Introduction

The death of Soviet leader Leonid Brezhnev in 1982 produced a change in Soviet attitudes towards foreign aid. Brezhnev's immediate successor as General Secretary of the Communist Party of the Soviet Union (CPSU), Iurii Andropov, viewed foreign aid skeptically, doubting that it provided proportional benefits to the Soviet Union. Neither he nor the next General Secretary, Konstantin Chernenko, lived long enough in the top job to make a significant difference, but the arrival of Mikhail Gorbachev as party leader in 1985 changed everything.

The evolution of Gorbachev's ideas eerily parallels that of Soviet development economists, albeit in a much truncated timeframe. Recognizing the Soviet Union's economic backwardness, Gorbachev began his leadership calling for economic acceleration (*uskorenie*), which in essence required increased capital investments. When this failed, he determined that the problem was structural, and demanded economic reform (*perestroika*). When this in turn failed, he decided that the problem was, after all, political and required a fundamental reform of the political institutions which blocked progress. This led to the policy of "openness" (*glasnost'*), which in due course brought total political and economic collapse.

Gorbachev wished to invest the Soviet Union's limited financial resources in the domestic Soviet economy, rather than disburse them to unpopular overseas regimes which provided little if any return on the investment and which, according to one Soviet commentator, were "notorious for their authoritarian or dictatorial methods of rule, the cults of their leaders, a ruthless suppression of the opposition, and for corruption."[1] Thus the March 1986 program of the CPSU qualified Soviet foreign aid by stating that the Soviet Union would continue to give aid only "to the extent of its abilities."[2]

The Soviet Union could not easily abandon Afghanistan, however. The USSR had invested too much of its prestige in the survival of the People's Democratic Party of Afghanistan (PDPA) to simply cut off all aid and risk the complete collapse of the Afghan government. Nevertheless, from the beginning of his leadership Gorbachev was determined to withdraw the Soviet Army from Afghanistan as soon as possible. This, to some extent, made economic and technical assistance even more important than before, as a means of propping up the government in the absence of Soviet troops.

Soviet leaders recognized that their earlier policies had failed. Marshal Sergei Akhromeev told the Politburo in November 1986: "We have lost. Most Afghans today support the counterrevolutionaries. We neglected the peasants. They did not gain anything from the revolution. Eighty percent of Afghan territory is in the hands of counterrevolutionaries, and the peasants live better there than in state-controlled territory."[3] The Politburo agreed. Prime Minister Nikolai Ryzhkov admitted that, "The revolution has led to a decline in living standards," and Foreign Minister Eduard Shevardnadze said, "Not one problem has been resolved in favor of the peasants. In fact, the war has been waged against the peasants. The state apparatus functions poorly. Our advisers' assistance is ineffective."[4]

Gorbachev therefore determined that "the regime must be transformed."[5] Seeking a political resolution of the Afghan problem, the Soviets replaced Afghan President Babrak Karmal with Najibullah, who in December 1986 introduced a "National Reconciliation Programme." This included "opening the lines of communication with the mujahidin commanders, resistance parties and former political figures, negotiating deals with the tribal chiefs and other local notables, and the creation of a coalition government ... [and] more investment in the rural economy."[6] At the same time, the Soviet Army reduced the tempo of its operations and began preparations to withdraw.

As part of the new strategy, Soviet economic and technical assistance increased substantially from 1986 to 1988, with expenditures reaching a peak of 179 million rubles in 1987 (see Annex VIII). As before, the emphasis was on infrastructure and natural resource exploitation. Nevertheless, the period from 1987 to 1991 saw three notable changes in Soviet aid policy in Afghanistan: first, for the very first time, the Soviets provided funds for the Afghan private sector; second, Soviet authorities delegated aid responsibilities from the central government to Soviet republics and regions (*oblasts*) and to individual organizations; and third, short-term humanitarian relief took increasing precedence over long-term development assistance.

Major Soviet Aid Agreements and Projects

In some respects, Soviet economic and technical assistance proved remarkably immune to the political and ideological changes going on around it. Much of it continued along the same lines as in the past, with largely unchanged priorities, as shown by an April 1988 Soviet radio broadcast, which announced:

Last year alone [1987] 11 facilities were put into operation in Afghanistan with Soviet aid. They include a foundry at the smelting plant in Jangalak, a broadcasting center, and a blood transfusion station in Kabul. A railway station was reconstructed and the plans provide for giving Soviet aid in the development of Afghanistan's health service, education, news media, communications, and the training of specialists.[7]

The Soviet Union and Afghanistan signed yet more treaties and agreements in this period. In January 1987, for instance, the Soviet Union agreed: to equip auto-transport enterprises in Herat, Balkh, Baghlan, Kandahar and Helmand provinces; to provide materials to build pumping stations on the Kunduz River in order to irrigate 4,000 hectares and create state farms for beet production; to provide equipment to bore twenty-five artesian wells and sixty shaft wells in the south-west of Afghanistan; to help improve water management organizations; to continue building a dam on the Kochka River; to renovate Turgundi rail station; and to carry out investigatory work for the building of the Bibi Mahru "mikroraion" in Kabul.[8] In connection with the last of these projects, a twenty-strong "student construction detachment" arrived in Kabul from Soviet higher education institutions in August 1987. According to Soviet television news, the detachment, appropriately named "Druzhba" (Friendship), was to work in the Kabul Housing Combine to "help reconstruction of the fixtures and fittings plant, which will help double the capacity of the combine."[9]

The Soviets continued to try to boost Afghan agriculture. A month after the January 1987 agreement, the Soviets and Afghans signed a contract to create a state cotton farm of some 2,000 hectares in the Kochka area.[10] And in March 1988 the Central Union of Consumer Societies of the USSR (Centrosoyuz) signed an agreement with the Union of Farmers' Cooperatives of Afghanistan to develop Afghan cooperatives, "training national personnel and expanding trade links... Centrosoyuz will also render assistance in building and fitting out with special refrigerating equipment a wholesale depot in Kabul intended for the storage of raw materials and consumer goods."[11] Also in the realm of agriculture, in January 1988 the State Agri-Industrial Committee of the USSR and the Afghan Ministry of Agriculture signed a protocol "for developing bilateral cooperation in farming." This was to include "increased Soviet supplies of tractors, harvesters, mineral fertilizers, and the seeds of wheat and other crops specially zoned for Afghanistan."[12] How much of any of these projects was completed is not clear, but it was probably very little, if any.

In February 1988, the Soviet Union also signed protocols to provide assistance in the sphere of communications and to postpone eighty million rubles of Afghan debt repayment for ten years.[13] Between 1988 and 1990, the Soviet Union was meant to help "in establishing four workshops in the provincial centers in order to repair communications equipment, as well as the construction of automatic telephone stations in the provinces with a capacity of 15,000 lines."[14] In the same month, the Soviet organization *Tekhnopromeksport* signed a contract to supply equipment to construct a power line in the region of Shir Khan. According to TASS, this project would "help to bring electricity to populated points, and also make it possible to build a power transmission line at the Kochka irrigation complex."[15]

In April 1988, the two countries signed an agreement for further cooperation in the energy field, in which the Soviets were to build the Sarobi-2 hydroelectric power station, to create a plan for the development of the Afghan energy sector until 2000, and to complete the power line from Pul-i-Khumri to Kabul.[16] Subsequently, Tashkent-based engineers began work on the Sarobi project, and the Uzbek Ministry of Power and Electrification, working through the organization Balkhenergo, provided Afghanistan with "long distance electric wires, transformers, pylons, insulators, instruments, and 12 rural substations," as well as training for Afghan electrical engineers.[17] Once again, though, little progress was made, and Sarobi-2 was never completed.

With regards to natural resource exploitation, in June 1988 the Soviet Union agreed to provide further assistance in prospecting work for gas and other minerals.[18] And in July 1988, the Union of Soviet Socialist Republics (USSR) signed an agreement on cooperation in the natural gas industry, under which it would develop the Bashikurd and Dzhuma gas fields.[19] Carrying out this work proved, however, to be impossible.

Such failures did not deter either the Soviets or the Afghans from pursuing dreams of additional development projects, but their aspirations proved to be increasingly detached from reality. Although by late 1988 the Soviet Union had firmly committed itself to withdrawing its military from Afghanistan (the withdrawal was completed in February 1989), it did not anticipate that the Afghan regime would fall, nor did it plan to terminate its economic relationship with Afghanistan. In fact, Soviet planners worked on the assumption that the Soviet Union would maintain a serious economic commitment to Afghanistan for the rest of the century. This assumption found reflection in a long-term program for economic, technical and trade cooperation between the USSR and the Democratic Republic of Afghanistan (DRA) until 2000, which was signed by both countries in September 1988. This made Soviet priorities clear, saying:

The current agreement is directed at developing and making concrete long[-]term cooperation on the basis of mutual advantage and the most rational use of the resources of raw materials, agricultural and forest industries, energy resources, light and foodstuffs industries, and the mining and refining of gas, oil and hard minerals, in the interests of both countries… The current agreement has the aim of developing economic, technical and trade cooperation by means of a) the help of the Soviet Union in restoring, modernizing, reconstructing and creating in Afghanistan mining, refining, agricultural, energy and other objects … b) mutual trade … c) the development of direct links between individual Soviet and Afghan ministries, departments, organizations and enterprises, and also between Union Republics and Oblasts of the USSR and provinces of Afghanistan d) the preparation, training, and internship of cadres [20]

The program then listed planned areas of cooperation under the headings of "agriculture and irrigation," "industry," "geology," "electrical energy," "transport," "communications, radio, and television," "objects with the participation of the private sector," and "preparation of national cadres." The Permanent Intergovernmental Commission on Economic Cooperation was to agree on specific projects to fulfill this plan.[21] In the light of future developments, this was an extraordinarily ambitious document, which seems completely out of touch with political realities, both in Afghanistan and in the Soviet Union.

The Soviet Union fell apart in 1991 and the regime in Afghanistan collapsed soon after. Some work was done before then, but few, if any, Soviet plans from this era came to fruition. The 1988 program was little more than wishful thinking.

Aid to the Private Sector

The provision in the 1988 program for aid to "objects with the participation of the private sector" represented an interesting new development in Soviet practice. From 1980 onwards the Soviets had advised the Afghan government to adopt a more positive attitude towards the private sector,[22] but the Soviets had never themselves provided much aid to private enterprises. The state sector received almost 100 percent of Soviet assistance (some humanitarian aid and some seeds and fertilizers for Afghan farmers being almost the sole exceptions).

A number of factors caused this shift in policy. In part, it revealed a much belated recognition that the private sector could not be ignored in a country as underdeveloped as Afghanistan. As Mikhail Gorbachev admitted, "When we went into Afghanistan, we were blinded by ideology and hoped that it was possible to skip three stages at once: from feudalism to socialism."[23] The failure of Soviet policy made Gorbachev and others, including the Afghan government, realize that some accommodation with capitalism was indeed necessary. As *Pravda* admitted in February 1988, "The Afghans do not hide the fact that the state sector still does not function as effectively as they wished," as a result of which it was necessary to stimulate the private sector.[24] Second, the new policy fit with the desire to reach out politically to private entrepreneurs as part of the National Reconciliation Programme. And third, it reflected a growing ideological flexibility within the Soviet Union as part of Gorbachev's policies of *perestroika* and *glasnost'*. Thus, in October 1985 Gorbachev told Babrak Karmal to "forget about socialism ... Protect private commerce, because it will take you a long time to create a different kind of economy."[25] Similarly, Gorbachev told Najibullah in April 1988: "all the impediments in Afghan society need to be removed and the road opened to private enterprise, primarily small property owners and tradesmen."[26]

One consequence of this new pragmatism was a Soviet-Afghan agreement, signed on 18 April 1987, which stated that the USSR and the DRA would "cooperate in creating and exploiting enterprises with the participation of the private sector." Soviet organizations were to provide equipment, materials, spare parts, and specialists, as well as train Afghan citizens. The USSR granted a credit of fifty million rubles to pay the costs of the Soviet organizations, repayable, as always, by deliveries of "natural gas, citrus fruits, and other Afghan goods," the prices of which were to be determined according to world markets.[27]

Following this, the newspaper *Sovetskaia Rossiia* claimed in August 1988 that, "Today Soviet foreign trade organizations maintain trade and economic operations with 250 private Afghan companies and national Afghan traders… In the past three years [1985–88] the private sector's share of Soviet-Afghan trade has doubled."[28] According to *Sovetskaia Rossiia*, two new Soviet-Afghan joint stock trading companies, *Aftorg* and *Aftento*, which were established in 1987, were "playing a considerable role in the development of cooperation with Afghanistan's private sector."[29] By December 1987 *Pravda* reported that the Soviet Union was already giving "economic and technical assistance to Afghan private businessmen in setting up enterprises." *Pravda* stated that:

To this end there are to be deliveries of Soviet equipment for two bakeries, four confectionery factories, and two salt purification shops. The USSR will give assistance in the setting up of four construction companies in Kabul, Konduz, Mazar-e-Sharif, and Sherberghan. The Soviet side is already helping with the construction of 15 bakeries in various regions of Afghanistan… Cooperation between private businessmen and Soviet organizations is a fact characteristic of the present situation in Afghanistan.[30]

According to TASS, by February 1988 the Soviet Union had signed contracts for the construction of twenty-eight facilities under the terms of the April 1987 agreement. This included "a bicycle assembly plant in Kabul, confectioneries, [and] bakeries."[31] *Pravda* reported in February 1988 that there had been "170 requests for Soviet assistance in starting new factories,"[32] indicating substantial potential for investment in the private sector. In August 1988 *Sovetskaia Rossiia* stated that another fifteen contracts were soon to be signed: "they include setting up in Afghanistan a number of major enterprises including a plant for producing rubber footwear, a textile factory, a motor transport enterprise, and a non-alcoholic drinks plant."[33]

The most significant of these projects was the bicycle assembly plant, named "Bakhtar." According to *Pravda*:

The Soviet external trade organization "Prommasheksport" and the Minsk motorcycle and bicycle factory have helped organize the production. By the end of last year [1987] the Soviet Union had provided subassemblies and technical equipment to assemble the first thousand bicycles. On the eve of the new year, engineer-mechanic Iurii Kovalenko arrived from Minsk to set up production.[34]

Bicycle production began in February 1988, but apparently things did not go well. In April of the same year, Gorbachev personally discussed the bicycle factory with Najibullah and complained that inflation was ruining business. Najibullah replied:

I invited the owner of this enterprise to my office ... and talked with him in detail. I asked him if he had any complaints or difficulties. He gave the same reply all the time, that he has no complaints or difficulties. Of course, I know that this is not so; he was simply afraid of the officials of the bureaucracy. Only at the very end of the conversation did he say that he had no telephone and that was hampering his work. I promised to help him.[35]

Clearly, despite the new politics, Afghanistan remained a difficult place for private business. No information is readily available to indicate what happened to the other projects funded under this initiative, but the overall sum of fifty million rubles assigned to help private enterprise was relatively small compared with the amounts that continued to be given to the state sector, and the projects were all small-scale. It seems unlikely that the attempt to help private industry had any noticeable impact on the Afghan economy. While the general direction may have made sense, it was too little too late.

Direct Soviet-Afghan Ties

A second Gorbachev-era initiative was to encourage direct ties between Soviet and Afghan organizations, and between Soviet republics and oblasts and Afghan provinces, bypassing the central governments through which all ties had previously been arranged. According to Bradsher, "Such ties apparently were intended to relieve the bureaucratic and financial burden on Moscow, permit more direct and specialized supervision of project implementation, and bypass the corruption and inefficiency of Kabul to get aid to the Afghan grass roots."[36] The policy thereby reflected Gorbachev's *perestroika*, which attempted to delegate authority in economic decision-making in order to enhance local initiative and bypass institutional bottle-necks which hampered progress.

To this end, Afghanistan and the Soviet Union signed a protocol in 1987 to promote the establishment of direct ties between elements of the two countries. This followed resolutions by the Central Committee of the Communist Party of the Soviet Union and the Soviet Council of Ministers in February 1987 to permit Soviet republics and oblasts to establish direct links with Afghan provinces without prior consultation with the Council of Ministers.[37] Within a short while, twelve of the fifteen Soviet republics and various oblasts within them, as well as the city of Moscow, had signed agreements with thirty Afghan provinces and the city of Kabul, as shown below in Table 2. Theoretically, these were akin to twinning arrangements providing mutual benefits, but in practice were rather more lopsided, with the Soviets giving far more than they received in return. In effect, they were a kind of sponsorship system under which Soviet organizations and republics sponsored their Afghan counterparts. While this was meant to be a form of delegation of authority, it does not seem as though the Soviet parties chose their roles freely. No record is available to show who decided which republic or oblast would sponsor which Afghan province, but according to Valerii Ivanov, "it was a decision from above," taken at the highest level, probably in either the Council of Ministers or the Party Central Committee.[38]

Table 2: Soviet-Afghan Direct Ties.

Soviet republic	Soviet oblast (if applicable)	Afghan province
Tajikistan	Gorno-Badakhshanskaia	Badakhshan
Tajikistan	Kuliabskaia	Takhar
Tajikistan	Kurgan-Tiubinskaia	Kunduz
Uzbekistan	Tashkentskaia	Samangan
Uzbekistan	Surkhan-Darinskaia	Balkh
Uzbekistan	Samarkandskaia	Baghlan
Uzbekistan	Ferganskaia	Jawzjan
Turkmenistan	Ashkhabadskaia	Herat
Turkmenistan	Chardzhouskaia	Faryab
Turkmenistan	Maryiskaia	Badghis
Russia	Astrakhanskaia	Farah
Russia	Orenburgskaia	Nangarhar
Russia	Saratovskaia	Helmand
Russia	Cheliabinskaia	Kabul
Ukraine	Khersonskaia	Nimroz
Ukraine	Kharkovskaia	Parwan
Kazakhstan	Alma-Altinskaia	Kandahar
Kazakhstan	Karagandinskaia	Uruzgan
Kazakhstan	Chimkentskaia	Zabul

Kyrgyzstan	Oshskaia	Bamian
Kyrgyzstan	Talasskaia	Wardak
Georgia		Kapisa
Belorussia	Minskaia	Kunar
Belorussia	Grodnenskaia	Laghman
Armenia		Logar and Ghor
Azerbaijan		Paktika, Paktia, and Khost
Moldavia		Ghazni
Russia	City of Moscow	City of Kabul

Source: Liakhovskii, *Tragediia*, pp. 447–8.

Izvestiia described the practical workings of these links, saying that, "Delegations from the Soviet oblasts and republics visiting the provinces have been familiarized on the spot with the state of affairs, have discussed cooperation prospects with the local authorities, and have outlined priority tasks."[39] These generally involved deliveries of agricultural, industrial and electrical equipment, support for education and training, medical assistance, and cultural exchanges.

The Soviet Central Asian republics seem to have been particularly active in their new roles. Kyrgyzstan, for instance, provided Bamian and Wardak provinces with agricultural machinery and training programs for Afghan agricultural workers. The Deputy Chairman of the Kyrgyz Council of Ministers, Mukun Aseyinov, announced in March 1988 that:

We have decided to build a school for 340 children of martyrs of the April Revolution in our Republic. Priority is given to children from Wardak and Bamian… There are at present 100 Afghan children of martyrs enrolled in a school in Kand city of our Republic. Teaching is done by Afghan teachers.[40]

Tajikistan also provided 600,000 rubles of equipment for electric power projects.[41]

Uzbekistan provided Afghanistan with "consumer goods, medicines, and other material and technical means worth more than R8 million" in 1987.[42] *Pravda* reported that in Fergana oblast:

An oblast branch of the Soviet-Afghan friendship society was created, and it was joined by collectives from more than 20 enterprises, organizations, and institutions. … [People from Fergana] shipped a consignment of gifts worth more than R500,000: tractors, a bus, a telephone exchange, construction materials, medicines, and medical equipment. They set up a language laboratory and supplied teaching aids to a school in the city of Sheberghan. About 100 children vacationed at the Fergana young pioneers' camp. Hospitals provide practical training for Afghan physicians, and schools for future Russian language teachers. The friends also exchange amateur artistic ensembles.[43]

The Uzbeks also provided substantial free assistance to the Afghan electrical industry, and the Uzbek Institute for Water Management helped to train Afghan irrigation specialists. *Izvestiia* described additional Uzbek aid in an article in February 1988:

Another delegation left Samarkand for Baghlan recently. With it and following it are clothing, sports goods, and cinematic equipment worth R1.5 million. In addition to a large selection of consumer industry goods and equipment, the Tashkent inhabitants decided to embellish a park in the center of Samangan Province with fairy tale towns and attractions. The Fergana machine operators have assembled three row-crop tractors, while teachers and pupils have prepared large selections of textbooks and a complete set of equipment for a school language laboratory. And 19 enterprises, organizations, and institutions in Termez and 52 in Samarkand have joined oblast societies of friendship with Afghanistan… Patronage ties have markedly enlivened border trade… In Tashkent the joint "Samangan" store has opened to customers. There is an agreement on creating a joint restaurant, a factory for processing and packaging sultanas, and an Afghan-Soviet commercial bureau for border trade.[44]

Turkmenistan was also active. *Pravda* claimed in June 1988 that the republic "as a whole has given Afghan provinces aid worth more than R3 million through direct sponsorship ties."[45] For instance, Ashkhabad oblast

"presented the Afghans with a mobile pumping station and power generating stations, tractors, trucks, and medical and construction equipment… An accord has been reached on regular book fairs in each other's country. The first fair of this kind was held recently in Ashkhabad and the second is planned for next fall in Kabul."[46] Meanwhile, Maryiskaia oblast arranged "to deliver to Baghdis province an agricultural technical college, cotton seeds and fertilizer, electrical equipment, and sporting equipment."[47]

Fewer details are available for aid given by other republics. Kherson and Kharkov oblasts provided some assistance in training and education to Nimroz and Parwan provinces. Ukrainians from Kherson, for instance, noted that there was a pumping station in Nimroz, but that no Afghans knew how to use it, an indication that years of Soviet training had not solved Afghanistan's human resource problems. Kherson therefore decided to provide help in training machine operators, as well as doctors and teachers. In 1987, according to *Sotsialisticheskaia Industriia*, "52 Afghans studied hydrologization, mechanization, and electrification of agriculture at the Novokakhovskii technical college," in Kherson oblast. In 1988, the newspaper continued, "The Kakhovskii state farm technical college is now ready to teach machine operators, metal workers, and welders, while medical workers will be able to improve their qualifications in the oblast's medical institutions, and children will be able to take holidays in pioneer camps."[48]

A number of Soviet press reports gave details of help provided by the city of Moscow to the city of Kabul. For instance, in December 1987 *Pravda* reported that:

Construction Factory no. 2 in Moscow will contribute to residential construction in Kabul, Moscow ATP [bus and trolleybus park] will collaborate with the center of public transportation of Kabul. MosSovet [Moscow City Council] will assist the municipality of Kabul with professional training, development of public transport, and the planning of water and sewage systems.[49]

For this purpose, a delegation of specialists organized by the Moscow city executive committee (*gorispolkom*) travelled to Kabul in January 1988.[50] *Sotsialisticheskaia Industriia* subsequently stated that, "Moscow has sent cranes, containers with medical equipment and medicines for two polyclinics, school desks and boards, furniture and linen for small children. Kabul specialists are coming to Moscow to familiarize themselves with their colleagues' work."[51]

Superficially, the aid provided through direct ties seems substantial. Unfortunately, when devising the plan to encourage direct ties, Soviet central authorities had given insufficient thought to the logistical problem of how the additional aid generated by the plan would be delivered. It appears that transport difficulties within Afghanistan prevented much of the aid from reaching the intended destinations and caused long delays. The Soviet railway system was able to deliver goods as far as the railhead on the Soviet-Afghan border at Termez, where by and large they then stayed. A report produced by the Soviet 40th Army in Afghanistan in November 1988 noted that 1,000 wagonloads of goods donated by Soviet republics and oblasts were sitting at Termez rail junction. Some had been there as long as eighteen months because of an almost complete halt in transport to Kabul caused "by the severe shortage of transport means"—the Afgano-Sovetskoe Transportno-Ekspeditsionnoe Obschestvo (AFSOTR) was said to be short of 75–80 percent of its requirements—and by the lack of security for transport columns.[52] General Aleksander Liakhovskii commented, however, that these were not the primary reasons for the failure to transport the goods. Rather he claimed that:

The main reason for this was the extremely poor organization of the most senior Afghans responsible for removing the provisions and other materials sent from the USSR. They were incapable of mobilizing the transport resources that they had. As a result only 250 trucks a day left Kabul for Hairaton rather than the 750 demanded. There were also insufficient means for loading and off-loading in both Kabul and Hairaton.[53]

Hearing this, the Soviet High Command decided to devote 250 military vehicles from among those already in Afghanistan as well as 150 heavy trucks from the Soviet Ministry of Defence to help eliminate the backlog. The Minister of Motor Transport of the Russian Soviet Federated Socialist Republic, Iurii Sukhin, was despatched to Afghanistan to supervise, and a series of measures were undertaken, including forming convoys of 100 vehicles each, paying drivers more, and giving part of the loads to locals en route to encourage them not to attack the convoys.[54] With the help of these measures and the additional trucks, the majority of the goods were shipped from Termez and Hairaton to Kabul during the winter of 1988/89, in time for the Soviet withdrawal from Afghanistan in February 1989. Whether the Soviets managed to deliver any goods to the more remote provinces of the country is unknown, but it seems unlikely, at least in any significant quantities.

Humanitarian Aid

By the winter of 1988/89 the Soviet involvement in Afghanistan had to a large extent deteriorated from long-term economic development and large-scale military operations into short-term emergency relief. Building communism was no longer the aim. Preventing the people from starving was the best the Soviets could do.

Humanitarian aid was part of Soviet activity throughout the 1980s, but became increasingly important as time went on, especially from 1987 onwards. In 1987, the Soviet Union granted an unprecedented 950 million rubles of "free aid," a substantial increase from the 203 million rubles spent in 1986 (See Annex IX). As shown in the previous chapter, the Soviets distributed seeds and fertilizers to Afghan farmers, and also delivered hundreds of thousands of tons of wheat as well as consumer goods. Iurii Sal'nikov described the arrival of such a delivery in Kandahar in the mid-

1980s, writing in his diary: "A column arrives in the city with material aid from the Soviet Union for the inhabitants of Kandahar. Here for a long time they have been awaiting salt, butter, galoshes, matches, and other necessary small items."[55]

The Soviet Army played an important role in the delivery of this aid. Despite its well-earned reputation for excessive violence, by the mid-1980s few if any Soviet generals believed the war could be won by military means[56] and at least some in the army gradually came to realize the importance of winning Afghan hearts and minds.[57]

Soviet troops had already made sporadic attempts to provide assistance to the Afghan population in the early 1980s. Many stories from that period involved the de-mining of villages which had been mined and booby-trapped by the rebels. A typical article in *Sovetskaia Rossiia* in March 1983 described the actions of a Soviet military detachment that cleared twenty mines placed by the rebels in a village school. "The soldiers," claimed the newspaper, "constantly come to the aid of the local population."[58] Similarly, Moscow World Service broadcast a report in August 1984 describing the actions of a dog-handler, Junior Sergeant Nikolai Svitsov, and his dog, Elsa, clearing mines from homes in an Afghan village. Svitsov and Elsa also removed fourteen mines "hidden in the walls and earthen floor" of the village school.[59]

The earlier report in *Sovetskaia Rossiia* also described another project undertaken by Soviet engineers in the mountain settlement of Kalay-Dala. After de-mining a village:

One of them, Sergeant Sabit Pugmanov, told his comrades of a wonderful custom existing from time immemorial back home in Uzbekistan. "When someone in our settlements decides to build a home, all the people come to help without being asked. This is called khashar. And people work without payment, from the goodness of their hearts." The entire company supported the sergeant who proposed to organize such a khashar in the Afghan settlement which had suffered heavily from the bandit attack. And work started. The walls of new homes grew like in a fairy tale. In one of them smoke even started pouring from the chimney. It was the grateful hosts who had started to cook supper for all those on the building sites. Thus they celebrated the new settlement together, Soviet soldiers and Afghan peasants.[60]

Soviet "agitprop" units were created to give a more organized form to such aid. Each division, brigade, and regiment eventually had one such unit. These would conduct non-combat "raids" in which they entered an Afghan village, broadcast propaganda from loudspeakers, spoke to village elders to convince them to support the government, distributed foodstuffs, kerosene, and other material goods, and provided medical aid to villagers. A 1988 article in *Sotsialisticheskaia Industriia* described a typical agitprop raid:

A raid with an agit detachment in a mountain village. This is the usual work of the twenty propagandists. Time after time they go out into Afghan settlements, in order to provide the inhabitants with products, to help the sick, and, above all, to tell them the truth about what is happening in the country... The boys waste no time. They turn on a loudspeaker. It broadcasts a communication about the *loya jirga* taking place in Kabul, and talks about the policy of national reconciliation. They start to give out kerosene... Nearby they give bread, salt, grain. Not far away the soldiers have put up a tent with a red cross. I look inside. An old man is complaining of a headache. He receives a couple of boxes of aspirin.[61]

A similar description by a Soviet interpreter appears in Svetlana Alexievich's book *Zinky Boys*:

Afghan songs blare out from the loudspeakers, which even the Afghans call "Alla Pugacheva" (a universally popular Russian singer). We soldiers hang our visual propaganda materials from our vehicles—flags, posters, slogans—and unfurl a screen for the film show. The medics put up tables and unpack their crates of medicines. A mullah in a long white robe and a white turban comes forward to read a *sura* from the Koran. Then he turns to Allah, begging him to protect believers from all the evils of the universe... The children do not listen to the speech—they're waiting for the film. As usual, we have cartoons in English, followed by two documentaries in Farsi and Pashtu... After the film show we distribute presents—today, toys and a bag of flour.[62]

Agitprop units appear to have begun in Afghanistan as a local initiative, the first unit being created by a Soviet political advisor, L.I. Shershnev, in 1981.[63] Over time, they spread throughout the Limited Contingent of Soviet Forces in Afghanistan (LCSFA), reaching a peak of activity in the years 1987–1988, when the Afghan government embarked on a new "National Reconciliation Program." In the first four months of the program alone, agitprop units distributed 100,000 bars of soap, 17,000 pairs of shoes, and other goods.[64]

Agitprop units played a key role in a new form of operation undertaken by the Soviet Army from late 1987 onwards. Some Soviet generals realized that rapid sweeps to clear areas of rebel forces were ineffective. The Afghan government lacked the capacity to govern the liberated areas, and the rebels rapidly moved back in as soon as Soviet forces left. In addition, as General Makhmut Gareev noted, "senseless bombing and rocket artillery strikes …

only made the local population hostile to the Soviet and government forces … while simultaneously causing large casualties among the peaceful population, the destruction of populated points, irrigation systems, crops, and gardens."[65]

In some places, Soviet troops began therefore to take a slower approach, designed to reduce both Soviet and Afghan casualties and to distribute aid to the liberated areas. The most notable effort took place in Kandahar province in 1987. Operations dragged on for several months, from April to October, in order, according to General Varennikov, "to avoid excessive casualties among our troops, the soldiers of the Afghan army, and, of course, the population."[66] Varennikov described the modus operandi as follows:

Through military or KGB scouts we established contacts with leaders of rebel bands and often reached agreement to decide all issues without battle. We sent material aid there—flour, rice, fats, canned goods, sugar, kerosene, soap, etc. In many regions, medical groups arrived, and looked at nearly all the inhabitants of the village on the spot and provided them with medicines—antibiotics for bowel diseases, analgesics, and, of course, large quantities of aspirin. These medical-humanitarian detachments had colossal success. In a number of regions we built bridges, roads and even wells; dug artesian bore-holes, and set up automatic diesel engines, which pumped water and simultaneously powered generators giving electric power.[67]

Varennikov believed that the new approach was successful: "By autumn 1987 in Kandahar and the great majority of districts of the province the situation had changed for the better in a fundamental way," he claimed.[68] Indeed, the months following the introduction of the National Reconciliation Program and the change in Soviet tactics witnessed a sharp increase in the number of mujahideen who surrendered to the government,[69] although it is not clear how much this was due to the new tactics and how longlasting the effect was.

Soviet troops also sometimes carried out construction work, such as building and repairing homes and schools. References to this occasionally appear in contemporary reports. Soviet reporter Artyom Borovik, for instance, recorded that "I came upon a hotel that has been restored from ruins by Soviet soldiers at a cost of eighty thousand rubles. The hotel, which has all the comforts of modern life, is intended to house the refugees who are streaming in from Pakistan."[70] TASS claimed in July 1988 that, "During the years of their deployment in Afghanistan, the troops have built and restored more than 80 schools, 25 hospitals, 26 kindergartens, 35 mosques and 325 residential houses. Hundreds of kilometers of ditches and canals have been dug and bore-holes drilled to supply fresh water for the population."[71] A few months later, in February 1989, Major General A. Zakharov, the head of the political department of the Limited Contingent of Soviet Forces in Afghanistan, issued similar, though slightly larger, figures: Soviet troops had, he said, built and repaired about 100 lycées, schools and colleges, more than twenty-five hospitals, around forty mosques, and many homes, and had dug or restored tens of kilometers of canals and irrigation ditches.[72] (Zakharov, of course, did not list how many objects the Soviet Army had destroyed.)

Both the Soviet Army and Soviet civilians provided medical assistance to Afghans. For instance, Soviet doctors worked at the Kabul Polyclinic and helped to set up five first-aid stations in industrial enterprises in the capital.[73] In 1987, Soviet medics also established the first blood transfusion center in Afghanistan.[74] The official history of the war produced by the Russian General Staff claimed that, "Soviet medical services … constantly provided consultative assistance to the local population and provided laboratory services, technical testing, electro-cardiograms, and X-ray examinations, as well as providing local medical facilities with medications, Soviet-made materials, and medical instruments."[75] "Sixty patients a day— that was the norm for the local population treated by Soviet medics," General Zakharov told the newspaper *Trud* in February 1989.[76] "Overall," claims Antonio Giustozzi, "in 1981–9 the Soviet forces gave medical assistance to 400,000 Afghans and material aid to over 1,000,000."[77]

Although the National Reconciliation Programme did allow the PDPA to make some progress in the countryside, most areas remained in rebel hands and the security situation continued to be very poor. Unable to take the major cities by storm, the rebels instead endeavored to strangle them to death, cutting the main roads to prevent the arrival of food, fuel, and other necessities. The situation became particularly bad in Kabul in the autumn and winter of 1988/89. To help alleviate conditions, the Soviet Union pledged in September 1988 to provide the Democratic Republic of Afghanistan (DRA) with an additional 300 million rubles of credit, half of which was to be given to the United Nations emergency aid program for Afghanistan which had been set up as part of the international agreement which led to the withdrawal of Soviet troops.[78] This was a clear indication of the new significance given to emergency aid.

Delivering this aid became one of the major tasks of the Soviet Army in its final months in Afghanistan. As TASS reported in January 1989:

People in many Afghan cities are having a hard time... Formerly crowded streets in Kabul's downtown shopping area now are empty... Roads linking Kabul with the country's south and east have been cut off by rebels, while the only operating road north through the Salang pass is posing a threat to traffic due to snow drifts. Each day, scores of Aeroflot and military-transport planes bring here foodstuffs and fuel which are later distributed free of charge among the most needy citizens. On January 19, Soviet and Afghan soldiers distributed more than 40 tons of flour and rice and nearly 30,000 liters of kerosene among hundreds of families.[79]

Similarly, in February 1989 Moscow Television news announced that:

A consignment of food has been delivered to Kabul from the USSR under the program for emergency aid to Afghanistan through the United Nations... the food situation in the Afghan capital has been deteriorating all the time. The situation has been intensified by the economic blockade... the Soviet Union's contribution to this [UN] program is valued at over US$600 million. Literally over the past few days we have completed deliveries, and handed over to the Afghans for the UN emergency aid program, food and other goods amounting to over US$165 million... Four aircraft have delivered 75 tons of wheat flour from the Soviet Union as a Soviet contribution to the program of emergency aid to Afghanistan through the United Nations.[80]

Even more supplies came in by road on convoys managed and escorted by the Soviet Army. In November-December 1988 alone, 27,500 tons of goods were transported from the Afghan border town of Hairaton to Kabul, half by vehicles of the Soviet Army.[81] The convoys and airlifts had the desired effect. While Kabul remained under siege, famine was avoided, and by May 1989, following the complete withdrawal of Soviet forces from Afghanistan, "the crisis was over."[82]

Artyom Borovik met one of the soldiers giving out the airlifted flour in Kabul. The soldier's words revealed the fundamental paradox of the Soviet involvement in Afghanistan. "This is some kind of international duty," he told Borovik, "You shoot them with one hand and put food in their mouths with the other."[83]

6

CONCLUSION

The Afghan economy, wrote *Pravda* in 1988, "has been destroyed by the war and cannot meet the basic needs of its population."[1] The withdrawal of the Soviet Army in February 1989 made matters even worse. Militarily, not much changed at first. Although many observers expected the People's Democratic Party of Afghanistan regime to fall, it was able to maintain control of the major population centers, and defeated a rebel offensive in the Jalalabad area in the spring and summer of 1989. However, the fact that the Soviet Army was no longer present to protect vital economic installations meant that production in those locations ground to a halt, bringing financial ruin on the government.

Most significantly, production of natural gas stopped following the Soviet withdrawal. Various explanations were given. *Pravda* blamed the lack of security, stating in October 1989 that "deliveries of natural gas, which used to constitute the main category of Soviet imports from Afghanistan in the past, have been suspended in connection with the complex military situation in the area of the gas fields."[2] According to Barnett Rubin, the Afghan government attributed the suspension "to inadequate maintenance of existing equipment, lack of skilled workers, shortage of diesel fuel and marketing problems," although the minister of mines stated that "the main reason that the wells were shut down was that the Soviet experts who actually ran the gas fields had left with the Soviet troops."[3]

This begs the question of what happened to the thousands of workers supposedly trained by the Soviets, who should, in principle, have been capable of running the gas fields without Soviet assistance. Anton Minkov and Gregory Smolynec suggest that the collapse of the gas industry points to a "failure to develop a domestic skilled labor pool able to operate the crucial gas and mining sectors,"[4] but this seems somewhat wide of the mark. There is no doubt that the Soviets did train thousands of Afghans. The problem was rather that they fled the country as soon as the Soviets were no longer there to protect them. As Valerii Ivanov put it:

In principle there were sufficient specialists at the objects we built. For example, the nitrogen fertilizer factory is a colossal enterprise, with a danger of explosion, and it is working to this day without Soviet specialists... The problem wasn't that. Simply, a large quantity of the specialists who studied in the Soviet Union and did not belong to any of the mujahideen movements had to leave... They threatened to kill them, and so they emigrated.[5]

Politics, it seems, is the determining factor in Afghanistan's economic failure. Afghanistan's economy could not develop without improvements in the quality of the country's human capital. But efforts to train and educate Afghans floundered in the face of a political situation which encouraged the educated to flee, leaving the country as devoid of trained personnel as if the training had never taken place.

The attempts from 1987 onwards to support private enterprise and to encourage direct ties between Soviet and Afghan regions represented a belated recognition of the institutional barriers blocking the country's progress. The Soviets also concentrated more of their efforts on providing humanitarian aid, rather than just military backing for the regime. But Soviet humanitarian aid could scarcely hope to win Afghan hearts and minds in the face of years of excessive violence, and however many schools, hospitals and other objects the Soviets built, they could not compare with the number destroyed by the war. At the last gasp, the Soviets sought to forge a new institutional arrangement, cemented by the National Reconciliation Program and the withdrawal of Soviet troops. It came too late. The situation was too bleak to be rescued.

The collapse of the gas industry, in particular, had a devastating impact on government finances. The products of Soviet economic assistance remained industrialized enclaves. Once these enclaves shut down, the government found it had nothing else on which to draw. Deprived of its largest source of revenue, Kabul resorted to printing money. As Rubin notes, "virtually 100 percent of expenditures had to be financed by distributing banknotes delivered weekly from Russia, where the afghani notes were printed."[6]

The result was that inflation, although officially estimated between 1987 and 1989 at 30–40 percent, sky-rocketed so that, "On the open market food prices increased 500% to 1,000%."[7]

Lacking any funds of its own, the government became even more dependent than before on subsidies from the Soviet Union. It could survive as long as it could support its army, but it could only do so if the Soviets paid the bills. The disintegration of the Soviet Union meant that they would not. Boris Yeltsin, the first president of the post-Soviet Russian Federation, decided that Russia, facing a financial crisis, drew no benefits from continuing to support Afghanistan. In 1992 the Russians turned off the tap, and fifty years of Soviet aid came to an end. With no more money, Najibullah's regime fell soon after. Before long, the victorious rebels turned on one another, and the resulting civil war destroyed much of what was left of the Afghan economy.

In 1955, when Soviet assistance began in earnest, Afghanistan was one of the poorest countries in the world. In 1991, when Soviet assistance came to an end, it was still one of the poorest. Regardless of how much the Soviets built over those forty-six years, the final assessment of Soviet economic and technical assistance to Afghanistan must be one of abject failure.

The story of this failure confirms many of the lessons learnt by development economists over the past few decades. The Soviets, like their Western counterparts, sought to promote development by injecting capital to jump-start the process of accumulation. They also sought to export their socialist methods of industrialization, including state ownership of the means of production and central economic planning. By the 1970s it was becoming clear that this had not worked. Somewhat earlier than their colleagues in the West, Soviet economists decided that the problem of development lay not solely in large-scale capital investments, but in the quality of the country's institutions. Many Soviet economists questioned the wisdom of slavishly copying socialist institutions in under-developed countries, pointing out the need for institutions to reflect local conditions. Effective economic planning was impossible in countries that lacked enough trained personnel to manage the economy, while industrialization merely created enclaves with little connection to the rest of the economy.

More significantly, the Soviets came to the conclusion that improving the economy's ability to efficiently allocate scarce resources at the margins was impossible unless there were fundamental cultural changes and political reforms. Soviet economists argued that countries such as Afghanistan needed to smash the existing social and political systems to clear the way for progress, similar to what Western free-market economists recommended former communist countries do after the fall of the Berlin Wall. In Eastern Europe, where the idea of abrupt institutional change had popular support, the result was a sharp economic slump; in Afghanistan, the result was popular resistance and war. Attempts at economic reform were made worse by the fact that the Afghan state governed poorly, being notoriously corrupt, incompetent and divided. Poor governance more than offset any benefits which Soviet assistance might have provided. In the face of an unreceptive culture, poorly functioning political institutions and bad governance, the failure of Soviet assistance was likely inevitable.

Political rather than economic motives drove the Soviet Union to provide economic and technical assistance to Afghanistan. The Soviets needed above all a stable and friendly Afghanistan. Contrary to Western Cold War myths, exploiting the country's national resources or creating dependence was not a conscious goal. The key to the desired stability was prosperity, and Soviet assistance was meant to stimulate economic growth. In this sense, the Soviets were more well intentioned than is popularly imagined. Their experience shows that good intentions are not enough.

ANNEX I

MAJOR DEVELOPMENT PROJECTS COMPLETED BY THE SOVIET UNION

1–8. Eight oil reservoirs with overall capacity of 8,300 cubic meters, 1952–58.

9. Asphalt factory in Kabul, 1955.

10. Bread factory, Kabul (grain elevator, two mills, and bakery), 1957.

11. Grain elevator, Pul-i-Khumri, 1957.

12. River port at Shir Khan, 1959; expanded in 1961.

13. Road bridge across the Khanabad river at Alchin, 1959.

14. Auto-repair factory in Kabul, 1960.

15. Bagram airport, 1961.

16–17. Two road bridges across the Salang and Gurband rivers, 1961.

18. Kabul international airport, 1962.

19. Pul-i-Khumri hydroelectric station, 9 megawatts. 1962.

20. Salang highway over Hindu Kush mountains, 1964.

21–23. Three road bridges in Nangarhar province, 1964.

24. Highway, Kushka-Herat-Kandahar (679 km), 1965.

25. Highway, Kabul-Jabel-us-Seraj (68.2 km), 1965.

26. Kabul house building combine, 1965.

27. Jalalabad irrigation canal, 1965.

28. Highway, Doshi-Shir Khan (216 km), 1966.

29. Road repair workshops, Herat, 1966.

30. Dam and Naghlu hydroelectric station on Kabul river, 100 megawatts, 1966.
31. Electric power line and substations from Pul-i-Khumri hydro-electric station to Baghlan and Kunduz (110 km), 1967.
32–33. 98 km gas pipeline from gas field to Soviet border, 1967. Addition of crossing over Amu-Darya River, 1974.
34. Completion of gas field in region of Shiberghan, 1968.
35. 88 km gas pipeline from gas field to Mazar-i-Sharif fertilizer plant, 1968.
36. Kabul Polytechnic Institute, 1968.
37. Geological, geophysical, and seismic work, and boring for oil and gas, in northern Afghanistan, 1968–77.
38. Surveying for hard mineral deposits, 1968–77.
39–40. Sarde dam and irrigation system, 1968–77.
41. Citywide electrical net, Jalalabad, 1969.
42–44. Two state farms, Gaziabad and Khalda, and land improvement in the zone of the Jalalabad irrigation canal, 1969–70.
45. Kindergarten, Kabul, 1970.
46. Maternity ward, Kabul, 1971.
47. Road, Pul-i-Khumri—Mazar-i-Sharif—Sherif—Shiberghan (329 km), 1972.
48. Road from the Pul-i-Khumri—Shiberghan highway to Hairaton (56 km), 1972.
49. Thermal energy power station at Mazar-i-Sharif, 36 megawatts. 1st phase, 1972, 2nd phase 1974. Capacity expanded to 48 megawatts, 1982.
50–52. Three veterinary laboratories in Jalalabad, Mazar-i-Sharif, and Herat, 1972.
53. Electric power line and substations from Mazar-i-Sharif thermal energy power station to the town of Mazar-i-Sharif (17.6 km), 1972.
54. Oil and mining technical college, Mazar-i-Sharif, 1973.
55. Auto-mechanical technical college, Kabul, 1973.
56–58. Electric substations in the north-western part of Kabul, and 25 km power line, 1974.
59–61. Nitrogen fertilizer plant at Mazar-i-Sharif, plus living quarters and construction base, 1974.
62–71. Ten meteorological stations and 25 meteorological posts, 1974.

72. Shindand airport, 1977.
73–74. Two suburbs in Kabul, 1978.
75–76. Citywide electrical nets in Mazar-i-Sharif and Balkh, 1979.
   77. 53 km of looping on gas pipeline, 1980.
   78. Construction of gas field at Jarkuduk, with gas purification plant, 1980.
   79. "Lotus" satellite communications station, 1980
   80. Expansion of the oil reservoir at Hariaton to 5,000 cubic meters, 1981.
   81. Compressor station at Khodzha-Gugerdag gas field, 1981.
   82. Bakery, Kabul, 1981.
   83. Oil reservoir at Mazar-i-Sharif with capacity of 12,000 cubic meters, 1982.
   84. Multichannel communications line from Mazar-i-Sharif to Hairaton, 1982.
   85. Expansion of capacity of house building combine, 1982.
   86. Road and rail bridge over Amu Darya River, 1982.
   87. Transshipment base on left bank of Amu Darya River at Hairaton, 1982.
   88. Mill, Pul-i-Khumri, 1982.
   89. Bakery, Mazar-i-Sharif, 1982.
   90. Mill, Mazar-i-Sharif, 1982.
91–98. Eight professional technical colleges, 1982–86.
   99. Oil reservoir in Logar with a capacity of 27,000 cubic meters, 1983.
  100. Oil reservoir in Pul-i-Khumri with a capacity of 6,000 cubic meters, 1983.
  101. Service station for Kamaz trucks in Hairaton, 1984.
  102. Boarding school on the site of Kabul kindergarten, 1984.
  103. Citrus fruit and olive oil factory, Jalalabad, 1984.
  104. Seed laboratory for grain cultures, Kabul, 1984.
105–107. Three soil laboratories in Kabul, Mazar-i-Sharif, and Jalalabad, 1984.
108–110. Three auto-transport enterprises in Kabul for servicing of 300 Kamaz trucks each per year, 1985.
  111. Auto-transport enterprise in Kabul for servicing oil tankers, 1985
  112. Laboratory for analysis of hard minerals, Kabul, 1985.

113. Grain elevator, Mazar-i-Sharif, 1985.
114. Truck service station, Pul-i-Khumri, 1985.
115–116. Two cotton seed laboratories, Kabul and Balkh, 1985.
117. Polyclinic for civil servants, Kabul, 1985.
118–120. Artificial insemination stations, Kabul, Mazar-i-Sharif, and Jalalabad, 1985.
121–122. Two cable cranes in region of Khorog and Kalaii-Khumb, 1985–1986.
123. Electric power line from the Soviet border near Shirkhan to the town of Kunduz, 1986.
124. Reconstruction of technical systems of Salang tunnel, 1986.
125. Electric power line from Soviet border to Mazar-i-Sharif, 1986.
126. Institute of social sciences for the Central Committee of the PDPA, 1986.
127. Exploratory work on the expediency of creating two state farms in the area of the Sarde irrigation system, 1986.
128. Electric power line from Soviet border in the region of Kushka to Turgundi, with substations, 1986.
129. Gas filling station, Kabul, 1986.
130. Base for unloading and preservation of special loads, Hairaton, 1986.
131. Reconstruction of Turgundi railway station, 1987.
132. Repair of bridge across Samangan river, 1987.
133. Gas filling station, Hairaton, 1987.
134. 50 km of looping on gas pipeline from USSR to Afghanistan, 1987.
135. Road repairs, 1987.
136. High school for 1,300 students, Kabul, 1987.
137. Plant to convert gas condensate into diesel, Jarkuduk, 1987.
138. Ministry of Internal Security base in Hairaton, 1987.
139–141. Three concrete platforms for open storage of loads, Hairaton, 1987.
142. Bicycle assembly plant, Kabul, 1988.

Source: Valerii Ivanov.

ANNEX II

KEY SOVIET-AFGHAN TREATIES, AGREEMENTS, PROTOCOLS, AND LETTERS, 1955–88

28 June 1955	Agreement on duty-free transit of Afghan goods through the USSR.
28 January 1956	Agreement on economic and technical cooperation.
1 March 1956	Agreement for Soviet specialists to be stationed in Afghanistan in connection with aid projects.
24 March 1956	Agreement on air links.
26 June 1956	Protocol for joint Soviet-Afghan efforts in establishing a hydroelectric irrigation project on the Amu Darya.
30 July 1957	Agreement on cooperation in geographic prospecting in northern Afghanistan, and granting of credit of US$15m for this purpose.
4 February 1959	Agreement on radio-telephone communications.
28 May 1959	Agreement on the construction a road from Turgundi to Kandahar, via Herat.
19 January 1960	Protocol on the exchange of goods between the two nations.
4 March 1960	Agreement on cultural exchanges.
16 October 1961	Agreement on economic and technical cooperation.

27 February 1963	Protocol to the trade Agreement, providing for Soviet cars, oil, cameras and watches to be delivered in exchange for Afghan wool, cotton and fresh and dried fruits.
23 March 1963	Agreement on second phase of Nangahar irrigation project.
20 May 1963	Agreement on hydroelectric work on the Pandj River.
25 July 1963	Protocol on economic and technical cooperation in the second five-year plan.
17 October 1963	Agreement on mining and gas exploration in northern Afghanistan.
19 July 1964	Agreement on the use of water and energy resources of the Pandj and Amu-Darya rivers.
19 August 1964	Agreement on the Kabul house-building combine.
16 September 1964	Exchange of letters on the provision of aid for the creation of an electric network in Jalalabad.
10 May 1967	Protocol on the gas industry.
6 February 1968	Agreement on Soviet help with the third Afghan five-year plan.
1 June 1969	Agreement on cooperation in the sphere of hydro-meteorology.
5 June 1969	Agreement on the mutual recognition of qualifications.
16 May 1970	Agreement on help in the creation of veterinary laboratories.
20 June 1970	Protocol on the struggle against cotton diseases.
5 August 1970	Protocol on the struggle against cattle plague.
11 July 1972	Agreement on Soviet help with the fourth five-year plan.
20 March 1974	Trade Agreement, based on the Most Favored Nation principle.
6 February 1975	Agreement on help in the creation of veterinary clinics.
27 February 1975	Agreement on economic and technical cooperation.

18 June 1975	Long-term trade Agreement.
23 December 1976	Treaty of friendship and cooperation.
14 April 1977	Treaty on economic cooperation
1 March 1979	Agreement on economic and technical cooperation.
30 August 1979	Agreement on machine-tractor stations.
30 October 1979	Agreement on preparation of national cadres.
November 1980	Agreement on cooperation of Soviet Journalists' Union and Afghan Journalists' Union.
24 December 1980	Agreement on economic and technical cooperation, with Protocol on the provision of free aid in preparation of national cadres.
22 January 1981	Protocol on provision of aid in the construction of professional technical training institutions.
3 April 1981	Trade Agreement for 1981–85.
2 June 1982	Agreement on cultural and scientific cooperation.
21 September 1982	Agreement to build soil-agronomy laboratories and other agricultural and veterinarian institutions.
2 June 1983	Agreement for the creation of three television studios in Kabul.
27 February 1985	Agreement on economic and technical cooperation.
18 June 1985	Protocol on provision of aid in creating technical training institutions.
27 August 1985	Agreement to continue geological prospecting and work in the gas industry.
22 April 1986	Treaty on the basic direction of Soviet-Afghan trade and economic cooperation.
16 January 1987	Agreement to equip auto-transport enterprises.
18 April 1987	Agreement on provision of aid to projects with the participation of the private sector.
4 September 1987	Agreement on the provision of agricultural supplies.
26 February 1988	Protocol on cooperation in the field of communications.
25 April 1988	Agreement on assistance in area of energy.
27 June 1988	Agreement on geological prospecting.

| 27 July 1988 | Agreement on cooperation in the gas industry. |
| 20 September 1988 | Agreement on economic and technical cooperation. |

Ministerstvo Inostrannykh Del SSSR, Sbornik deistvuiushchikh dogovorov, soglashenii i konventsii, zakliuchennykh SSSR s inostrannymi gosudastvami, vypuski XVII-XVIII, XXI, XXII, XXIII, XXIV, XXV, XXVI, XXX, XXXI, XXXIII, & XXXV (Moscow: Mezhdunarodnye Otnosheniia, various dates 1960–1981)

Ministerstvo Inostrannykh Del SSSR, Deistvuiushchie dogovory, soglasheniia i konventsii, vypuski XXXVI, XXXVII, XXXVIII, XXXIX, XLI, XLII, XLIII, & XLIV (Moscow: Mezhdunarodnye Otnosheniia, various dates 1982–1990).

Naik, J.A. (ed.), Russia's Foreign Policy Documents: Russia in Asia and Africa (Kolhapur: Avinash Reference Publications, 1979).

ANNEX III

PROFITS OF ENTERPRISES BUILT WITH THE ASSISTANCE OF THE USSR, 1976–77

Name of Enterprise or Object	1976 (millions of afghanis)	1977 (millions of afghanis)	1977 (as a percentage of 1976)
Gas production, Shirbirghan	1755.44	1683.44	95.8
Fertilizer factory, Mazar-i-Sharif	77.64	108.48	139.7
Hydroelectric station, Naghlu	174.43	151.17	86.6
Hydroelectric station, Fuli-Khumri-2	17.97	23.27	129.5
Auto-repair workshop, Jangalak	12.5	15.0	120.0
Bread combine, Kabul	36.97	59.71	161.5
House building combine, Kabul	7.75	4.25	54.8
Total	2082.7	2045.32	98.2

Source: Review of the Afghan economy in 1977, RGAE, f. 413, o. 31, d. 9134, l. 84.

ANNEX IV

CREDITS GRANTED BY THE SOVIET UNION FOR ECONOMIC DEVELOPMENT

Date of agreement	Repayment period (years)	Annual interest rate (%)	Amount of credit (millions of rubles)
27 January 1954	8	3	3.2
1 March 1956	30	2	69.5
30 July 1957	50	0	13.5
16 October 1961	50	0	95.1
	30	2	75.5
17 May 1962	30	2	18.0
5 September 1963	30	2	0.2
19 August and 15 November 1964	10	2	6.5
6 February 1968	15	2	64.0
11 July 1972	15	2	80.0
27 February 1975	30	2	108.0
	15	2	95.0
	8	2	105.0
31 March 1977	30	2	9.0
1 March 1979	12	2	200.0
	15	2	70.0
24 December 1980	12	3	200.00

27 February 1985	12	3	168.0
18 April 1987	15	3	50.0
26 February 1988	12	3	20.0
7 March 1988	12	3	15.0
25 April 1988	12	3	40.0
27 July 1988	12	3	50.0
27 July 1988	12	3	40.0
20 September 1988	12	3	150.0
			200.00*
		Total	1945.0

*Special credit of 200 million rubles designed to balance clearing accounts, but never used in full by Afghanistan.
Source: Valerii Ivanov (Interview).

ANNEX V

POSTPONEMENTS OF DEBT REPAYMENTS, 1965–91

Date of agreement to postpone payments	Amount of postponed payment (millions of rubles)	Period of postponement	New timescale for repayment of postponed debts
26 July 1965	11.0	1965–1967	1992–1994
11 July 1972	25.0	1972–1976	1977–1986
27 February 1975	100.0	1975–1980	1986–1995
16 August 1979	200.0	1979–1988	1989–1998
5 July 1983	80.0	1984–1985	1986–1995
22 April 1986	350.0	1986–1990	1991–2000
27 July 1987	70.0	1987	1997–2006
26 February 1988	80.0	1988	1998–2007
4 January 1989	220.0	1989	1999–2008
28 February 1990	218.0	1990	2000–2010
5 April 1991	462.0	1991	1996–2006
Totals	1816.0	1965–1990	1977–2010

Source: Valerii Ivanov.

ANNEX VI

MAJOR DEVELOPMENT PROJECTS CANCELLED
BY THE SOVIET UNION, 1980–85

Cancelled in July 1980

1. Construction of Kosh-Tepe canal.
2. Dam and reservoir in the region of Kashmai-Shafa on the river Balkh.
3. Dam and Kelagai hydroelectric station on the Kunduz River.
4. Cartographic work.

5–10. Construction of six local airports in north-eastern provinces.

11. Work on the Hadjigak iron desposits.
12. Construction of roads from Shiberghan to Herat and from Kunduz to Keshm.
13. Creation of additional capabilities in production of nitrogen fertilizers.
14. Surveying for hard mineral deposits.

15–7. Cotton factories in Baghlan, Balkh, and Takhar provinces.

18. Reconstruction of existing cotton factories.
19. "Otdelochnaia" factory, Pul-i-Khumri.
20. Fabric spinning factory, Pul-i-Khumri.
21. Fabric spinning factory, Talukan.
22. Bakery, Herat.
23. Mill, Herat.
24. Electric power line from Naghlu hydroelectric station to Jalalabad, with substations.

25. Electric power line from Jebel-Seradj to the Salang tunnel.
26. 200-bed hospital in the north of the country.
27. Construction of a mining enrichment combine at the Aynak copper deposits.
28. Construction of oil fields at Angot, Akdaria and Kashkari.
29. Construction of oil refinery.
30. Reconstruction of Gulbakhar textile combine.
31. Exploratory work for exploitation of water energy resources of the Kochka River.
32. Exploratory work for the construction of a thermal energy electric power station.

Cancelled in November 1983

33. Multichannel communications line from kabul to Mazar-i-Sharif.
34. Organization of production of simple agricultural appliances at the Herat workshops.
35. Reconnaissance of coal deposits at Shebashek.

Cancelled in November 1985

36. Construction of bird incubator station in Balkh province.

Source: Valerii Ivanov (Interview).

ANNEX VII

CREDITS GRANTED BY THE SOVIET UNION FOR THE PURCHASE OF CONSUMER GOODS

Date of agreement	Conditions of repayment	Amount granted (million of rubles)	Amount used by 1 January 1991 (millions of rubles)
13 January 1962	30 years at 2%	10.8	10.8
18 January 1965, 10 May 1965, & 14 December 1966	30 years at 2%	10.0	9.9
6 February 1968	10 years at 2%	17.0	16.9
11 July 1972	10 years at 2%	20.0	19.7
28 July 1977	10 years at 2%	37.5	37.5
1 March 1979	10 years at 2%	14.0	14.0
13 September 1984	10 years at 4%	100.0	97.4
	Totals	209.3	206.2

Note: Mainly wheat, sugar, and oil products.
Source: Valerii Ivanov.

ANNEX VIII

COSTS OF SOVIET TECHNICAL ASSISTANCE
TO AFGHANISTAN, 1981–91

Year	Deliveries of equipment and materials (millions of rubles)	Other costs, including personnel (millions of rubles)	Total
1981	77.8	9.6	87.4
1982	70.3	10.8	81.1
1983	69.6	9.0	78.6
1984	79.1	13.0	92.1
1985	105.3	12.9	118.2
1986	134.5	17.5	152.0
1987	158.1	20.9	179.0
1988	122.3	16.9	139.2
1989	30.5	5.1	35.6
1990	25.0	3.0	28.0
1991	26.0	2.0	28.0
Totals	898.5	120.7	1019.2

Source: Valerii Ivanov (Interview).

ANNEX IX

ECONOMIC ASSISTANCE AND OTHER EXPENSES, 1986–1987 (IN MILLIONS OF RUBLES)

	1986	*1987*
Free Aid	203	950
Economic assistance through Gosudarstvennyi komitet po vneshnim ekonomicheskim sviazam (GKEHS) (State Committee for Foreign Economic Relations) channels	152	166
Through Ministry of Foreign Trade channels, export above import	28	67
Aid through preferential prices for Afghan goods delivered to the USSR: natural gas, wool, etc.	70	65
Deliveries within the framework of sponsored aid	–	10
Total economic aid	453	1,258

Source: State Planning Committee Memorandum, in *Cold War International History Project Bulletin*, Issue 14/15.

NOTES

1. INTRODUCTION

1. Andrew Wilder, "A 'weapons system' based on wishful thinking," *Boston Globe*, 16 September 2009. For similar comments, see: Mark Moyar, "Development in Afghanistan's Counterinsurgency: A New Guide," *Small Wars Journal*, March 2011, p. 3, available online at, http://smallwarsjournal.com/documents/development-in-afghanistan-coin-moyar.pdf; and Mathieu Aikins, "Last Stand in Kandahar," *The Walrus*, December 2010, available online at: http://www.walrusmagazine.com/articles/2010.12-international-affairs-last-stand-in-kandahar/

2. Anthony Hyman, *Afghanistan under Soviet Domination, 1964–91*, third edition (Basingstoke: Macmillan, 1992), p. 30.

3. Amartya Sen, *Development as Freedom* (New York: Alfred Knopf, 1999).

4. India's Jawaharlal Nehru was particularly fond of Soviet central planning. For an historical take on the appeal of the Soviet model, see David Engerman, *Modernization from the Other Shore: American Intellectuals and the Romance of Russian Development* (Harvard University Press, 2003).

5. Dani Rodrik, "Institutions for High-Quality Growth: What They Are and How to Acquire Them," *Studies in Comparative International Development*, vol. 35, no. 3, Fall 2000.

6. Henry S. Bradsher, *Afghan Communism and Soviet Intervention* (Oxford: Oxford University Press, 1999), pp. 169–171.

7. Gregory Feifer, *The Great Gamble: The Soviet War in Afghanistan* (New York: Harper, 2009), pp. 146.

8. Rodric Braithwaite, *Afgantsy: The Russians in Afghanistan 1979–89* (London: Profile Books, 2011), especially Chapter 7 "The Nationbuilders," pp. 146–168.

9. Anton Minkov & Gregory Smolynec, *Economic Development in Afghanistan During the Soviet Period, 1979–1989: Lessons Learned from the Soviet Experience in*

Afghanistan (Ottawa: DRDC Centre for Operational Research and Analysis, 2007), p. 1.

10. Ibid.

11. A.A. Liakhovskii, *Doblest i tragediia Afgana* (Moscow: GPI Iskona, 1995).

12. The Russian General Staff, *The Soviet-Afghan War: How a Superpower Fought and Lost*, trans. and ed. Lester W. Grau & Michael A. Gress (Lawrence: University Press of Kansas, 2002).

13. For instance, L.B. Teplinskii, *Istoriia sovetsko-afganskikh otnoshenii* (Moscow: Mysl, 1988), pp. 325–337.

14. J. Bruce Amstutz, *Afghanistan: The First Five Years of Soviet Occupation* (Washington, DC: National Defense University, 1986).

15. Richard F. Nyrop & Donald M. Seekins, *Afghanistan Country Study*, available online at: http://www.gl.iit.edu/govdocs/afghanistan.

16. For instance, M.S. Noorzoy, "Long-Term Economic Relations between Afghanistan and the Soviet Union: An Interpretative Study," *International Journal of Middle East Studies*, vol. 17, no. 2, May 1985, pp. 151–173, and various chapters in Rosanne Klass (ed.), *Afghanistan: The Great Game Revisited* (Lanham, MD: Freedom House, 1990).

17. Martin Kipping, *Two Interventions: Comparing Soviet and US-led State-building in Afghanistan*, AAN Thematic Report 01/2010, available online at: http://aan-afghanistan.com/uploads/AAN_Two_Interventions.pdf.

18. Minkov & Smolynec, *Economic Development*.

19. L.B. Teplinskii, "Sovetsko-Afganskie otnosheniia za sorok let sushchestvovaniia nezavisimogo Afganistana," in R.T. Akhramovich (ed.), *Nezavisimaia Afganistan. 40 let nezavisimosti: sbornik statei* (Moscow: Izdatel'stvo Vostochnoi Literatury, 1958), pp. 32–33.

20. Lev Nikolaev, *Afghanistan Between the Past and Future* (Moscow: Progress, 1986).

21. R.B. Gaur, *Afghanistan: Expanding Social Base of Revolution* (New Delhi: Allied, 1987), pp. 22–23.

22. *Za Rubezhom*, no. 30 (1151), 1982, p. 13.

23. A. Chertkov, "Etazhi Kabula," *Sotsialisticheskaia Industriia*, 26 April 1986, p. 3.

24. B. Shabaev, "Dorogi muzhestva," *Sotsialisticheskaia Industriia*, April 1986.

25. "Doklad V.G. Korguna, zaveduiushchego kaphedroi Afganistana v Institute vostokovedeniia RAN," *AZIAINFORM*, 16 January 2006, available online at: http://www.asiainform.ru/rusdoc/9600.htm.

26. Braithwaite, *Afgantsy*, p. 149.

27. Ibid.

28. Interview of Valerii Ivanov with Paul Robinson, 8 December 2008 (henceforth: Ivanov, interview).

29. For instance, Amstutz, p. 257.

30. M.S. Noorzoy, "Long-Term Economic Relations between Afghanistan and the

Soviet Union: An Interpretative Study," *International Journal of Middle East Studies*, vol. 17, no. 2, 1985, p. 161.

31. Martin Ewans, *Afghanistan: A Short History of Its People and Politics* (New York: Perennial, 2001), p. 155.

32. Amstutz, p. 25.

33. Dupree, p. 638.

34. Ibid. p. 640.

35. Ibid. p. 514.

36. Rosanne Klass, "The Great Game Revisited," in Rosanne Klass (ed.), *Afghanistan: the Great Game Revisited* (Lanham, MD: Freedom House, 1990), p. 11.

37. John F. Shroder Jr. and Abdul Tawab Assifi, "Afghan Resources and Soviet Exploitation," in Rosanne Klass (ed.), *Afghanistan: the Great Game Revisited* (Lanham, MD: Freedom House, 1990), p. 97.

38. Leon B. Poullada, "The Road to Crisis, 1919–1980," in Rosanne Klass (ed.), *Afghanistan: the Great Game Revisited* (Lanham, MD: Freedom House, 1990), p. 45.

39. M.S. Noorzoy, "Long-Term Economic Relations," p. 163.

40. For expressions of this theory, see, Noorzoy, op cit, passim, and also M.S. Noorzoy, "Soviet Economic Interests and Policies in Afghanistan," in Rosanne Klass (ed.), *Afghanistan: the Great Game Revisited* (Lanham, MD: Freedom House, 1990), pp. 71–95.

41. Poullada, op cit., p. 46.

42. Hyman, *Afghanistan*, p. 209.

2. MODELS OF DEVELOPMENT AND SOVIET THEORIES

1. John F. Shroder and Abdul Tawab Assifi, "Afghan Mineral Resources and Soviet Exploitation," in Rosanne Klass (ed.), *Afghanistan: The Great Game Revisited* (Lanham, MD: Freedom House, 1990), p. 116.

2. The table is drawn from several sources, most notably: information provided by Valerii Ivanov; Gustavson Associates, *Islamic Republic of Afghanistan: Preparing the Natural Gas Development Project* (Boulder, CO: Gustavson Associates, 2007), p. 3, available online at http://www.adb.org/Documents/Reports/Consultant/37085-AFG/37085-TACR-AFG.pdf, accessed 11 January 2010; M.S. Noorzoy, "Soviet Economic Interests and Policies in Afghanistan," in Klass (ed.), *Afghanistan*, p. 95; and Shroder & Assifi, "Afghan Mineral Resources," pp. 110–122.

3. Richard F. Nyrop & Donald M. Seekins, *Afghanistan Country Study and Government Publications* (Washington, DC: The American University, 1986), p. 143.

4. Ibid.

5. Ibid.

6. Barnett Rubin, *The Fragmentation of Afghanistan: State Formation and Collapse in the International System* (New Haven: Yale University Press, 1995), p. 34.

7. Ibid. p. 146.

8. Ibid. p. 65.

9. Antonio Giustozzi, *Afghanistan: Transition without End. An Analytical Narrative on State-Making*, Crisis State Research Centre, Working Paper 40 (London: LSE, 2008), p. 19.

10. Ibid. p. 20.

11. Ibid. p. 17,

12. Rubin, *Fragmentation*, p. 65.

13. Ibid. p. 130.

14. The basis of growth shifted in the 1850s in the industrialized countries with the Industrial Revolution, but Malthusian growth still prevails in many parts of the world. For details of the transition, see Gary D. Hansen & Edward C. Prescott, "Malthus to Solow," *American Economic Review*, vol. 92, no. 4, 2002, pp. 1205–1217.

15. In this chapter, we will use capital to refer collectively to both physical and human capital.

16. Metaphorically speaking: in practice, after Khrushchev's secret speech denouncing Stalin, brute force did not mean the overt violence of the Soviet experience. In fact, the Soviets often advised their clients to compromise with the peasantry and bourgeois classes. To their frustration, they were often ignored, with unfortunate consequences.

17. de Soto, Hernando, "The Myserty of Capital."

18. William Easterly & Ross Levine, "It's Not Factor Accumulation: Stylized Facts and Growth Models," in Norman Loayza, Raimundo Soto & Klaus Schmidt-Hebbel (eds), *Economic Growth: Sources, Trends, and Cycles*, edition 1, volume 6 (Central Bank of Chile, 2002), pp. 61–114.

19. John Williamson coined the phrase to describe ten reforms that formed the lowest common denominator of official Washington's advice (the International Monetary Fund (IMF), World Bank, US Department of the Treasury). For details, see Williamson, John. "Did the Washington Consensus Fail?," Outline of Remarks at CSIS (Washington DC: Institute for International Economics, 6 November 2002).

20. Adam Smith, "Lecture in 1775," quoted in Dugald Stewart, *Account of the Life and Writings of Adam Smith LLD*, section IV, p. 25.

21. D. Rodrik, A. Subramanian & F. Trebbi, "Institutions Rule: The Primacy of Institutions over Geography and Integration in Economic Development," *Journal of Economic Growth*, vol. 9, no. 2 (June 2004), pp. 131–165.

22. Douglass North, *Understanding the Process of Economic Change* (Princeton University Press, 2005).

23. Thomas Hobbes, *Leviathan*.

24. John Williamson, "The New Institutional Economics: Taking Stock, Looking Ahead," *Journal of Economic Literature*, vol. 38, 2000, pp. 595–613.

25. In fact, the issue may instead be that economists still know too little about traditions and their relationship to day-to-day affairs. They are in any case more the focus of other disciplines.

26. Adapted from Williamson, "The New Institutional Economics."

27. One is tempted to say that they are absent in places like Afghanistan or Somalia, but despite an absence of formal institutions, there are still rules that permit some economic activity.

28. See, for example, Paolo Mauro, "Corruption and Growth," *The Quarterly Journal of Economics*, vol. 110, no. 3, 1995, pp. 681–712.

29. There is a large literature documenting the tendency for countries to be worse off as a result of their resource wealth. See Alan Gelb, *Oil Windfalls: Blessing or Curse? A Comparative Study of Six Developing Exporters* (Oxford: Oxford University Press, 1990) for a seminal analysis of the "resource curse."

30. Aaron Tornell & Phillip Lane use the term "voracity" to describe the tendency of large rents to generate an even larger demand for them: "The voracity effect," *American Economic Review*, vol. 89, p. 2246.

31. See Joseph E. Stiglitz, *Whither Socialism?* (MIT Press, 1996), edition 1, volume 1, for some of the more trenchant critiques.

32. Charles R. Dannehl, *Politics, Trade, and Development: Soviet Economic Aid to the Non-Communist Third World, 1955–89* (Aldershot: Dartmouth, 1995), pp. 10–11.

33. Ibid. p. 19.

34. Ibid. p. 45.

35. Ibid. pp. 118–119.

36. Ivanov, interview.

37. Dannehl, *Politics, Trade, and Development*, p. 36.

38. For a discussion of the importance of consumption under Khrushchev, see David C. Engerman, "The Romance of Economic Development and New Histories of the Cold War," *Diplomatic History*, vol. 28, no. 1, 2004, pp. 41–42; for references on the ideological importance of consumption during the Stalinist era, see fn 64.

39. A. Sandakov, "Razvivaiushchiesia strany Afriki: problemy nakopleniia," *Narody Azii i Afriki*, no. 3, 1970, pp. 25–26.

40. See Robert S. Jaster, "Foreign Aid and Development: The Shifting Soviet View," *International Affairs*, vol. 45, no. 3, 1969, pp. 452–464, and Donald S. Carlisle, "The Changing Soviet Perception of the Development Process in the Afro-Asian World," *Midwest Journal of Political Science*, vol. 8, no. 4, 1964, pp. 385–407.

41. Carlisle, "Changing Soviet Perception," p. 386.

42. Engerman notes that they were caught in what he calls the "romance of development." The term refers to the belief in the government's apparent ability to create a plan that would lead the country to industrial prosperity: Engerman, "The Romance of Economic Development," pp. 23–54.

43. For a discussion of the concept's evolution, see Jerry F. Hough, *The Struggle for the Third World: Soviet Debates and American Options* (Washington, D. C.: The Brookings Institution, 1986); and Paul Bellis, "The Non-Capitalist Road and Soviet Development Theory Today: A Critique of Some Recent Accounts," *Journal of Communist Studies and Transition Politics*, vol. 4, no. 3, 1988, pp. 258–281.

44. The innovation was not without cost to the Soviets' standing in the communist world. As Carlisle notes these "post-Stalinist ideological and policy innovations … [bred] dissatisfaction among communist militants and played a special role in the Sino-Soviet conflict." Carlisle, "The Changing Soviet Perception," p. 386.

45. Roger E. Kanet, "The Recent Soviet Reassessment of Developments in the Third World," *Russian Review*, vol. 27, no. 1, 1968, p. 29.

46. A.Iu. Shpirt, "Nauchno-tekhnicheskaia revolutsiia i razvivaiushchiesia strany Azii i Afriki," *Narody Azii i Afriki*, no. 2, 1971, p. 9; & A.I. Dinkevich, "O strategii ekonomicheskogo razvitiia stran 'tret'ego mira'," *Narody Azii i Afriki*, no. 1, 1975, p. 7.

47. Sandakov, 1970, p. 23.

48. Ibid.

49. Morrison 1973, p. 126. Most economists now believe that "it is not factor accumulation." See: William Easterly & Ross Levine, *It's Not Factor Accumulation: Stylized Facts and Growth Models*, Working Papers Central Bank of Chile 164, Central Bank of Chile, 2002.

50. For a typical comment on the importance of training and educating "national cadres," see: G.M. Prokhorov, "Industrializatsiia razvivaiushchikhsia stran i znachenie opyta i pomoshchi SSSR," *Narody Azii i Afriki*, no. 6, 1974, p. 22.

51. This is known as the Prebisch-Singer Thesis. Revised estimates of commodity price trends now cast doubt on the hypothesis of a pronounced secular decline.

52. Sandakov, 1970, p. 21.

53. "Finansirovanie ekonomiki razvivaiushchikhsia stran Azii", *Narody Azii i Afriki*, no. 1, 1968, p. 3.

54. For instance, S.A. Bylniak, review of H. Spetter, "Inward-Looking and Export-Oriented Industrialization in Developing Countries (The Case for Export-Oriented Industries)," *Narody Azii i Afriki*, no. 4, 1971, pp. 177–182.

55. For instance, Iu.F. Shamrai, "Nekotorye voprosy rynochnykh otnoshenii mezhdu sotsialisticheskimi i razvivaiuishchimi stranami," *Narody Azii i Afriki*, no. 2, 1969, pp. 19–21.

56. V.V. Rymalov, "Razvivaiushchiesia strany: tendentsii i problem ekonomichesk-ogo rosta," *Narody Azii i Afriki*, no. 3, 1967, p. 7.
57. R.M. Avakov et al., *The Third World and Scientific and Technical Progress* (Moscow: Nauka, 1976), p. 125.
58. Shpirt, "Nauchno-tekhnicheskaia revolutsiia," p. 3.
59. For instance, Avakov et al, *The Third World*, pp. 23, 37, & 118.
60. Ibid. p. 141.
61. Ibid. p. 137.
62. Ibid. p. 283.
63. See Morrison, p. 129.
64. Avakov et al., *The Third World*, pp. 283–4.
65. Ibid. p. 143.
66. Prokhorov, "Industrializatsiia," p. 22.

3. SOVIET ASSISTANCE TO AFGHANISTAN PRIOR TO 1979

1. Teplinskii, "Sovetsko-Afganskie otnosheniia za sorok let sushchestvovaniia neza-visimogo Afganistana," in R.T. Akhromovich (ed.), *Nezavisimyi Afganistan, 40 let nezavistimosti: sbornik statei* (Moscow: Izdatel'stvo Vostochnoi Literatury, 1958), pp. 7–9.
2. Ibid. p. 11.
3. J. Bruce Amstutz, *Afghanistan: The First Five Years of Soviet Occupation* (Washington, DC: National Defense University, 1986), p. 12.
4. Ibid. p. 15.
5. Iu.M. Golovin, "Piatiletnii plan i perspectivy razvitiia ekonomiki Afganistana," in R.T. Akhromovich, (ed.), *Nezavisimaia Afganistan, 40 let nezavisimosti: sbornik statei* (Moscow: Izdatel'stvo Vostochnoi Literatury, 1958), p. 41. M.N. Khod-zhaev, "Sotrudnichestvo SSSR i respublika Afganistana v oblasti energetiki," in Iu. V. Gankovskii (ed.), *Afganistan: Istoriia, ekonomika, kul'tura: sbornik statei* (Moscow: Nauka, 1989), p. 93.
6. Nake M. Kamrany, *Peaceful Competition in Afghanistan: American & Soviet Models For Economic Aid* (Washington, DC: Communication Service Corporation, 1969), p. 11.
7. M.S. Noorzoy, "Long-Term Economic Relations Between Afghanistan and the Soviet Union: An Interpretative Study," *International Journal of Middle East Studies*, vol. 17, no. 2, May 1985, p. 157.
8. Teplinskii, "Sovetsko-Afganskie otnosheniia," pp. 20–21.
9. Golovin, 'Piatiletnii plan," p. 41.
10. Henry S. Bradsher, *Afghanistan and the Soviet Union* (Durham, NC: Duke Press Policy Studies, 1983), p. 23, & Martin Ewans, *Afghanistan: A Short History of Its People and Politics* (New York: Perennial, 2001), p. 154.

11. Nick Cullather, "Damming Afghanistan: Modernization in a Buffer State," *Journal of American History*, vol. 89, 2002, pp. 512–37.

12. Eric Newby, *A Short Walk in the Hindu Kush* (Melbourne: Lonely Planet, 1998. Originally published, 1958), p. 72.

13. Cullather, "Damming Afghanistan."

14. Omar Zakhilwal, *The Helmand Valley Project*, http://www.institute-for-afghan-studies.org/Foreign%20Affairs/us-afghan/helmand_0.htm.

15. Anthony Hyman, *Afghanistan Under Soviet Domination* (Basingstoke: Macmillan, 1992), p. 27.

16. Anthony Arnold, *Afghanistan: The Soviet Invasion in Perspective*, revised and enlarged edition (Stanford: Hoover International Studies, 1985), p. 30.

17. Golovin, "Piatiletnii plan," p. 44.

18. L.B. Teplinskii, *SSSR i Afganistan, 1919–1981* (Moscow: Glavnaia Redaktsiia Vostochnoi Istorii, 1982), p. 145.

19. Pierre Metge, *L'URSS en Afghanistan: De la coopération à l'occupation: 1947–1984* (Paris: CIRPES, 1984), p. 57.

20. Barnett R. Rubin, *The Fragmentation of Afghanistan: State Formation and Collapse in the International System* (New Haven: Yale University Press, 1995), p. 65.

21. Teplinskii, *SSSR i Afganistan*, p. 135.

22. Newby, *Short Walk*, p. 73.

23. Henry S. Bradsher, *Afghanistan and the Soviet Union* (Durham, NC: Duke Press Policy Studies, 1983), p. 25.

24. Kamrany, *Peaceful Competition*, p. 47.

25. "Zapis' peregovorov mezhdu afganskoi torgovoi delegatsii i ekspertami Sovetsomu Soiuzu po protokolu o tovarooborote na 1970 god, sostoiavshikhsia 23. XII. 1969 g.," Rossiiskii Gosudarstvennyi Arkhiv Ekonomiki (henceforth RGAE), f. 413, o. 31, d. 3282, l. 25.

26. Martin Ewans, *Afghanistan: A Short History of Its People and Politics* (New York: Perennial, 2001), p. 157.

27. Ivanov, interview.

28. Andrzej Korbonski and Francis Fukuyama, *The Soviet Union and the Third World: The Last Three Decades* (Ithaca & London: Cornell University Press, 1987), p. 81.

29. Bradsher, *Afghanistan*, p. 24.

30. Iu.F. Shamrai, "Problemy sovershenstvovaniia ekonomicheskogo sotrudnichestva sotsialisticheskikh i razvivaiushchikhsia stran," *Narody Azii i Afriki*, no. 4, 1968, p. 3.

31. Ibid. p. 8.

32. V.I. Berezin, "Ekonomicheskoe i tekhnicheskoe sotrudnichestvo SSSR so stranami Tropicheskoi Afriki," *Narody Azii i Afriki*, no. 5, 1973, p. 138.

33. Korbonski & Fukuyama, *The Soviet Union and the Third World*, p. 81, footnote 24.

34. "Nefteprodukty," 29 June 1971, RGAE, f. 413, o. 31, d. 4734, l. 21.

35. Anthony Hyman, *Afghanistan under Soviet Domination, 1964–91*, Third Edition (Basingstoke: Macmillan, 1992), p. 27.

36. Amstutz, *Afghanistan*, p. 27.

37. "Dopolnenie k spravke o rynke traktorov i sel'skokhoziastvennykh mashin Afganistana," 6 June 1971, RGAE, f. 413, o. 31, d. 4734, l. 87.

38. Noorzoy, "Long-Term Economic Relations," p. 163.

39. Abdul Tawak Assifi, "The Russian Rope: Soviet Economic Motives and the Subversion of Afghanistan," *World Affairs*, vol. 145, no. 3, Winter 1982/83, pp. 253–266. For a similar viewpoint, see also, Leon B. Poullada, "The Road to Crisis, 1919–1980," in Rosanne Klass (ed.), *Afghanistan: The Great Game Revisited* (Lanham, MD: Freedom House, 1990), p. 46.

40. Ivanov, interview.

41. Dupree, Louis, *Afghanistan*, 1980 edition (Princeton: Princeton University Press, 1980), p. 640.

42. "Finansirovanie ekonomiki razvivaiushchikhsia stran Azii," *Narody Azii i Afriki*, no. 1, 1968, p. 18.

43. Shamrai, "Problemy," p. 9.

44. V.M. Kollontai, "Novye iavleniia v imperialisticheskoi politike pomoshchi slaborazvitym stranam," *Narody Azii i Afriki*, no. 4, 1961, p. 27.

45. Shamrai, "Problemy," p. 9.

46. Kollontai, "Novye iavleniia," p. 23.

47. Ibid.

48. E.g. Teplinskii, *SSSR i Afganistan*, pp. 176, 180, & 183

49. For instance, "Zapis' besedy s ministrom gornykh del i promyshlennosti Afganistana Dastegirom Azizi," 14 February 1973, RGAE, f. 413, o. 31, d. 6201; & "Zapis' besedy s ministrom planirovaniia Afganistana Abdul Vakhedom Sorabi," 25 February 1973, RGAE, f. 413, o. 31, d. 6201, l. 3.

50. Ivanov, interview.

51. Ibid. Also, John F. Shroder & Abdul Tawab Assifi, "Afghan Mineral Resources and Soviet Exploitation," in Klass (ed.), *Afghanistan*, pp. 110–11.

52. "Nefteprodukty", RGAE, f. 413, o. 31, d. 4734, ll. 26–27.

53. Amstutz, *Afghanistan*, p. 26.

54. Hyman, *Afghanistan under Soviet Domination*, p. 27.

55. For instance, "Finansirovanie," p. 5.

56. E.R. Makhmudov, "Afganistan. Osnovnye etapy evoliutsii gosudarstvennoi politiki v oblasti industrializatsii (1919–1978)," in *Afganistan. Istoriia, ekonomika, kul'tura: sbornik statei* (Moscow: Nauka, 1989), p. 139.

57. Metge, *L'URSS en Afghanistan*, p. 59.
58. Makhmudov, "Afganistan," p. 137.
59. Ibid. p. 140.
60. Teplinskii, "Sovetsko-Afganskie otnosheniia," p. 32.
61. See for instance, A. Sandakov, "Razvivaiushchiesia strany Afriki: problemy nakopleniia," *Narody Azii i Afriki*, no. 3, 1970, p. 16.
62. "Finansirovanie," p. 3.
63. Ibid.
64. Makhmudov, "Afganistan," p. 141.
65. L.Z. Zevin, review of A.Ia. El'ianov, "Razvivaiushchiesia strany: problemy ekonomicheskogo razvitiia i rynok," *Narody Azii i Afriki*, no. 1, 1977, pp. 167–8. Zevin argued in favor of "a gradual, *organic* inclusion of export production in the national economic complex," (emphasis in original) and wrote positively of the theory of "endogenous development."
66. S.A. Byliniak, review of H. Spetter, "Inward-Looking and Export-Oriented Industrialization in Developing Countries (The Case for Export-Oriented Industries)," *Narody Azii i Afriki*, no. 4, 1971, p. 177. For a similar comment, see Dinkevich, "O strategii ekonomicheskogo razvitiia stran 'tret'ego mira'," *Narody Azii i Afriki*, no. 1, 1975, p. 9.
67. Dinkevich, "O strategii," p. 12.
68. Iu.F. Shamrai, "Nekotorye voprosy rynochnykh otnoshenii mezhdu sotsialisticheskimi i razvivaiushchimisia stranami," *Narody Azii i Afriki*, no. 2, 1969, pp. 20–21.
69. R.N. Andreasian and L.N. Vinogradova, "Razvivaiushchiesia strany: gornodobyvaiushchaia promyshlennost' i problemy industrializatsii," *Narody Azii i Afriki*, no. 5, 1970, p. 29.
70. L.B. Teplinskii, *Istoriia sovetsko-afganskikh otnoshenii* (Moscow: Mysl, 1988), p. 325.
71. Dupree, *Afghanistan*, pp. 508–8.
72. "Finansirovanie," p. 4.
73. V.V. Rymalov, "Razvivaiuishchie strany: tendentsii i problemy ekonomicheskogo rosta," *Narody Azii i Afriki*, no. 3, 1967, p. 7.
74. Makhmudov, "Afganistan," p. 146.
75. Report on the Afghan economy, 1973, RGAE, f. 413, o. 31, d. 6203, l. 104.
76. Golovin, "Piatiletnii plan," p. 52.
77. Teplinskii, *SSSR i Afganistan*, p. 182.
78. Teplinskii, *Istoriia*, p. 332.
79. Untitled report on the Afghan economy, RGAE, f. 413, o. 31, d. 4734, l. 148.
80. Untitled report on the Afghan economy, RGAE, f. 413, o. 31, d. 4734, l. 150, & Teplinskii, *SSSR i Afganistan*, p. 183.
81. Ibid.

82. "Organizatsiia zashchity i karantina rastenii v Afganistane," RGAE, f. 413, o. 31, d. 5471, ll. 54–76.

83. "Dopolnenie k spravke o rynke traktorov i sel'skokhoziaistvennykh mashin v Afganistane," 6 September 1971, RGAE, f. 413, o. 31, d. 4734, ll. 87–93.

84. Teplinskii, *SSR i Afganistan*, p. 180.

85. Khodzhaev, "Sotrudnichestvo," p. 93.

86. G.P. Ezhov, "Sovetsko-Afganskoe ekonomicheskoe sotrudnichestvo (1978–1987 gg.)," in M.A. Babakhodzhaev (ed.), *Respublika Afganistan: opyt i tendentsii razvitii* (Tashkent: Fan, 1990), p. 62.

87. Teplinskii, *SSR i Afganistan*, p. 147.

88. Ibid. p. 177.

89. "Nefteprodukty," RGAE, f. 413, o. 31, d. 4734, ll. 21–22.

90. "Zapis' besedy zamestitelia ministra tov. Osipova N.G. s poslom Afganistana v SSSR g-nom Arefom, sostoiavsheisia 9 oktiabria 1969," RGAE, f. 413, o. 31, d. 2214, ll. 15–17.

91. "O perspektivakh sovetsko-afganskoi torgovli v 1974–1980 g.g.," RGAE, f. 413, o. 31, d. 7002, ll. 15–16.

92. "Zapis' besedy Torgovogo Predstavitelia SSSR v Respublike Afganistan tov. Bulakha Iu.G. s ministrom torgovli Respubliki Afganistan Mukhammedom Khanom Dzhalalarom, sostoiavsheisia v zdanii Ministerstva Torgovli 28 aprelia 1974 goda," RGAE, f. 413, o. 31, d. 6201, ll. 2–3.

93. Teplinski, *SSR i Afganistan*, p. 148.

94. For a description of the activities undertaken at Jangalak, see Report on the Afghan economy, 1972, RGAE, f. 413, o. 31, d. 5471, ll. 170–171.

95. E.R. Makhmudov, "Rol' gosudarstvennogo i chastnogo sektorov v razvitii avtomobil'nogo transporta Afganistana," in Babakhodzhaev (ed.), *Respublika*, p. 108.

96. Shamrai, "Problemy," p. 9.

97. "Anniversary of 1978 Soviet-Afghan Treaty Observed," in *Foreign Broadcast Information Service* (henceforth *FBIS*), USSR International Affairs. 4 December 1981; & Dupree, *Afghanistan*, p. 637.

98. Asne Seierstad, *The Bookseller of Kabul* (London: Virago, 2002), p. 116.

99. Teplinskii, *SSR i Afganistan*, p. 177.

100. Andreasian & Vinogradova, "Razvivaiushchiesia strany," p. 30.

101. Ibid. p. 35.

102. Shpirt, "Razvivaiushchiesia strany," p. 19.

103. Teplinskii, *SSR i Afganistan*, pp. 143 & 145.

104. Ibid. p. 180.

105. Teplinskii, *Istoriia*, p. 330.

106. Ivanov, interview.

107. Teplinskii, *SSR i Afganistan*, p. 181.

108. "Nefteprodukty," 29 June 1971, RGAE, f. 413, o. 31, d. 4734, l. 17.
109. G.M. Prokhorov, "Industrializatsiia razvivaiushchikhsia stran i znachenie opyta i pomoshci SSSR," *Narody Azii i Afriki*, no. 6, 1974, p. 22.
110. V.A. Kondrat'ev, "Utechka nastional'nykh kadrov: prichiny i sledstviia," *Narody Azii i Afriki*, no. 4, 1970, p. 3.
111. Ibid. p. 30.
112. Teplinskii, *SSSR i Afganistan*, p. 184.
113. Nabi Misdaq, *Afghanistan: Political Frailty and External Interference* (London: Routledge, 2006), p. 129. Amstutz, *Afghanistan*, p. 24.
114. Report on the Afghan economy, 1977, RGAE, f. 413, o. 31, d. 9134, ll. 77–78.
115. Golovin, "Piatiletnii plan," p. 55.
116. Ibid. p. 64.
117. Teplinskii, *SSSR i Afganistan*, p. 148.
118. Ibid. p. 177.
119. Ibid. p. 185.
120. Ibid. p. 148.
121. For instance, A. Kondrat'ev, "Industrializatsiia razvivaiushchikhsia stran i formirovanie natsional'nykh kadrov," *Narody Azii i Afriki*, no. 4, 1971, p. 11.
122. R.M. Avakov et al., *The Third World and Scientific and Technical Progress* (Moscow: Nauka, 1976), p. 88.
123. Ibid. p. 111.
124. Teplinskii, *SSSR i Afganistan*, p. 186.
125. L.B. Aristova, "Sotsial'naia infrastruktura Afganistana," in Iu.V. Gankovskii (ed.), *Afganistan. Istoriia, ekonomika, kul'tura: sbornik statei* (Moscow: Nauka, 1989), p. 100.
126. Report on the Afghan economy, 1977, RGAE, f. 413, o. 31, d. 9134, l. 80.
127. Avakov et al., *The Third World*, pp. 53 & 60.
128. Teplinskii, "Sovetsko-Afganskie otnosheniia," pp. 36–7.
129. Bradsher, *Afghanistan*, p. 25.
130. Teplinskii, *SSSR i Afganistan*, p. 202.
131. Ibid. pp. 147 & 184.
132. Ibid. pp. 199–200.
133. Moscow Domestic Service, 4 December 1982, in *FBIS*, 6 December 1982, p. D1.
134. "Spravka o fabrike 'Hamlet Sausage Factory'," RGAE, f. 413, o. 31, d. 4734, l. 30.
135. Ibid.
136. "Spravka po rynke tovarov V/O 'Mezhdunarodnaia kniga' v Afganistane," RGAE, f. 413, o. 31, d. 4734, l. 58.
137. Ibid.
138. Khodzhaev, "Sotrudnichestvo," p. 95.

139. Report on the Afghan economy, 1971, RGAE, f. 413, o. 31, d. 4734, l. 124.

140. Report on the Afghan economy, 1976, RGAE, f. 413, o. 31, d. 8530, l. 71.

141. "Zapis' besedy Zam. Torgpreda SSSR v Afganistane t. Drusakova V.M. s Prezidentom zavoda 'Dzhangalak' g-nom Abdul Rakhim Chinzai," 29 May 1973, RGAE, f. 413, o. 31, d. 6201, l. 10.

142. Report on the Afghan economy, 1973, RGAE, f. 413, o. 31, d. 6203, l. 111.

143. "Pishchevaia promyshlennost' Afganistana," December 1972, RGAE, f. 413, o. 31, d. 5471, l. 122.

144. Report on the Afghan economy, 1971, RGAE, f. 413, o. 31, d. 4734, l. 142.

145. Report on the Afghan economy, 1977, RGAE, f. 413, o. 31, d. 9134, l. 23.

146. N.M. Gurevich, "Problemy sel'skokhoziastvennogo proizvodstva v Afganistane," *Narody Azii i Afriki*, no. 2, 1979, pp. 36–7.

147. A.D. Davydov, "Bor'ba za agrarnuiu reformu v Afganistane," *Narody Azii i Afriki*, no. 5, 1979, p. 8.

148. Gilles Dorronsoro, *Revolution Unending. Afghanistan: 1979 to the Present* (New York: Columbia University Press, 2005), p. 65.

149. Davydov, "Bor'ba," p. 8.

150. Richard F. Nyrop, & Donald M. Seekins, *Afghanistan Country Study and Government Documents* (Washington, DC: The American University, 1986), p. 151.

151. Ibid. p. 141.

152. Amstutz, *Afghanistan*, p. 235.

153. Aristova, "Sotsial'naia infrastruktura," p. 100.

154. V.E. Gankovskii, "Razvivaiushchiesia strany Azii i mezhdunarodnyi kapitalisticheskii kredit (analiz vneshnei zadolzhennosti)," *Narody Azii i Azii*, no. 6, 1976, pp. 23–8.

155. Nake M. Kamrany, "The Continuing Soviet War in Afghanistan," *Current History*, vol. 85, no. 513, October 1986, p. 334.

156. Quoted in Henry S. Bradsher, *Afghan Communism and Soviet Intervention*, Oxford: Oxford University Press (1999), p. 2.

157. Prokhorov, "Industrializatsiia," p. 23.

158. Gankovskii, "Razvivaiushchie strany Azii," p. 19.

159. John F. Shroder Jr., "Afghanistan Resources and Soviet Policy in Central and South Asia," in Milan Hauner & Robert L. Canfield (eds), *Afghanistan and the Soviet Union: Collision and Transformation* (Boulder: Westview, 1989), p. 107.

160. Shpirt, "Razvivaiushchiesia strany," p. 20.

161. A.I. Dinkevich, "Nekotorye voprosy ekonomicheskogo razvitiia stran 'tret'ego mira'," *Narody Azii i Afriki*, no. 5, 1969, p. 10.

162. Dupree, *Afghanistan*, p. 548.

163. Noorzoy, "Long-Term Economic Relations," p. 161.

164. "Zapis' besedy zamestitelia ministra vneshnei torgovli SSSR tov. Grishina I.T. i zamestitelem prem'er-ministra Respubliki Afganistan goktorom Mukhammedom Khasanom Sharkom, sostoiavsheisia 2 fevralia 1975," RGAE, f. 413, o. 31, d. 7422, l. 3.

165. Ibid.

166. Ibid.

167. Note from the Afghan Ministry of Foreign Affairs to the Soviet Embassy in Kabul, 30 March 1976, RGAE, f. 413, o. 31, d. 8530, ll. 18–19.

168. "Zapis' besedy zamestitelia Ministra vneshnei torgovli Kuz'mina M.R. s ministrom torgovli Afganistana Dzhalalarom, sostoiavsheisia 13 aprelia 1977," RGAE, f. 413, o. 31, d. 8840, ll. 1–2.

169. Rubin, *Fragmentation*, Table 5.1.

170. Assifi, "The Russian Rope," p. 262.

171. Ibid. p. 264.

172. Ibid. p. 265.

173. Shamrai, "Problemy," p. 8.

174. Andreasian & Vinogradova, "Razvivaiuishchiesia strany," p. 37.

175. Ibid. pp. 38–9.

176. Shpirt, "Razvivaiushchiesia strany," p. 24.

177. Ibid. p. 31.

178. Shroder & Assifi, "Afghan Mineral Resources," p. 110.

179. Shpirt, "Razvivaiuishchiesia strany," p. 20.

180. Ivanov, interview.

181. Ibid.

182. Leslie Dienes, "Central Asia and the Soviet 'Midlands': Regional Position and Economic Integration," in Hauner & Canfield (eds), *Afghanistan and the Soviet Union*, p. 77.

183. Metge, *L'URSS en Afghanistan*, p. 39.

184. Dupree, *Afghanistan*, p. 638.

185. Untitled report on the Afghan economy in 1971, RGAE, f. 413, o. 31, d. 4734, ll. 180–181. See also "Nefteprodukty," RGAE, f. 413, o. 31, d. 4734, l. 26.

186. Shroder & Assifi, "Afghan Mineral Resources," p. 102.

187. Assifi, "The Russian Rope," p. 258.

188. Dupree, *Afghanistan*, p. 637.

189. Ibid. pp. 637, 640 & 645.

190. R. Tursunov, "Pomoshch' sovetskikh sredneaziatkikh respublik Afganistanu," *Narody Azii i Afriki*, no. 4, 1971, p. 127.

191. Metge, *L'URSS en Afghanistan*, p. 38.

192. Eden Naby, "The Ethnic Factor in Soviet-Afghan Relations," *Asian Survey*, vol. 20, no. 3, 1980, p. 250.

193. Dupree, *Afghanistan*, pp. 527–8.
194. Ibid. p. 527.
195. Amstutz, *Afghanistan*, p. 24.
196. Ibid.
197. Ibid.
198. Joel Hafvenstein, *Opium Season: A Year on the Afghan Frontier* (Guilford, CT: The Lyons Press, 2007), p. 147.
199. Kamrany, *Peaceful Competition*, p. 65.
200. Makhmudov, "Afganistan," p. 159.
201. Amstutz, *Afghanistan*, p. 24.
202. Review of the Afghan economy in 1977, RGAE, f. 413, o. 31, d. 9134, ll. 83–84.
203. Untitled report on the Afghan economy, RGAE, f. 413, o. 31, d. 4734, l. 126.
204. Report on the Afghan economy in 1976, RGAE, f. 413, o. 31, d. 8530, l. 83.
205. Ibid.
206. Report on the Afghan economy, 1977, RGAE, f. 413, o. 1, d. 9134, ll. 43–44.
207. Report on the Afghan economy, 1971, RGAE, f. 413, o. 31, d. 4734, l. 126.
208. Report on the Afghan economy, 1976, RGAE, f. 413, o. 31, d. 8530, l. 102.
209. "Dopolnenie k spravke o rynke traktorov i sel'skokhoziaistvennykh mashin v Afganistane," 6 September 1971, RGAE, f. 413, o. 31, d. 4734, l. 91.
210. "Sostoianie tekhnicheskogo obsluzhivaniia avtomobiliei sovetskogo proizvodstva v Afganistane (spravka)," 19 July 1972, RGAE, f. 413, o. 31, d. 5471, l. 40.
211. "Transport Respubliki Afganistan," RGAE, f. 413, o. 31, d. 6203, l. 65.
212. Report on the Afghan economy, 1977, RGAE, f. 413, o. 31, d. 9134, l. 74.
213. "Sostoianie tekhnicheskogo obsluzhivaniia avtomobiliei sovetskogo proizvodstva v Afganistane (spravka)," 19 July 1972, RGAE, f. 413, o. 31, d. 5471, l. 38.
214. "Organizatsiia zashchity i karantina rastenii v Afganistane," 26 September 1972, RGAE, f. 413, o. 31, d.
215. "Dopolnenie k spravke o rynke traktorov i sel'skoskhoziastvennykh mashin Afganistana," RGAE, f. 413, o. 31, d. 4734, l. 91.
216. "Finansirovanie," p. 6.
217. Dinkevich, "Nekotorye voprosy," p. 8.
218. R.N. Andreaisan, "Protivorechiia i kriterii nekapitalisticheskogo razvitiia," *Narody Azii i Afriki*, no. 2, 1974, p. 43.
219. Dinkevich, "O strategii," p. 9.
220. For instance, A.I. Dinkevich, "Nekotorye voprosy," p. 3.
221. L.Z. Zevin, "Razvivaiushchiesia strany: problemy ekonomicheskogo razvitiia i rynok," *Narody Azii i Afriki*, no. 1, 1977, p. 166.

222. P.I. Pol'shikov, "Problema nakopleniia v razvivaiushchikhsia stranakh Afriki," *Narody Azii i Afriki*, no. 4, 1977, p. 56.

223. Zevin, review of A.Ia. El'ianov, p. 166.

224. P.I. Pol'shikov, "Problema nakopleniia," p. 56.

225. G.V. Smirnov, "Rol' gosudarstva v reshenii problemy nakopleniia v ANDR," *Narody Azii i Afriki*, no. 5, 1973, p. 13.

226. Sandakov, "Razvivaiushchiesia strany Afriki," p. 27.

227. L.I. Reisner, "Zapadnye burzhiaznye teorii razvitiia molodykh natsional'nykh gosudastv (kriticheskii obzor literatury)," *Narody Azii i Afriki*, no. 5, 1969, p. 42.

228. "Transport Respubliki Afganistan," RGAE, f. 413, o. 31, d. 6203, l. 65.

229. Rubin, *Fragmentation*, p. 78.

230. Dinkevich, "Nekotorye voprosy," p. 12.

231. Hyman, *Afghanistan*, p. 33.

232. Makhmudov, "Afganistan," p. 154.

233. Ibid. p. 154.

234. R.T. Akhramovich, "K kharakteristike etapov obshchestvennoi evolutsii Afganistana posle vtoroi mirovoi voiny," *Narody Azii i Afriki*, no. 3, 1967, p. 55.

235. Andreasian & Vinogradova, "Razvivaiushchiesia strany," p. 36.

236. Ibid. p. 159.

237. Ibid.

238. For instance, Dinkevich, "O strategii," p. 16.

239. Sandakov, "Razvivaiushchiesia strany," p. 22.

240. Dinkevich, "O strategii," p. 8.

241. Prokhorov, "Industrializatsiia," p. 22.

242. Sandakov, "Razvivaiushchiesia strany Afriki," pp. 25–6.

243. Pol'shikov, "Problema nakopleniia," p. 57.

244. Report on the Afghan economy, 1971, RGAE, f. 413, o. 31, d. 4734, l. 143. For similar comments, see also Report on the Afghan economy, 1973, RGAE, f. 413, o. 31, d. 6203, l. 96.

245. Report on the Afghan economy, 1976, RGAE, f. 413, o. 31, d. 850, l. 53.

246. Antonio Giustozzi, *Afghanistan: Transition without End. An Analytical Narrative on State-Making*, Crisis State Research Centre, Working Paper 40 (London: LSE, 2008), p. 19.

247. "Finansirovanie," p. 20.

248. Sandakov, "Razvivaiushchiesia strany Afriki," p. 27.

249. Nyrop & Seekins, *Afghanistan: Country Study*, p. 151.

250. Ibid. p. 150.

251. Makhmudov, "Afganistan," p. 145.

252. Ibid. p. 154.

253. Gurevich, 'Problemy," p. 31.

254. Davydov, "Bor'ba," p. 10.
255. Makhmudov, "Afganistan," p. 147.
256. Davydov, "Bor'ba," p. 5.
257. V.V. Basov, "Voprosy sotsial'no-ekonomicheskogo razvitiia Afganistana (po materialam afganskoi pechati)," *Narody Azii i Afriki*, no. 3, 1971, p. 159.
258. Ibid. p. 160.
259. Davydov, "Bor'ba," p. 9.
260. Report on the Afghan economy, 1976, RGAE, f. 413, o. 31, d. 8530, l. 56. See also, Report on the Afghan economy, 1975, RGAE, f. 413, o. 31, d. 7814, ll. 42–43.
261. E. Urazova & L. Teplinskii, review of N.M. Gurevich, "Ekonomicheskoe razvitie Afganistana (finansovye voprosy)," *Narody Azii i Afriki*, no. 1, 1969, p. 153.
262. Ibid. p. 160.
263. Dorronsoro, *Revolution Unending*, p. 64.

4. SOVIET ASSISTANCE TO AFGHANISTAN: 1979–86

1. "Zapis' besedy zamestitelia vneshnei torgovli SSSR tov. Grishin I.T. s ministrom torgovli DRA M.Kh. Dzhalalarom," 6 August 1980, RGAE, f. 413, o. 32, d. 739, l. 2.
2. A.D. Davydov, "Bor'ba za agrarnuiu reform v Afganistane," *Narody Azii i Afriki*, no. 5, 1979, pp. 11–12.
3. Henry S. Bradsher, *Afghan Communism and Soviet Intervention* (Oxford: Oxford University Press, 1999), pp. 44–45.
4. *Treaty of Friendship, Good-Neighbourliness and Co-operation Between the Union of Soviet Socialist Republics and the Democratic Republic of Afghanistan*, in J.A. Naik (ed.), *Russia's Foreign Policy Documents. Russia in Asia and Africa* (Kolhapur: Avinash Reference Publications, 1979), p. 52.
5. Ibid.
6. "Soglashenie mezhdu pravitel'stvom soiuza sovetskikh sotsialisticheskikh respublik i pravitel'stvom demokraticheskoi respubliki afganistan ob ekonomicheskom i tekhnicheskom sotrudnichestve," in Ministerstvo Inostrannykh Del SSSR, *Deistvuiushchie dogovory, soglasheniia i konventsii, vstupivshie v silu mezhdu 1 ianvaria i 31 dekabria 1979 goda*, vypusk XXXV (Moscow, Mezhdunarodnye Otnosheniia, 1981), pp. 191–195.
7. "Soglashenie mezhdu pravitel'stvom soiuza sovetskikh sotsialisticheskikh respublik i pravitel'stvom demokraticheskoi respubliki afganistan ob okazanii afganistanu tekhnicheskogo sodeistviia v sozdanii mashinno-traktornykh stantsii," in Ministerstvo Inostrannykh Del SSSR, *Deistvuiushchie dogovory*, vypusk XXXV, pp. 195–197.

8. "Protokol mezhdu pravitel'stvom soiuza sovetskikh sotsialisticheskikh respublik i pravitel'stvom demokraticheskoi respubliki afganistan ob ekonomicheskom i tekhnicheskom sotrudnichestve v podgotovke afganskikh natsional'nykh kadrov," in Ministerstvo Inostrannykh Del SSSR, *Deistvuiushchie dogovory*, vypusk XXXV, pp. 197–198.

9. B.V. Gromov, *Ogranichenyi kontingent* (Moscow: Progress, 1994), p. 25.

10. Ibid. pp. 41–3.

11. A.A. Liakhovskii, *Tragediia i doblest' Afgana* (Moscow: GPI Iskona, 1995), p. 110.

12. John F. Shroder Jr., "Afghanistan Resources and Soviet Policy in Central and South Asia," in Milan Hauner & Robert L. Canfield (eds), *Afghanistan and the Soviet Union: Collision and Transformation* (Boulder: Westview, 1989), p. 101.

13. Abdul Tawak Assifi, "The Russian Rope: Soviet Economic Motives and the Subversion of Afghanistan," *World Affairs*, vol. 145, no. 3, Winter 1982/83, p. 264.

14. Milan Hauner, *The Soviet War in Afghanistan: Patterns of Russian Imperialism* (Philadelphia: University Press of America, 1991), p. 135.

15. See Gromov, *Ogranichenyi kontingent*, pp. 18–82 for an analysis and transcripts of Politburo and Central Committee discussions.

16. Ivanov, interview.

17. E.R. Makhmudov, "Rol' gosudarstvennogo i chastnogo sektorov v razvitii avtomobil'nogo transporta Afganistana," in M.A. Babakhodzhaev (ed.), *Respublika Afganistan: opyt i tendentsii razvitii* (Tashkent: Fan, 1990), p. 111.

18. Anton Minkov & Gregory Smolynec, *Economic Development in Afghanistan During the Soviet Period: Lessons Learned from the Soviet Experience in Afghanistan*, Technical Memorandum TM 2009–017 (Ottawa: DRDC Centre for Operational Research and Analysis, 2007), p. 9.

19. Richard F. Nyrop & Donald M. Seekins, *Afghanistan Country Study and Government Documents* (Washington, DC: The American University, 1986), p. 153.

20. Transcript of meeting of Gorbachev with Najibullah, 20 July 1987, in *Cold War International History Project Bulletin*, Issue 14/15, p. 157.

21. L.B. Teplinskii, *Istoriia sovetso-afganskikh otnoshenii* (Moscow: Mysl, 1988), p. 326.

22. Ivanov, interview.

23. Marshall Goldman, "A Balance Sheet of Soviet Foreign Aid," *Foreign Affairs*, vol. 43, no. 2, 1965, p. 354. Goldman cites the example of a US$2 million loan given by the Soviets to build a sports stadium in Guinea. According to the Soviet ambassador, "Guinea was in such a state of economic and psychological shock, we felt we could not refuse her requests." A similar logic may sometimes have applied in Afghanistan.

24. Ivanov, interview.

25. Ivanov, interview.

26. TASS, 3 March 1983, in *FBIS*, 7 March 1983, p. D2.

27. See for instance Ministerstvo Inostrannykh Del SSSR, *Deistvuiushchie dogovory*, vypusk XXXV, p. 193.

28. TASS, 5 July 1983, in *FBIS*, 6 July 1983, p. D2.

29. Nyrop & Seekins, *Afghanistan Country Study*, p. 152.

30. The Russian General Staff, *The Soviet-Afghan War: How a Superpower Fought and Lost*, trans. and ed. Lester W. Grau and Michael A. Gress (Lawrence: University Press of Kansas, 2002), p. 5.

31. *Pravda*, 4 October 1982, p. 4, in *FBIS*, 15 October 1982, p. D1.

32. R.B. Gaur, *Afghanistan: Expanding Bases of Social Revolution* (New Delhi: Allied, 1987), p. 26.

33. *Moscow News*, no. 13, 19 March 1987, in *FBIS*, 3 April 1987, p. D3.

34. L.B. Teplinskii, *SSSR i Afganistan, 1919–1981* (Moscow: Glavnaia Redaktsiia Vostochnoi Istorii, 1982), p. 264.

35. *Moscow Domestic Service*, 31 October 1984, in *FBIS*, 9 November 1984.

36. In 1988 Teplinskii was still writing that Soviet organizations had developed "technical plans for the dam and canal on the Kochka river," but did not mention any substantial work resulting from these. Teplinskii 1988, *Istoriia*, p. 332.

37. Ministerstvo Inostrannykh Del SSSR, *Deistvuiushchie dogovory*, vypusk XXXV, pp. 195–197.

38. *Za Rubezhom*, 30 (1151), 1982, p. 12. Confusingly, this report states that four more were planned, for a total of eight MTSs. This appears to be an error.

39. TASS, 9 January 1988, in *FBIS*, 12 January 1988, p. 34.

40. TASS, 12 October 1988, in *FBIS*, 19 October, p. 25.

41. *Pravda*, 13 October 1980, p. 4.

42. Antonio Giustozzi, *War, Politics and Society in Afghanistan, 1978–1992* (London: C. Hurst, 2000), p. 24.

43. TASS, 24 April 1986, in *FBIS*, 1 May 1986.

44. Barnett R. Rubin, *The Fragmentation of Afghanistan: State Formation and Collapse in the International System* (New Haven: Yale University Press, 1995), p. 145.

45. *Za Rubezhom*, 30 (1151), 1982, p. 12.

46. "Soglashenie mezhdu pravitel'stvom soiuza sovetskikh sotsialisticheskikh respublik i pravitel'stvom demokraticheskoi respubliki afganistan ob okazanii afganistanu tekhnicheskogo sodeistviia v oblasti sel'skogo khoziaistva," in Ministerstvo Inostrannykh Del SSSR, *Deistvuiushchie dogovory, soglasheniia i konventsii, vstupivshie v silu s 1 ianvaria po 31 dekabria 1982 goda*, vypusk XXX-VIII (Moscow, Mezhdunarodnye Otnosheniia, 1984), pp. 194–196.

47. *Pravda*, 27 April 1982, p. 4, in *FBIS*, 5 May 1982, p. D1.

48. *Tashkent International Service*, 4 January 1984, in *FBIS*, 9 January 1984, p. D6.

49. Giustozzi, *War, Politics and Society*, p. 25.

50. TASS, 24 April 1986, in *FBIS*, 1 May 1986.

51. Rubin. *Fragmentation*, p. 173.

52. See Annex 1.

53. *Demokraticheskaia respublika Afganistan: spravochnik* (Moscow: Nauka, 1981), p. 95.

54. Ivanov, interview.

55. Iurii A. Sal'nikov, *Kandagar: zapiski sovetnika posol'stva* (Volgograd: Volgogradskii Komitet po Pechati, 1995), p. 64.

56. TASS, 27 February 1983, in *FBIS*, 1 March 1983, p. D9.

57. Tashkent International Service, 14 January 1982, in *FBIS*, 18 January 1982, p. F9.

58. TASS, 26 April 1986, in *FBIS*, 30 April 1986, p. D7; also Teplinskii, *Istoriia*, p. 329.

59. Giustozzi, *War, Politics and Society*, p. 105.

60. Lee O. Coldren, "Afghanistan in 1984: The Fifth Year of the Russo-Afghan War," *Asian Survey*, vol. 25, no. 2, February 1985, p. 177.

61. G.P. Ezhov, "Sovetsko-Afganskoe ekonomicheskoe sotrudnichestvo (1978–1987 gg.)," in M.A. Babakhodzhaev (ed.), *Respublika Afganistan: opyt i tendentsii razvitii* (Tashkent: Fan, 1990), p. 65.

62. *New Times*, no. 23, June 1983, pp. 7–9, in *FBIS*, 22 June 1983, p. D3.

63. *Demokraticheskaia respublika Afganistan*, p. 99.

64. Nyrop & Seekins, *Afghanistan Country Study*, p. 153.

65. *Pravda*, 31 May 1985, first edition, p. 5, in *FBIS*, 5 June 1985, p. D4.

66. See Annex 1.

67. "Zapis' besedy s ministrom torgovli Respubliki Afganistan M.Kh. Dzhalalarom," 22 January 1978, RGAE, f. 413, o. 31, d. 9421, l. 2.

68. "Zapis' besedy zamestitelia vneshnei torgovli SSSR tov. Grishin I.T. s ministrom torgovli DRA M.Kh. Dzhalalarom," 6 August 1980, RGAE, f. 413, o. 32, d. 739, l. 7.

69. TASS, 27 February 1983, in *FBIS*, 1 March 1983, p. D9.

70. *Pravda*, 18 February 1980, p. 6.

71. *Za Rubezhom*, 37 (1158), 1982, p. 9.

72. "Nefteprodukty," 29 June 1971, RGAE, f. 413, o. 31, d. 4734, l. 21.

73. Report on the Afghan economy, 1976, RGAE, f. 413, o. 31, d. 8530, l. 89.

74. "Zapis' besedy s ministrom torgovli Respubliki Afganistan M.Kh. Dzhalalarom," 22 January 1978, RGAE, f. 413, o. 31, d. 9421, l. 6.

75. The Russian General Staff, *The Soviet-Afghan War*, p. 248; for a specific example of Soviet forces repairing a bridge on the route from Kabul to the Salang pass, see *Krasnaia Zvezda*, 11 August 1984, 2nd edition, p. 3, in *FBIS*, 13 August 1984, p. D3.

76. *Moscow World Service*, 15 August 1985, in *FBIS*, 16 August 1985.
77. TASS International Service, 25 December 1986, in *FBIS*, 31 December 1986, p. D4.
78. Makhmudov. "Rol'," p. 113.
79. Moscow Television Service, *Vremia* broadcast, 22 October 1985, in *FBIS*, 23 October 1985, p. D5.
80. *Sotsialisticheskaia Industriia*, 29 March 1988, p. 3.
81. Makhmudov, "Rol'," p. 113.
82. TASS, 27 February 1983, in *FBIS*, 1 March 1983, p. D9; Gaur, *Afghanistan*, p. 26.
83. See Annex 1.
84. *Pravda*, 9 August 1985, p. 5.
85. *Sotsialisticheskaia Industriia*, 26 April 1987, p. 3.
86. *Pravda*, 9 August 1985, p. 5.
87. "Anniversary of 1978 Soviet-Afghan Treaty Observed," *Novoe Vremia*, 4 December 1981, in *FBIS*.
88. *Sovetskaia Rossiia*, 20 December 1981, p. 5, in *FBIS*, 30 December 1981, p. D4;
89. *Pravda*, 5 December 1984, p. 5, & 1 July 1985, p. 6.
90. *Sotsialisticheskaia Industriia*, 26 April 1986, p. 3.
91. Teplinskii, *Istoriia*, p. 327.
92. "Soglashenie mezhdu pravitel'stvom soiuza sovetskikh sotsialisticheskikh respublik i pravitel'stvom demokraticheskoi respubliki afganistan ob ekonomi-cheskom i tekhnicheskom sotrudnichestve," in Ministerstvo Inostrannykh Del SSSR, *Deistvuiushchie dogovory, soglasheniia i konventsii, vstupivshie v silu s 1 ianvaria po 31 dekabria 1985 goda*, vypusk XLI (Moscow, Mezhdunarodnye Otnosheniia, 1987), pp. 134–136
93. *Za Rubezhom*, no. 34 (1051), 1980, p13.
94. "Primer sotrudnichestva," *Pravda*, 13 May 1980.
95. TASS International Service, 27 August 1985, in *FBIS*, 28 August 1985, p. D2.
96. See Annex 1.
97. Ibid.
98. TASS, 27 February 1983, in *FBIS*, 1 March 1983, p. D9
99. Teplinskii, *Istoriia*, p. 331.
100. Library of Congress, *Country Study*, p. 2.
101. Ibid. p. 3.
102. See Annex 1.
103. Assifi, "The Russian Rope," p. 265.
104. Ivanov, interview.
105. Bradsher, *Afghan Communism*, p. 87.
106. Gaur, *Afghanistan*, p. 26.

107. Ezhov, "Sovetsko-Afganskoe ekonomicheskoe sotrudnichestvo," p. 69.

108. "Decree of the Secretariat of the Central Committee of the Communist Party of the Soviet Union, 195/59, 29 January 1980" and other related papers. For English translations, see *Cold War International History Project Virtual Archive*, http://www.wilsoncenter.org/index.cfm?topic_id=1409&fuseaction=va2.bro wse&sort=Collection&item=Soviet%20Invasion%20of%20Afghanistan, accessed 12 January 2010.

109. See Annex 1.

110. *Pravda*, 27 April 1982, in *FBIS*, 5 May 1982, p. D1.

111. *Izvestiia*, 26 November 1984, morning edition, p. 4, in *FBIS*, 30 November 1984, p. D4.

112. Sal'nikov, *Kandagar*, p. 29.

113. Rasul A. Amin, "The Sovietization of Afghanistan," in Rosanne Klass (ed.), *Afghanistan: The Great Game Revisited* (Lanham, MD: Freedom House, 1990), p. 311.

114. Central Committee of the Communist Party of the Soviet Union, "Vypiska iz protokola no. 198," 19 February 1980. For an English translation, see *Cold War International History Project Virtual Archive*.

115. Ibid.

116. L.B. Aristova, "Sotsial'naia infrastruktura Afganistana," in Iu.V. Gankovskii (ed.), *Afganistan. Istoriia, ekonomika, kul'tura: sbornik statei* (Moscow: Nauka, 1989), p. 100.

117. Ibid, p. 101.

118. Giustozzi, *War, Politics and Society*, p. 23.

119. Sal'nikov, *Kandagar*, p. 52.

120. Statement by General Zakharov, "Vozvrashchenie," *Trud*, 7 February 1989, p. 3; see also TASS, 15 February 1988, in *FBIS*, 18 July 1988, p. 35.

121. Amstutz, *Afghanistan*, pp. 303–304.

122. Eden Naby, "The Ethnic Factor in Soviet-Afghan Relations," *Asian Survey*, vol. 20, no. 3, 1980, p. 241–2.

123. Ibid. p. 251.

124. For instance, see Jeri Laber, "Afghanistan's Other War," *The New York Review of Books*, vol. 33, no. 20, 18 December 1980, and Amin, "The Sovietization of Afghanistan."

125. Central Committee, "Vypiska."

126. Foreign and Commonwealth Office, *Sovietization of Afghanistan*, Background Brief 80–0998, 1980.

127. Amstutz, *Afghanistan*, p 312.

128. Bradsher, *Afghan Communism*, p. 143.

129. Foreign and Commonwealth Office, *Sovietization*.

130. Laber, "Afghanistan's Other War," p. 3.

131. *Pravda*, 28 March 1984, p. 5.

132. "Protokol mezhdu pravitel'stvom soiuza sovetskikh sotsialisticheskikh respublik i pravitel'stvom demokraticheskoi respubliki afganistan ob ekonomicheskom i tekhnicheskom sotrudnichestve v podgotovke afganskikh natsional'nykh kadrov," in Ministerstvo Inostrannykh Del, *Deistvuiushchie dogovory, soglasheniia i konventsii, vstupivshie v silu mezhdu 1 ianvaria i 31 dekabria 1979 goda*, vypusk XXXV (Moscow: Izdatel'stvo Mezhdunarodnye Otnosheniia, 1981), p. 197.

133. "Protokol mezhdu pravitel'stvom soiuza sovetskikh sotsialisticheskikh respublik i pravitel'stvom demokraticheskoi respubliki afganistan ob okazanii afganistanu bezvozmezdnoi pomoshchi v oblasti podgotovki natsional'nykh kadrov," in Ministerstvo Inostrannykh Del SSSR, *Deistvuiushchie dogovory, soglasheniia i konventsii, vstupivshie v silu s 1 ianvaria po 31 dekabria 1980 goda*, vypusk XXXVI (Moscow, Mezhdunarodnye Otnosheniia, 1982), pp. 98–99.

134. Jeri Laber & Barnett R. Rubin, *A Nation is Dying: Afghanistan Under the Soviets 1979–1987* (Evanston, Il: Northwest University Press, 1988), p. 118.

135. Amstutz, *Afghanistan*, p. 311; *Demokraticheskaia Respublika Afganistan*, p. 111.

136. *Moscow News*, 2 September 1984, in *FBIS*, 5 September 1984, p. D1.

137. Bradsher, *Afghan Communism*, p. 142.

138. Amin, "Sovietization," p. 323.

139. Monica Whitlock, *Beyond the Oxus: The Central Asians* (London: John Murray, 2002), p. 126.

140. Anton Oleinik, "Lessons of Russian in Afghanistan," *Society*, vol. 45, no. 3, 2008, p. 290

141. TASS International Service, 29 July 1988, in *FBIS*, 3 August 1988, p. 26.

142. TASS, 4 June 1985, in *FBIS*, 5 June 1985, p. D4.

143. "Protokol mezhdu pravitel'stvom soiuza sovetskikh sotsialisticheskikh respublik i pravitel'stvom demokraticheskoi respubliki afganistan ob okazanii afganistanu tekhnicheskogo sodeistviia v sozdanii uchebnykh zavedenii," in Ministerstvo Inostrannykh Del SSSR, *Deistvuiushchie dogovory, soglasheniia i konventsii, vstupivshie v silu s 1 ianvaria po 31 dekabria 1985 goda*, vypusk XLI (Moscow, Mezhdunarodnye Otnosheniia, 1987), pp. 132–134.

144. Mohammad Yousaf & Mark Adkin, *The Bear Trap: Afghanistan's Untold Story* (London: Leo Cooper, 1992), p. 146.

145. Ibid.

146. TASS, 27 February 1982, in *FBIS*, 1 March 1982, p. D3.

147. *Za Rubezhom*, no. 15 (1032), 1980, p. 13.

148. *Moscow News*, no. 13, 19 March 1987, in *FBIS*, 3 April 1987.

149. Nyrop & Seekins, *Afghanistan Country Study*, p. 154.

150. Rubin, *Fragmentation*, p. 125.

151. Amstutz, *Afghanistan*, p. 140 (Amstutz's figure of 8–10,000 includes accompanying wives); & Bradsher 1999, p. 122.

152. Mikhail Gorbachev gave a figure of 2,500 advisors in 1986: see Anatolii Cherniaev, "The Afghanistan Problem," *Russian Politics and Law*, vol. 42, no. 5, September-October 2004, p. 34. Valerii Ivanov stated that there were "up to 3,000 specialists" (interview with Paul Robinson). British author Martin Ewans writes that by 1980, "1,000 or so were working in the armed forces and between 2,000 and 2,500 in civilian posts": Martin Ewans, *Conflict in Afghanistan: Studies in Asymmetric Warfare* (London: Routledge, 2005), p. 112. A report by the British Foreign and Commonwealth Office gave a figure of 5,000 advisors, half military and half civilian: Foreign and Commonwealth Office, *Sovietization*.

153. Ivanov, interview. Rodric Braithwaite states that Soviet specialists in Afghanistan received an income of about US$700 a month, "significantly more than they would have received back home": Braithwaite, *Afgantsy*, p. 150.

154. Whitlock, *Beyond the Oxus*, p. 127. See also Naby, "The Ethnic Factor," p. 252.

155. Braithwaite, *Afgantsy*, p. 159.

156. Ivanov, interview.

157. Braithwaite, *Afgantsy*, p. 160.

158. Sal'nikov, *Kandagar*, p. 100.

159. Ivanov, interview.

160. Braithwaite, *Afgantsy*, p. 160.

161. Amstutz, *Afghanistan*, p. 140.

162. Sal'nikov, *Kandagar*, pp. 180–1.

163. Gregory Feifer, *The Great Gamble: The Soviet War in Afghanistan* (New York: Harper, 2009), p. 207.

164. "Komandirovany v Afganistan," *Sovetskaia Rossiia*, 2 May 1982, p. 5.

165. Ivanov, interview.

166. Braithwaite, *Afgantsy*, p. 45.

167. Feifer, *The Great Gamble*, p. 30.

168. M. Hassan Kakar, *Afghanistan: The Soviet Invasion and the Afghan Response, 1979–1982* (Berkeley: University of California Press, 1995), p. 205.

169. Braithwaite, *Afgantsy*, p. 160.

170. Yousaf & Adkin, *The Bear Trap*, p. 146.

171. Braithwaite, *Afgantsy*, p. 161.

172. Ivanov, interview.

173. Braithwaite, *Afgantsy*, p. 300.

174. Ivanov, interview.

175. Gaur, *Afghanistan*, p. 24.

176. *Pravda*, 27 January 1986, first edition, p. 6, in *FBIS*, 3 February 1986, pp. D3–D5.

177. Teplinskii, *Istoriia*, p. 328. For details of the projects built in the 1980s, see

Annex 1 and also Ezhov, "Sovetsko-Afganskoe ekonomicheskoe sotrudnichestvo," pp. 68–72.

178. Nyrop & Seekins, *Afghanistan Country Study*, p. 141.
179. Ibid. p. 162.
180. Nake M. Kamrany, "The Continuing Soviet War in Afghanistan," *Current History*, vol. 85, no. 513, October 1986, p. 333.
181. Amstutz, *Afghanistan*, p. 233.
182. *Pravda*, 27 April 1982, in *FBIS*, 5 May 1982, pp. D1–D2.
183. Ezhov, "Sovetsko-Afganskoe ekonomicheskoe sotrudnichestvo," p. 68.
184. Nyrop & Seekins, *Afghanistan Country Study*, p. 181.
185. Giustozzi, *War, Politics and Society*, p. 233.
186. Library of Congress, *Country Study*, p. 4.
187. Amstutz, *Afghanistan*, p. 245.
188. For instance Amstutz, *Afghanistan*, p. 145, & Mark Galleotti, *Afghanistan: The Soviet Union's Last War* (London: Frank Cass, 1995), p. 17
189. Liakhovskii, *Tragediia*, pp. 163–4.
190. Sal'nikov, *Kandagar*, p. 45.
191. Ibid. p. 66.
192. *Cold War International History Project Bulletin*, Issue 14/15, p. 175.
193. *Za Rubezhom*, no. 30 (1151), 1982, p. 12.
194. *Za Rubezhom*, no. 34 (1051), 1980, pp. 12–13.
195. *Za Rubezhom*, no. 30 (1151), 1982, p. 12.
196. Sal'nikov, *Kandagar*, p. 66.
197. Ibid. p. 148.
198. Ibid. p. 152.
199. Bradsher, *Afghan Communism*, p. 170.
200. Sal'nikov, *Kandagar*, p. 115.
201. Nyrop & Seekins, *Afghanistan Country Study*, p. 171; Gaur, *Afghanistan*, p. 24.
202. M.N. Khodzhaev, "Sotrudnichestvo SSSR i respublika Afganistan v oblasti energii," in Iu.V. Gankovskii (ed.), *Afganistan. Istoriia, ekonomika, kul'tura: sbornik statei* (Moscow: Nauka, 1989), p. 94.
203. Sal'nikov, *Kandagar*, p. 64; Khodzhaev, "Sotrudnichestvo," p. 96.
204. Khodzhaev, "Sotrudnichestvo," p. 96.
205. Nyrop & Seekins, *Afghanistan Country Study*, p. 171.
206. See Victor L. Mote, "Afghanistan and the Transport Infrastructures of Turkestan," p. 147, & Shroder, "Afghanistan Resources," p. 107, both in Hauner & Canfield (eds), *Afghanistan*, for details of the projects.
207. V.I. Varennikov, *Nepovtorimoe*, vol. 5 (Moscow: Sovetskii Pisatel', 2001), p. 332.
208. Makhmudov, "Rol'," p. 112.
209. Amstutz, *Afghanistan*, p. 246.

210. Note by Prime Minister Ryzhkov to Gorbachev, attaching State Planning Committee memorandum of Soviet expenditures in Afghanistan, January 1988, *Cold War International History Project Bulletin*, Issue 14/15, p. 256.

211. M.S. Noorzoy, "Long-Term Economic Relations between Afghanistan and the Soviet Union: An Interpretative Study," *International Journal of Middle East Studies*, vol. 17, no. 2, May 1985, pp. 161–2.

212. Ibid. p. 162.

213. Amstutz, *Afghanistan*, p. 470, f. 91.

214. Namik Yakubov, head of the Main Administration for Economic Links with Asian Countries at the Ministry of Foreign Affairs, cited by TASS International Service, 29 July 1988, in *FBIS*, FBIS-SOV-88-149, p. 26.

215. "Memorandum besedy Ministra t. Aristova B.I. s ministrom DRA M.Kh. Dzhalalarom, sostoiavsheisia 13 fevralia 1986 g.," 4 April 1986, RGAE, f. 413, o. 32, d. 4607, l. 5.

216. Nyrop & Seekins, *Afghanistan Country Study*, p. 156.

217. *Pravda*, 27 April 1982, in *FBIS*, 5 May 1982, pp. D1–D2.

218. Shroder, "Afghanistan Resources," p. 109.

219. Amstutz, *Afghanistan*, p. 260.

220. Aristova, "Sotsial'naia infrastruktura," p. 101.

221. Giustozzi, *War, Politics and Society*, p. 23.

222. Amstutz, *Afghanistan*, p. 303.

223. Laber, "Afghanistan's Other War"; see also Laber & Rubin, *A Nation is Dying*, p. 130.

224. Rubin, *Fragmentation*, p. 141.

225. Laber & Rubin, *A Nation is Dying*, p. 127.

226. Rubin, *Fragmentation*, p. 141.

227. Liakhovskii, *Tragediia*, Annex 8.

228. Laber & Rubin, *A Nation is Dying*, p. 116.

229. Rosanne Klass, "The Great Game Revisited," in Klass (ed.), *Afghanistan*, p. 13.

230. Bradsher, *Afghan Communism*, p. 142.

231. Sal'nikov, *Kandagar*, p. 114.

232. Amstutz, *Afghanistan*, p. 304.

233. Amin, "Sovietization," p. 319; also Rubin, *Fragmentation*, p. 140.

234. Bradsher, *Afghan Communism*, p. 3.

235. Aristova, "Sotsial'naia infrastruktura," p. 105.

236. Laber & Rubin, *A Nation is Dying*, p. 122.

237. Giustozzi, *War, Politics and Society*, p. 13.

238. Amstutz, *Afghanistan*, p. 240.

239. Sal'nikov, *Kandagar*, p. 46.

240. Alex Marshall, "Managing Withdrawal: Afghanistan as the Forgotten Exam-

ple in Attempting Conflict Resolution and State Reconstruction," *Small Wars and Insurgencies*, vol. 18, no. 1, 2007, pp. 71–2.

241. Ivanov, interview.

242. Ibid.

243. Rubin, *Fragmentation*, p. 129.

244. "Memorandum besedy Ministra t. Aristova B.I. s Ministrom torgovli DRA M.Kh. Dzhalalarom, sostoiavsheisia 13 fevralia 1986 g.," 4 April 1986, RGAE, f. 413, o. 32, d. 4607, l. 2.

245. Ivanov, interview.

246. "Zapis' besedy Nachal'nika Upravleniia torgovli so stranami Azii tov. Kiseleva M.A. s Nachal'nikom Glavnogo Upravleniia grazhdanskoi aviatsii DRA M.N. Adzhmalem, sostoiavsheisia 13 fevralia 1985 g.," 5 April 1985, RGAE, f. 413, o. 32, d. 4122, l. 7.

247. Ibid.

248. *Cold War International History Project Bulletin*, Issue 14/15, p. 165.

249. Although Valerii Ivanov reckoned that corruption in the central government was probably not as great as it is at present, if only because "we had full control of the economic ministries, our advisers were everywhere, and although none of them were accountants they could still keep an eye on things": Ivanov, interview.

250. Gilles Dorronsoro, *Revolution Unending. Afghanistan: 1979 to the Present* (New York: Columbia University Press, 2005), p. 176.

251. *Cold War International History Project Bulletin*, Issue 14/15, p. 144.

252. Bradsher, *Afghan Communism*, p. 124.

253. M.A. Gareev, *Afganskaia strada (s sovetskimi voiskami i bez nikh)* 2nd edition (Moscow: Insan, 1999), p. 26.

254. Rubin, *Fragmentation*, p. 125.

255. Rubin, *Fragmentation*, p. 128.

256. Liakhovskii, *Tragediia*, Annex 8.

257. Oleinik, "Lessons," p. 291.

258. Nabi Nisdaq, *Afghanistan: Political Frailty and External Interference* (London: Routledge, 2006), p. 138.

259. Cherniaev, "The Afghanistan Problem," p. 37.

260. Feifer, *The Great Gamble*, p. 207.

261. Gromov and Varennikov, cited in Bradsher, *Afghan Communism*, p. 123.

262. Fred Halliday, & Zahir Tanin, "The Communist Regime in Afghanistan 1978–1992: Institutions and Conflicts," *Europe-Asia Studies*, vol. 50, no. 8, 1998, p. 1373.

263. Rubin, *Fragmentation*, p. 125.

264. Anton Minkov, *Soviet Counterinsurgency and Development Efforts in Afghanistan: Implications for US Strategy in Iraq*, Technical Memorandum TM 2009–

017 (Ottawa: DRDC Centre for Operational Research and Analysis, 2009), p. 32.

265. Halliday & Tanin, "The Communist Regime," p. 1376.

266. Ibid, p. 1373.

267. Dambisa Moyo, *Dead Aid: Why Aid is Not Working and How There is a Better Way for Africa* (New York: Farrar, Straus and Giroux, 2009), p. 143.

268. Ibid. p. 57.

269. Giustozzi, *War, Politics and Society*, p. 234.

270. Bradsher, *Afghan Communism*, p. 169.

5. SOVIET ASSISTANCE TO AFGHANISTAN: 1987–91

1. Henry S. Bradsher, *Afghan Communism and Soviet Intervention* (Oxford: Oxford University Press, 1999), p. 255.

2. Bradsher, *Afghan Communism*, p. 255.

3. Anatolii Cherniaev, "The Afghanistan Problem," *Russian Politics and Law*, vol. 42, no. 5, September-October 2004, p. 36.

4. Ibid. pp. 37–8.

5. Ibid. p. 40.

6. Anton Minkov, *Soviet Counterinsurgency and Development Efforts in Afghanistan: Implications for US Strategy in Iraq*, Technical Memorandum TM 2009–017 (Ottawa: DRDC Centre for Operational Research and Analysis, 2009), p. 23.

7. Broadcast in English from Moscow to North America, 7 April 1988, in *FBIS*, FBIS-SOV-88-069, p. 40.

8. "Soglashenie mezhdu pravitel'stvom soiuz sovetskikh sotsialisticheskikh respublik i pravitel'stvom demokraticheskoi respubliki afganistana ob ekonomicheskom i tekhnicheskom sotrudnichestve," in Ministerstvo Inostrannykh Del SSSR, *Deistvuiushchie dogovory, soglasheniia i konventsii, vstupivshie v silu s 1 ianvaria po 31 dekabria 1987 goda*, vypusk XLIII (Moscow: Mezhdunarodnye Otnosheniia, 1989), pp. 183–4.

9. Moscow Television Service, 31 August 1987, in *FBIS*, 1 September 1987, p. 21.

10. L.B. Teplinskii, *Istoriia sovetsko-afganskikh otnoshenii* (Moscow: Mysl, 1988), p. 332.

11. TASS, 31 March 1988, in *FBIS*, 5 April 1988, p. 21.

12. TASS, 9 January 1988, in *FBIS*, 12 January 1988, p. 34.

13. Kabul Domestic Service, 27 February 1988, in *FBIS*, 29 February 1988, p. 36.

14. Ibid.

15. TASS International Service, 23 February 1988, in *FBIS*, 24 February 1988.

16. "Soglashenie mezhdu pravitel'stvom soiuz sovetskikh sotsialisticheskikh respublik i pravitel'stvom respubliki afganistan ob okazanii sodeistviia afganistanu v

oblasti energetiki," in Ministerstvo Inostrannykh Del SSSR, *Deistvuiushchie dogovory, soglasheniia i konventsii, vstupivshie v silu s 1 ianvaria po 31 dekabria 1988 goda*, vypusk XLIV (Moscow: Mezhdunarodnye Otnosheniia, 1990), pp. 265–8.

17. *Izvestiia*, 16 February 1988, morning edition, p. 4, in *FBIS*, 17 February 1988, pp. 36–7.

18. "Soglashenie mezhdu pravitel'stvom soiuz sovetskikh sotsialisticheskikh respublik i pravitel'stvom respubliki afganistan o sotrudnichestve v provedenii geologorazvedochnykh rabot," in Ministerstvo Inostrannykh Del SSSR, *Deistvuiushchie dogovory, soglasheniia i konventsii, vstupivshie v silu s 1 ianvaria po 31 dekabria 1988 goda*, vypusk XLIV (Moscow: Mezhdunarodnye Otnosheniia, 1990), pp. 271–3.

19. "Soglashenie mezhdu pravitel'stvom soiuz sovetskikh sotsialisticheskikh respublik i pravitel'stvom respubliki afganistan ob ekonomicheskom i tekhnicheskom sotrudnichestve v oblasti gazovoi promyshlennosti," in Ministerstvo Inostrannykh Del SSSR, *Deistvuiushchie dogovory*, vypusk XLIV, pp. 268–71.

20. "Dolgosrochnaia programma ekonomicheskogo, tekhnicheskogo i torgogo sotrudnichestva mezhdu soiuza sovetskikh sotsialisticheskikh respublik i respublikoi afganistan na period do 2000 goda," in Ministerstvo Inostrannykh Del SSSR, *Deistvuiushchie dogovory*, vypusk XLIV, p. 274.

21. Ibid. pp. 274–5.

22. "Zapis' besedy zamestitelia vneshnei torgovli SSSR tov. Grishin I.T. s ministrom torgovli DRA M.Kh. Dzhalalarom," 6 August 1980, RGAE, f. 413, o. 32, d. 739, ll. 5–6.

23. Cherniaev "The Afghanistan Problem," p. 39.

24. V. Okulov, "Pervye Afganskie," *Pravda*, 17 February 1988, p. 5.

25. Cherniaev, "The Afghanistan Problem," pp. 32–3.

26. *Cold War International History Project Bulletin*, Issue 14/15, p. 175.

27. "Soglashenie mezhdu pravitel'stvom soiuz sovetskikh sotsialisticheskikh respublik i pravitel'stvom demokraticheskoi respubliki afganistan ob ekonomicheskom i tekhnicheskom sotrudnichestve v sooruzhenii v demokraticheskoi respublike afganistan ob''ektov s uchastiem afganskogo chastnogo sektora," in Ministerstvo Inostrannykh Del SSSR, *Deistvuiushchie dogovory, soglasheniia i konventsii, vstupivshie v silu s 1 ianvaria po 31 dekabria 1987 goda*, vypusk XLIII (Moscow: Mezhdunarodnye Otnosheniia, 1989), pp. 184–7.

28. *Sovetskaia Rossiia*, 25 August 1988, second edition, p. 3, in *FBIS*, 7 September 1988, p. 27.

29. Ibid.; see also *Pravda*, 8 October 1989, second edition, p. 4, in *FBIS*, 12 October 1989, p. 8.

30. *Pravda*, 23 December 1987, second edition, p. 4, in *FBIS*, 30 December 1987, p. 28.

31. TASS, 26 February 1988, in *FBIS*, 29 February 1988, p. 36.

32. Okulov, "Pervye Afganskie."

33. *Sovetskaia Rossiia*, 25 August 1988, second edition, p. 3, in *FBIS*, 7 September 1988, p. 27; see also *Pravda*, 8 October 1989, second edition, p. 4, in *FBIS*, 12 October 1989, p. 8.

34. Okulov, "Pervye Afganskie."

35. *Cold War International History Project Bulletin*, Issue 14.15, p. 180.

36. Bradsher, *Afghan Communism*, p. 170.

37. A.A. Liakhovskii, *Tragediia i doblest' Afgana* (Moscow: GPI Iskona, 1995), p. 447.

38. Ivanov, interview.

39. *Izvestiia*, 9 April 1988, morning edition, in *FBIS*, 11 April 1988, p. 41.

40. Kabul Bakhtar, 4 March 1988, in *FBIS*, 4 March 1988, p. 19.

41. Moscow Domestic Service, 31 January 1988, in *FBIS*, 1 February 1988, p. 28.

42. *Pravda*, 29 May 1988, first edition, p. 5, in *FBIS*, 7 June 1988, p. 32.

43. *Pravda*, 29 May 1988, first edition, p. 5, in *FBIS*, 7 June 1988, p. 32.

44. *Izvestiia*, 16 February 1988, morning edition, p. 4, in *FBIS*, 17 February 1988, p. 37.

45. *Pravda*, 28 June 1988, second edition, p. 5, in *FBIS*, 30 June 1988, p. 23.

46. Ibid.

47. "Pomosch' druzei," *Sotsialisticheskaia Industriia*, 9 July 1988, p. 1.

48. "Zhdem v gosti afganskikh rebiat," *Sotsialisticheskaia Industriia*, 23 March 1988, p. 3.

49. "Druzei znaiut v litso," *Pravda*, 20 December 1987, p. 5.

50. TASS International Service, 11 January 1988, in *FBIS*, 12 January 1988, p. 34.

51. "Moskva-Kabulu," *Sotsialisticheskaia Industriia*, 8 March 1988, p. 3.

52. Liakhovskii, *Tragediia*, pp. 439–41.

53. Ibid. p. 441.

54. Ibid. pp. 442–3.

55. Iurii A. Sal'nikov, *Kandagar: zapiski sovetnika posol'stva* (Volgograd: Volgogradskii Komitet po Pechati, 1995), p. 115.

56. For statements to this effect, see B.V. Gromov, *Ogranichennyi kontingent* (Moscow: Progress, 1994), p. 174; V.I. Varennikov, *Nepovtorimoe*, vol. 5 (Moscow: Sovetskii Pisatel', 2001), p. 203; & Cherniaev, "The Afghanistan Problem," p. 38.

57. For more on this change in Soviet attitudes and tactics, see Paul Robinson, "Soviet Hearts-and-Minds Operations in Afghanistan," *The Historian*, vol. 72, no. 1, 2010, pp. 1–22.

58. *Sovetskaia Rossiia*, 12 March 1983, First Edition, 3, in *FBIS*, 17 March 1983, p. D1.

59. *Moscow World Service*, 11 August 1984, in *FBIS*, 13 August 1984, p. D3.

60. *Sovetskaia Rossiia*, 12 March 1983, First Edition, p. 3, in *FBIS*, 17 March 1983, p. D1.

61. "Afganistan, god 1366-i," *Sotsialisticheskaia Industriia*, 29 March 1988, p. 3.

62. Svetlana Alexievich, *Zinky Boys: Soviet Voices from a Forgotten War* (London: Chatto & Windus, 1992), p. 143.

63. Antonio Giustozzi, *War, Politics and Society in Afghanistan, 1978–1992* (London: C. Hurst, 2000), p. 41.

64. Ibid. p. 44.

65. M.A. Gareev, *Afganskaia strada (s sovetskimi voiskami i bez nikh)* 2nd edition (Moscow: Insan, 1999), p. 52.

66. Varennikov, *Nepovtorimoe*, 333.

67. Ibid. 331.

68. Ibid. 334.

69. Giustozzi, *War, Politics and Society*, p. 296.

70. Artyom Borovik, *The Hidden War: A Russian Journalist's Account of the Soviet War in Afghanistan* (London: Faber and Faber, 1991), p. 48.

71. TASS, 15 July 1988, in *FBIS*, 18 July 1988, p. 35.

72. "Vozvrashchenie," *Trud*, 7 February 1989, p. 3.

73. L. Mironov & B. Tret'iachenko, "Komandirovanyi v Afganistan," *Sovetskaia Rossiia*, 2 May 1982, p. 5.

74. TASS International Service, 6 January 1987, in *FBIS*, 17 January 1988.

75. The Russian General Staff, *The Soviet-Afghan War: How a Superpower Fought and Lost*, trans. and ed. Lester W. Grau & Michael A. Gress (Lawrence: University Press of Kansas, 2002), p. 296.

76. "Vozvrashchenie," *Trud*, 7 February 1989, p. 3.

77. Giustozzi, *War, Politics and Society*, p. 44.

78. "Soglashenie mezhdu pravitel'stvom soiuz sovetskikh sotsialisticheskikh respublik i pravitel'stvom respubliki afganistan ob ekonomicheskom i tekhnicheskom sotrudnichestve," in Ministerstvo Inostrannykh Del SSSR, *Deistvuiushchie dogovory, soglasheniia i konventsii, vstupivshie v silu s 1 ianvaria po 31 dekabria 1988 goda*, vypusk XLIV (Moscow: Mezhdunarodnye Otnosheniia, 1990), pp. 278–81.

79. TASS, 20 January 1989, in *FBIS*, 23 January 1989, p. 36.

80. Moscow Television News, *Vremia*, 17 February 1989, in *FBIS*, 21 February 1988, p. 35.

81. Liakhovskii, *Tragediia*, p. 445.

82. Barnett Rubin, *The Fragmentation of Afghanistan: State Formation and Collapse in the International System* (New Haven: Yale University Press, 1995), p. 171.

83. Borovik, *Hidden War*, p. 240.

6. CONCLUSION

1. Bradsher, *Afghan Communism*, p. 167.
2. *Pravda*, 8 October 1989, second edition, p. 4, in *FBIS*, 12 October 1989, p. 8.
3. Rubin, *Fragmentation*, p. 16.
4. Anton Minkov & Gregory Smolynec, *Economic Development in Afghanistan during the Soviet Period: Lessons Learned from the Soviet Experience in Afghanistan*, Technical Memorandum TM 2007–35 (Ottawa: DRDC Centre for Operational Research and Analysis, 2007), p. 18.
5. Ivanov, interview.
6. Rubin, *Fragmentation*, p. 164.
7. Minkov & Smolynec, *Economic Development*, p. 16.

BIBLIOGRAPHY

Interview

Valerii Ivanov, 8 December 2008.

Archives

Cold War International History Project, Virtual Archive 2.0, Soviet Invasion of Afghanistan.

Rossiiskii Gosudarstvennyi Arkhiv Ekonomiki (RGAE), fond 413 (Ministerstvo Vneshnei Torgovli SSSR).

Published Documents

Cold War International History Project Bulletin, Issue 14/15, Winter 2003–Spring 2004.

Ministerstvo Inostrannykh Del SSSR, *Sbornik deistvuiushchikh dogovorov, soglashenii i konventsii, zakliuchennykh SSSR s inostrannymi gosudastvami,* vypuski XVII-XVIII, XXI, XXII, XXIII, XXIV, XXV, XXVI, XXX, XXXI, XXXIII, & XXXV, Moscow: Mezhdunarodnye Otnosheniia, various dates 1960–1981.

Ministerstvo Inostrannykh Del SSSR, *Deistvuiushchie dogovory, soglasheniia i konventsii,* vypuski XXXVI, XXXVII, XXXVIII, XXXIX, XLI, XLII, XLIII, & XLIV, Moscow: Mezhdunarodnye Otnosheniia, various dates 1982–1990.

Naik, J.A. (ed.), *Russia's Foreign Policy Documents: Russia in Asia and Africa,* Kolhapur: Avinash Reference Publications, 1979.

Newspapers & Other Media

Foreign Broadcast Information Service, 1979–1989.
Pravda.
Pravda Vostoka.
Sotsialisticheskaia Industriia.

BIBLIOGRAPHY

Sovetskaia Rossiia.

Trud.

Za Rubezhom.

Books and Articles

Aikins, Mathieu, "Last Stand in Kandahar," *The Walrus*, December 2010, http://www.walrusmagazine.com/articles/2010.12-international-affairs-last-stand-in-kandahar/.

Akhramovich, R.T., "K kharakteristike etapov obshchestvennoi evoliutsii Afganistana posle vtoroi mirovoi voiny," *Narody Azii i Afriki*, no. 3 (1967), pp. 48–61.

Alexievich, Svetlana, *Zinky Boys: Soviet Voices from a Forgotten War*, London: Chatto & Windus, 1992.

Amin, A. Rasul, "The Sovietization of Afghanistan," in Rosanne Klass, ed., *Afghanistan: The Great Game Revisited*, Lanham, MD: Freedom House, 1990, pp. 301–333.

Amstutz, J. Bruce, *Afghanistan: The First Five Years of Soviet Occupation*, Washington, DC: National Defense University, 1986.

Andreasian, R.N., "Protivorechia i kriterii nekapitalisticheskogo razvitiia," *Narody Azii i Afriki*, no. 2 (1974), pp. 38–49.

Andreasian, R.N. and Vinogradova, L.N., "Razvivaiushchiesia strany: gornodobyvaiushchaia promyshlennost' i problemy industrializatsii," *Narody Azii i Afriki*, no. 5 (1970), pp. 29–40.

Aristova, L.B., "Sotsial'naia infrastruktura Afganistana," in Iu.V. Gankovskii (ed.), *Afganistan. Istoriia, ekonomika, kul'tura: sbornik statei*, Moscow: Nauka, 1989, pp. 99–106.

Arnold, Anthony, *Afghanistan: The Soviet Invasion in Perspective*, revised and enlarged edition, Stanford, CA: Hoover International Studies, 1985.

Assifi, Abdul Tawak, "The Russian Rope: Soviet Economic Motives and the Subversion of Afghanistan," *World Affairs*, vol. 145, no. 3 (Winter 1982/83), pp. 253–266.

Avakov, R.M. et al., *The Third World and Scientific and Technical Progress*, Moscow: Nauka, 1976.

Basov, V.V., "Voprosy sotsial'no-ekonomicheskogo razvitiia Afganistana (po materialam afganskoi pechati)," *Narody Azii i Afriki*, no. 3 (1971), pp. 154–164.

Becker, Abraham S., "The Soviet Union and the Third World: the Economic Dimension," in Andrzej Korbonski & Francis Fukuyama (eds), *The Soviet Union and the Third World: the Last Three Decades*, Ithaca, London: Cornell University Press, 1987, pp. 67–93.

Bellis, Paul, "The Non-Capitalist Road and Soviet Development Theory Today: A Critique of Some Recent Accounts," *Journal of Communist Studies and Transition Politics*, vol. 4, no. 3 (1988), pp. 258–281.

BIBLIOGRAPHY

Berezin, V.I., "Ekonomicheskoe i tekhnicheskoe sotrudnichestvo SSSR so stranami Tropicheskoi Afriki," *Narody Azii i Afriki*, no. 5 (1973), pp. 133–138.

Borovik, Artyom, *The Hidden War: A Russian Journalist's Account of the Soviet War in Afghanistan*, London: Faber and Faber, 1991.

Bradsher, Henry S., *Afghanistan and the Soviet Union*, Durham, NC: Duke Press Policy Studies, 1983.

———, *Afghan Communism and Soviet Intervention*, Oxford: Oxford University Press, 1999.

Braithwaite, Rodric, *Afgantsy: The Russians in Afghanistan 1979–89*, London: Profile Books, 2011.

Byliniak, S.A., review of H. Spetter, "Inward-Looking and Export-Oriented Industrialization in Developing Countries (The Case for Export-Oriented Industries)," *Narody Azii i Afriki*, no. 4 (1971), pp. 177–182.

Carlisle, Donald S., "The Changing Soviet Perception of the Development Process in the Afro-Asian World," *Midwest Journal of Political Science*, vol. 8, no. 4 (1964), pp. 385–407.

Chaffetz, David, "Afghanistan in Turmoil," *International Affairs*, vol. 56, no. 1 (January 1980), pp. 15–36.

Cherniaev, Anatolii, "The Afghanistan Problem," *Russian Politics and Law*, vol. 42, no. 5 (September-October 2004), pp. 29–49.

Coldren, Lee O., "Afghanistan in 1984: The Fifth Year of the Russo-Afghan War," *Asian Survey*, vol. 25, no. 2 (February 1985), pp. 169–179.

Cullather, Nick, "Damming Afghanistan: Modernization in a Buffer State," *Journal of American History*, vol. 89 (September 2002), pp. 512–537.

Dannehl, Charles R., *Politics, Trade, and Development: Soviet Economic Aid to the Non-Communist Third World, 1955–89*, Aldershot: Dartmouth, 1995.

Davydov, A.D., "Bor'ba za agrarnuiu reformu v Afganistane," *Narody Azii i Afriki*, no. 5 (1979), pp. 3–12.

Demokraticheskaia respublika Afganistan: spravochnik, Moscow: Nauka, 1981.

Dinkevich, A.I., "Nekotorye voprosy ekonomicheskogo razvitiia stran 'tret'ego mira'," *Narody Azii i Afriki*, no. 5 (1969), pp. 3–15.

———, "O strategii ekonomicheskogo razvitiia stran 'tret'ego mira'," *Narody Azii i Afriki*, no. 1 (1975), pp. 7–19.

"Doklad V.G. Korguna, zaveduiushchego kaphedroi Afganistana v Institute vostokovedeniia RAN," *AZIAINFORM*, 16 January 2006, http://www.asiainform.ru/rusdoc/9600.htm.

Dorronsoro, Gilles, *Revolution Unending. Afghanistan: 1979 to the Present*, New York: Columbia University Press, 2005.

Dupree, Louis, *Afghanistan*, 1980 edition, Princeton NJ: Princeton University Press, 1980.

BIBLIOGRAPHY

Easterly, William and Levine, Ross, *It's Not Factor Accumulation: Stylized Facts and Growth Models*, Working Papers Central Bank of Chile 164, Central Bank of Chile, 2002.

Edwards, David B., *Before Taliban: Genealogies of the Afghan Jihad*, Berkeley: University of California Press, 2002.

Engerman, David C., *Modernization from the Other Shore: American Intellectuals and the Romance of Russian Development*, Harvard University Press, 2003.

————, "The Romance of Economic Development and New Histories of the Cold War," *Diplomatic History*, vol. 28, no. 1 (2004), pp. 23–54.

Ewans, Martin, *Afghanistan: A Short History of Its People and Politics*, New York: Perennial, 2001.

————, *Conflict in Afghanistan: Studies in Asymmetric Warfare*, London: Routledge, 2005.

Ezhov, G.P., "Sovetsko-Afganskoe ekonomicheskoe sotrudnichestvo (1978–1987 gg.)," in M.A. Babakhodzhaev (ed.), *Respublika Afganistan: opyt i tendentsii razvitii*, Tashkent: Fan, 1990), pp. 61–73.

Feifer, Gregory, *The Great Gamble: The Soviet War in Afghanistan*, New York: Harper, 2009.

"Finansirovanie ekonomiki razvivaiushchikhsia stran Azii," *Narody Azii i Afriki*, no. 1 (1968), pp. 3–20.

Foreign and Commonwealth Office, *Sovietization of Afganistan*, Background Brief 80–0998, 1980.

Franck, Peter G., "Economic Progress in an Encircled Land," *Middle East Journal*, vol. 10, no. 1 (Winter 1956), pp. 43–59.

Galeotti, Mark, *Afghanistan: The Soviet Union's Last War*, London: Frank Cass, 1995.

Gankovskii, V.E., "Razvivaiushchiesia strany Azii i mezhdunarodnyi kapitalisticheskii kredit (analiz vneshnei zadolzhennosti)," *Narody Azii i Azii*, no. 6 (1976), pp. 19–32.

Gareev, M.A., *Afganskaia strada (s sovetskimi voiskami i bez nikh)* 2nd edition, Moscow: Insan, 1999.

Gaur, R.B., *Afghanistan: Expanding Bases of Social Revolution*, New Delhi: Allied, 1987.

Gelb, Alan, *Oil Windfalls: Blessing or Curse? A Comparative Study of Six Developing Exporters*, Oxford: Oxford University Press, 1990.

Giustozzi, Antonio, *Afghanistan: Transition Without End. An Analytical Narrative on State-Making*. Crisis States Research Centre, Working Paper 40, London: LSE, 2008.

————, *War, Politics and Society in Afghanistan, 1978–1992*, London: C. Hurst, 2000.

BIBLIOGRAPHY

Goldman, Marshall, "A Balance Sheet of Soviet Foreign Aid," *Foreign Affairs*, vol. 43, no. 2 (1965), pp. 349–360.

Golovin, Iu. M., "Piatiletnii plan i perspectivy razvitiia ekonomiki Afganistana," in R.T. Akhramovich, ed., *Nezavisimaia Afganistan. 40 let nezavisimosti: sbornik statei*, Moscow: Izdatelstvo Vostochnoi Literatury, 1958, pp. 39–77.

Grau, Lester W., *The Bear Went Over the Mountain: Soviet Combat Tactics in Afghanistan*, London: Frank Cass, 1998.

Gromov, B.V., *Ogranichennyi kontingent*, Moscow: Progress, 1994.

Gurevich, N.M., *Gosudarstvennyi sektor v ekonomike Afganistana*, Moscow: Izdatel'stvo vostochnoi literatury, 1962.

———, "Problemy selskokhoziastvennogo proizvodstva v Afganistane," *Narody Azii i Afriki*, no. 2 (1979), pp. 29–40.

———(ed.), *Voprosy ekonomiki Afganistana*, Moscow: Izdatel'stvo vostochnoi literatury, 1963.

Gustavson Associates, *Islamic Republic of Afghanistan: Preparing the Natural Gas Development Project*, Boulder, CO: Gustavson Associates, 2007, available online at http://www.adb.org/Documents/Reports/Consultant/37085-AFG/37085-TACR-AFG.pdf.

Hafvenstein, Joel, *Opium Season: A Year on the Afghan Frontier*, Guilford, CT: The Lyons Press, 2007.

Hall, Robert E., and Jones, Charles I., *Why Do Some Countries Produce So Much More Output per Worker than Others?*, Stanford University Working Paper No. 98–007, available at: http://ssrn.com/abstract=3595.

Halliday, Fred, & Tanin, Zahir, "The Communist Regime in Afghanistan 1978–1992: Institutions and Conflicts," *Europe-Asia Studies*, vol. 50, no. 8 (1998), pp. 1357–1380.

Hansen, Gary D., & Prescott, Edward C., "Malthus to Solow," *American Economic Review*, vol. 92, no. 4 (2002), pp. 1205–1217.

Hauner, Milan, *The Soviet War in Afghanistan: Patterns of Russian Imperialism*, Philadelphia: University Press of America, 1991).

Hauner, Milan, & Canfield, Robert L. (eds), *Afghanistan and the Soviet Union: Collision and Transformation*, Boulder: Westview, 1989.

Hobbes, Thomas, "Leviathan, or the Matter, forme & Power of a Commonwealth Ecclesiasticall and Civill," London: Andrew Crooke, 1651, p. 62.

Hough, Jerry F., *The Struggle for the Third World: Soviet Debates and American Options*, Washington, D.C.: The Brookings Institution, 1986.

Hyman, Anthony, *Afghanistan under Soviet Domination, 1964–91*, Third Edition, Basingstoke: Macmillan, 1992.

Jaster, Robert S., "Foreign Aid and Development: The Shifting Soviet View," *International Affairs*, vol. 45, no. 3 (1969), pp. 452–464.

BIBLIOGRAPHY

Kakar, M. Hassan, *Afghanistan: The Soviet Invasion and the Afghan Response, 1979–1982*, Berkeley: University of California Press, 1995.

Kamrany, Nake M., "The Continuing Soviet War in Afghanistan," *Current History*, vol. 85, no. 513 (October 1986), pp. 333–336.

————, *Peaceful Competition in Afghanistan: American & Soviet Models For Economic Aid*, Washington, DC: Communication Service Corporation, 1969.

Kanet, Roger E., "The Recent Soviet Reassessment of Developments in the Third World," *Russian Review*, vol. 27, no. 1 (1968), pp. 27–41.

Khodzhaev, M.N., "Sotrudnichestvo SSSR i respublika Afganistan v oblasti energii," in Iu.V. Gankovskii (ed.), *Afganistan. Istoriia, ekonomika, kul'tura: sbornik statei*, Moscow: Nauka, 1989, pp. 92–106.

Khrushchev, Nikita, *Khrushchev Remembers*, London: Andre Deutsch, 1971.

Kipping, Martin, *Two Interventions: Comparing Soviet and US-led State-building in Afghanistan*, AAN Thematic Report 01/2010, http://aan-afghanistan.com/uploads/AAN_Two_Interventions.pdf.

Klass, Rosanne, "The Great Game Revisited," in Rosanne Klass (ed.), *Afghanistan: The Great Game Revisited*, Lanham, MD: Freedom House, 1990, pp. 1–29.

Kollontai, V.M., "Novye iavleniia v imperialisticheskoi politike pomoshchi slaborazvitym stranam," *Narody Azii i Afriki*, no. 4 (1961), pp. 13–28.

————, review of V.B. Rybakov & L.V. Stepanov, "Pomoshch' osvobodivshimsia stranam v politike i strategii imperializma," *Narody Azii i Afriki*, no. 4 (1965), pp. 186–188.

Kondrat'ev, V.A., "Utechka nastional'nykh kadrov: prichiny i sledstviia," *Narody Azii i Afriki*, no. 4 (1970), pp. 3–14.

Korbonski, Andrzej and Fukuyama, Francis, *The Soviet Union and the Third World: The Last Three Decades*, Ithaca & London: Cornell University Press, 1987.

Korgun, Viktor, "Doklad V.G. Korguna zaveduiushchego kafedroi Afganistana v Institute vostovedeniia PAN,' http://www.asiainform.ru/rusdoc/9600.htm.

Krugman, Paul, "The Myth of Asia's Miracle," *Foreign Affairs*, vol. 73, no. 6 (November/December 1994), pp. 62–79.

Laber, Jeri, "Afghanistan's Other War," *The New York Review of Books*, vol. 33, no. 20 (18 December 1980).

Laber, Jeri, & Rubin, Barnett R., *A Nation is Dying: Afghanistan Under the Soviets 1979–1987*, Evanston, Il: Northwest University Press, 1988.

Lanine, Nikolai, "We're Still Dying in Afghanistan," *Globe and Mail*, 13 January 2007.

Liakhovskii, A.A., *Tragediia i doblest Afgana*, Moscow: GPI Iskona, 1995.

Makhmudov, E.R., "Afganistan. Osnovnye etapy evoliutsii gosudarstvennoi politiki v oblasti industrializatsii (1919–1978)," in *Afganistan. Istoriia, ekonomika, kul'tura: sbornik statei*, Moscow: Nauka, 1989, pp. 137–163.

BIBLIOGRAPHY

————, "Rol' gosudarstvennogo i chastnogo sektorov v razvitii avtomobil'nogo transporta Afganistana," in M.A. Babakhodzhaev (ed.), *Respublika Afganistan: opyt i tendentsii razvitii*, Tashkent: Fan, 1990, pp. 103–116.

Maprayil, Cyriac, *The Soviets and Afghanistan*, London: Cosmic, 1982.

Marshall, Alex, "Managing Withdrawal: Afghanistan as the Forgotten Example in Attempting Conflict Resolution and State Reconstruction," *Small Wars and Insurgencies*, vol. 18, no. 1 (2007), pp. 68–89.

Mauro, Paolo, "Corruption and Growth," *The Quarterly Journal of Economics*, vol. 110, no. 3 (1995), pp. 681–712.

McClosky, Deirdre, "The Bourgeois Reevaluation: How Innovation Became Virtuous," 2010, pp. 1600–1848, www.deirdremccloskey.org.

Metge, Pierre, *L'URSS en Afghanistan: De la coopération à l'occupation: 1947–1984*, Paris: CIRPES, 1984).

Minkov, Anton, *Soviet Counterinsurgency and Development Efforts in Afghanistan: Implications for US Strategy in Iraq*, Technical Memorandum TM 2009–017, Ottawa: DRDC Centre for Operational Research and Analysis, 2009.

Minkov, Anton & Smolynec, Gregory, *Economic Development in Afghanistan During the Soviet Period: Lessons Learned from the Soviet Experience in Afghanistan*, Technical Memorandum TM 2007–35, Ottawa: DRDC Centre for Operational Research and Analysis, 2007.

————, *Social Development and State Building in Afghanistan During the Soviet Period, 1979–1989: Lessons Learned from the Soviet Experience in Afghanistan*, Technical Memorandum TM 2009–033, Ottawa: DRDC Centre for Operational Research and Analysis, 2009.

Moyar, Mark, "Development in Afghanistan's Counterinsurgency: A New Guide," *Small Wars Journal*, March 2011, http://smallwarsjournal.com/documents/development-in-afghanistan-coin-moyar.pdf.

Moyo, Dambisa, *Dead Aid: Why Aid is not Working and How There is a Better Way for Africa*, New York: Farrar, Straus and Giroux, 2009.

Naby, Eden, "The Ethnic Factor in Soviet-Afghan Relations," *Asian Survey*, vol. 20, no. 3 (March 1980), pp. 237–256.

Newby, Eric, *A Short Walk in the Hindu Kush*, Melbourne: Lonely Planet, 1998.

Nikolayev, Lev, *Afghanistan: Between the Past and Future*, Moscow: Progress, 1986.

Nisdaq, Nabi, *Afghanistan: Political Frailty and External Interference*, London: Routledge, 2006.

Noorzoy, M.S., "Long-Term Economic Relations between Afghanistan and the Soviet Union: An Interpretative Study," *International Journal of Middle East Studies*, vol. 17, no. 2 (May 1985), pp. 151–173.

————, "Soviet Economic Interests and Policies in Afghanistan," in Rosanne Klass, ed., *Afghanistan: The Great Game Revisited*, Lanham, MD: Freedom House, 1990, pp. 71–95.

BIBLIOGRAPHY

Nyrop, Richard F. & Seekins, Donald M., *Afghanistan Country Study and Government Publications*, Washington, DC: The American University, 1986, available online at http://www.gl.iit.edu/govdocs/afghanistan.

Oleinik, Anton, "Lessons of Russian in Afghanistan," *Society*, vol. 45, no. 3 (2008), pp. 288–293.

Papp, Daniel S., *Soviet Policies Toward the Developing World During the 1980s*, Maxwell Air Force Base: Air University Press, 1986.

Pol'shikov, P.I., "Problema nakopleniia v razvivaiushchikhsia stranakh Afriki," *Narody Azii i Afriki*, no. 4 (1977), pp. 55–66.

Poullada, Leon B., "The Road to Crisis, 1919–1980," in Rosanne Klass, ed., *Afghanistan: The Great Game Revisited*, Lanham, MD: Freedom House, 1990, pp. 37–69.

Prokhorov, G.M., "Industrializatsiia razvivaiushchikhsia stran i znachenie opyta i pomoshci SSSR," *Narody Azii i Afriki*, no. 6 (1974), pp. 21–32.

Rashid, Ahmed, "Graveyard of Analogies," *The National*, 30 January 2009, http://www.thenational.ae/article/20090130/REVIEW/458735663/1008.

————, "Highway Lifeline," *Far Eastern Economic Review*, vol. 146, no. 43 (26 October 1989), pp. 22–23.

Reisner, L.I., "Zapadnye burzhiaznye teorii razvitiia molodykh natsional'nykh gosudarstv (kriticheskii obzor literatury)," *Narody Azii i Afriki*, no. 5 (1969), pp. 30–42.

Robinson, Paul, "Soviet Hearts-and-Minds Operations in Afghanistan," *The Historian*, vol. 72, no. 1 (2010), pp. 1–22.

Rodrik, Dani, "Institutions for High Quality Growth: What They Are and How to Acquire Them," *Studies in Comparative International Development*, vol. 35, no. 3 (2000).

Rodrik, Dani, Subramanian, Arvind, and Trebbi, Francesco, "Institutions Rule: The Primacy of Institutions over Geography and Integration in Economic Development," *Journal of Economic Growth*, vol. 9, no. 2 (2004), pp. 131–165.

Rubin, Barnett R., *The Fragmentation of Afghanistan: State Formation and Collapse in the International System*, New Haven: Yale University Press, 1995.

The Russian General Staff, *The Soviet-Afghan War: How a Superpower Fought and Lost*, trans. and ed. Lester W. Grau & Michael A. Gress, Lawrence: University Press of Kansas, 2002.

Rymalov, V.V., "Razvivaiushchiesia strany: tendentsii i problemy ekonomicheskogo rosta," *Narody Azii i Afriki*, no. 3 (1967), pp. 5–23.

Sal'nikov, Iurii A., *Kandagar: zapiski sovetnika posol'stva*, Volgograd: Volgogradskii Komitet po Pechati, 1995.

Sandakov, A., "Razvivaiushchiesia strany Afriki: problemy nakopleniia," *Narody Azii i Afriki*, no. 3 (1970), pp. 16–27.

Seierstad, Asne, *The Boookseller of Kabul*, London: Virago, 2002.

BIBLIOGRAPHY

Sen, Amartya, *Development as Freedom*, New York: Alfred Kopf, 1999.

Shamrai, Iu.F., "Nekotorye voprosy rynochnykh otnoshenii mezhdu sotsialisticheskimi i razvivaiuishimi stranami," *Narody Azii i Afriki*, no. 2 (1969), pp. 15–25.

————, "Problemy sovershenstvovaniia ekonomicheskogo sotrudnichestva sotsialisticheskikh i razvivaiuishikhsia stran," *Narody Azii i Afriki*, no. 4 (1968), pp. 3–14.

Shleifer, Andrei, Glaeser, Edward L., Lopez de Silanes, Florencio, La Porta, Rafael, and Djankov, Simeon, *The New Comparative Economics*, Harvard Institute of Economic Research Discussion Paper No. 2002, Yale SOM Working Paper No. ES-24, World Bank Policy Research Working Paper No. 3054, available at: http://ssrn.com/abstract=390760.

Shpirt, A.Iu., "Razvivaiuishchiesia strany Azii i Afriki i mineral'noe syr'e," *Narody Azii i Afriki*, no. 4 (1968), pp. 15–26.

Shroder, John F. & Assifi, Abdul Tawab, "Afghan Mineral Resources and Soviet Exploitation," in Rosanne Klass (ed.), *Afghanistan: The Great Game Revisited*, Lanham, MD: Freedom House, 1990, pp. 97–134.

Smirnov, G.V., "Rol' gosudarstva v reshenii problemy nakoplenii v ANDR," *Narody Azii i Afriki*, no. 5 (1973), pp. 13–22.

de Soto, Hernando, "The Mystery of Capital: Why Capitalism Triumphs in the West and Fails Everywhere Else," New York: Basic Books, 2000.

Stiglitz, Joseph E., *Whither Socialism?*, Cambridge, Mass.: MIT Press, 1996.

Teplinskii, L.B., *Istoriia sovetsko-afganskikh otnoshenii*, Moscow: Mysl, 1988.

————, "Sovetsko-Afganskie otnosheniia za sorok let sushchestvovaniia nezavisimogo Afganistana," in R.T. Akhramovich, ed., *Nezavisimaia Afganistan. 40 let nezavisimosti: sbornik statei*, Moscow: Izdatelstvo Vostochnoi Literatury, 1958, pp. 5–38.

————, *SSSR i Afganistan, 1919–1981*, Moscow: Glavnaia Redaktsiia Vostochnoi Istorii, 1982.

Tornell, Aaron & Lane, Phillip "The voracity effect," *American Economic Review*, vol. 89, no. 1 (1999), pp. 22–46.

Tursunov, R., "Pomoshch' sovietskikh sredneaziatskikh respublik Afganistanu," *Narody Azii i Afriki*, no. 4 (1971), pp. 177–182.

Urazova, E. & Teplinskii, L., review of N.M. Gurevich, "Ekonomicheskoe razvitie Afganistana (finansovye voprosy)," *Narody Azii i Afriki*, no. 3 (1967), pp. 152–153.

USSR Academy of Sciences, Department of Economics, *The Third World and Scientific and Technical Progress*, Moscow: Nauka, 1976.

Varennikov, V.I., *Nepovtorimoe*, Moscow: Sovetskii Pisatel', vol. 5 (2001).

Volchek, N.Z., review of "Razvivaiushchiesia strany v bor'be za nezavisimuiu natsional'nuiu ekonomiku (usloviia, faktory, perspektivy)," *Narody Azii i Afriki*, no. 1 (1969), pp. 191–193.

BIBLIOGRAPHY

Whitlock, Monica, *Beyond the Oxus: The Central Asians*, London: John Murray, 2002.

Wilder, Andrew, "A 'weapons system' based on wishful thinking," *Boston Globe*, 16 September 2009.

Williamson, John, "Did the Washington Consensus Fail?," Outline of Remarks at CSIS (Washington DC: Institute for International Economics, 6 November 2002).

——, "The New Institutional Economics: Taking Stock, Looking Ahead," *Journal of Economic Literature*, vol. 38 (2000), pp. 595–613.

Young, Alwyn, "The Tyranny of Numbers: Confronting the Statistical Realities of the East Asian Growth Experience," *The Quarterly Journal of Economics*, vol. 110, no. 3 (1995), pp. 641–680.

Yousaf, Mohammad & Adkin, Mark, *The Bear Trap: Afghanistan's Untold Story*, London: Leo Cooper, 1992.

Zevin, L.Z, review of A.Ia. El'ianov, "Razvivaiushchiesia strany: problemy ekonomicheskogo razvitiia i rynok," *Narody Azii i Afriki*, no. 1 (1977), pp. 164–168.

INDEX